SPEED AT THE
TT RACES

FASTER
AND
FASTER

>>>>>>>>>>>>>

DUNLOP TYRES
NEWSAGENTS
DUNLOP TYRES
Arai
Belstaff
BARRY
LOCTITE
METZELER
96

SPEED AT THE TT RACES

AT THE

FASTER AND FASTER

>>>>>>>>>>>

DAVID WRIGHT

THE CROWOOD PRESS

First published in 2017 by
The Crowood Press Ltd
Ramsbury, Marlborough
Wiltshire SN8 2HR

www.crowood.com

British Library Cataloguing-in-Publication Data
A catalogue record for this book is available from the British Library.

ISBN 978 1 78500 298 4

Frontispiece: Barry Woodland rounds Quarter Bridge on his 400cc Yamaha on his way
to victory in 1988 Production Race D.

Typeset by Jean Cussons Typesetting, Diss, Norfolk

Printed and bound in Malaysia by Times Offset (M) Sdn Bhd

CONTENTS

INTRODUCTION AND ACKNOWLEDGEMENTS

Every year in late May and early June, tens of thousands of people journey to the Isle of Man to be present at an event known the world over simply as 'The TT'. For two weeks, the roads that make up the 37¾ miles of the famed Isle of Man Mountain Course are given over to top motorcycle racers, to ride the fastest bikes of the day in pursuit of one of the most highly coveted prizes in motorcycle racing: a Tourist Trophy.

This is the way it has been for 110 years, during which time the annual event has evolved from a single race into a festival of motorcycling. But however varied the interests on show, the main reason for the high-octane atmosphere that envelops the Island during those two weeks is the unfettered spectacle of raw speed generated by racing over the public roads of the TT Mountain Course.

It was the opportunity to break free from the shackles of mainland Britain's then 20mph speed limit and to ride faster than the next man that brought the first motorcycle TT to the Isle of Man in 1907. Recognized from the outset as being one of motorcycling's greatest challenges, for over a century the island has attracted the very best road racers, while successive generations of followers have crowded the roadside banks and marvelled at the way in which riders have gone ever faster at this unique event.

In the following pages you can read about the attraction of speed to competitors and spectators, and how faster motorcycles have caused the time required to lap the Mountain Course to shrink from 45 minutes to under 17 minutes. Also considered are how changes to the roads and the rules of racing have affected race speeds, plus the many factors in the development of racing motorcycles that have

contributed to lap speeds growing from an average of just over 40mph to well in excess of 130mph. All this is interwoven with the history of the event and will leave you in no doubt that it is speed that has shaped most aspects of the now legendary TT races.

ACKNOWLEDGEMENTS

A book like this cannot be written without assistance across many areas and I am grateful for the support provided by Stan Basnett, David and Joan Crawford, Ralph Crellin, Tony East, Geoff Judges, Paul Wright, Manx National Heritage and the VMCC Library. The database on www.iomtt.com was consulted on several occasions and found to be very useful.

Photographs to illustrate the theme of 'Speed' have been supplied by Stan Basnett, Ron Clark, David and Joan Crawford, Juan Cregeen, John Dalton, Paul Ingham, Alan and Mike Kelly of Mannin Collections, Ray Knight Archives, Brian Maddrell, Doug Peel, Geoff Preece, Richard Radcliffe, Elwyn Roberts, Rob Temple, Paul Wright, Bill Snelling of FoTTofinders and Mortons Media.

The author has made every effort to locate and credit the source of the hundreds of photographs used in the book. If any have not been properly acknowledged, please accept my apologies.

Special thanks go to Vic Bates for providing considerable input to this project, drawing maps of the several TT courses, taking photographs to illustrate riders at particular locations on the course and making his photo archive available for use.

CHAPTER ONE

GATHERING MOMENTUM

Followers of the Isle of Man Tourist Trophy races are interested in many aspects of the annual event, but the dominant attraction to most of them has always been the spectacle of raw and unbridled speed on offer over the roads of the famed and feared Mountain Course. Through successive generations of TT racing, spectators have marvelled as riders have exhibited their skills and courage over those public roads, while extracting maximum performance from their machines. Each will have given their all, but history confirms that it has always been the fastest riders who commanded the most attention, received the greatest publicity and entered the record books.

Much has been written to explain man's wish to travel ever faster, but just one week after the first TT race in 1907, when the event faced criticism from some quarters, *The Motor Cycle* magazine neatly summarized the situation with the words: 'It is useless to say that fast speeds are not to be encouraged, human nature being what it is.'

Top motorcycle racers have always demanded the very best motorcycles to ride and over a century of effort has now been committed to developing more powerful racing engines, together with improved transmissions, suspension, brakes, tyres, electrics and the like, all with the aim of putting better machines into the hands of riders, to travel ever faster around the 37¾-mile lap of the TT Mountain Course. Has all that effort been successful? Well, in the first running of the race for the Tourist Trophy over the Mountain Course in 1911, winner Oliver Godfrey thrilled spectators with speeds they had never before experienced, as he rode his c10bhp Indian to first place at a race average speed of 47.63mph, reaching perhaps 65mph in the process. In 2016 Michael Dunlop did exactly the same with his 220-plus bhp BMW as he rode to victory at a race average speed of 130.68mph, while hitting close to 200mph. That simple comparison reflects over 100 years' growth in power and speed, substantial technical progress and an awful lot of excitement.

EARLY TT RACES

The first Tourist Trophy race for motorcycles was run in 1907, over ten laps of a 15½-mile circuit in the west of the island called the St John's Course.

It presented a challenge for motorcycles of the era, for they were still in an early stage of development. Though billed as a race, out and out speed was not the main target

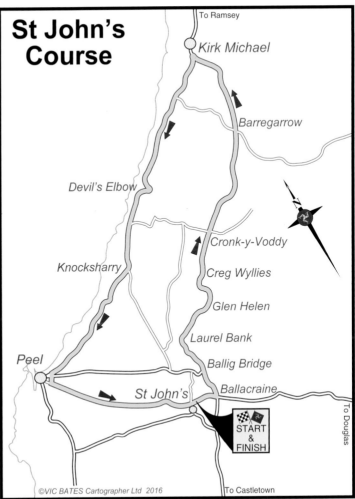

This is the St John's Course, used from 1907 to 1910.

Riders tackle the sharp downhill turn at Douglas Road Corner, Kirk Michael, on the St John's Course.

of the first event: in words of the day, the Tourist Trophy race was created 'for the development of the ideal touring motorcycle'. To help achieve that ideal, machines were equipped with silencers, had to carry a specified minimum weight of tools, be fitted with a proper saddle and use touring-type mudguards. The regulation that had most influence on speeds, however, was the one that specified fixed allocations of fuel for the race. This was limited to 1 gallon for every 90 miles of race distance for single-cylinder machines and 1 gallon per 75 miles for those with more than one cylinder. For many competitors the effect of that regulation was to govern the speed at which they could 'race', because trying to run at maximum throttle would see them use up their fuel before completion of the 158-mile total distance.

After spending their practice sessions seeking the right balance between speed and economy, twenty-five riders lined up in front of the historic Tynwald Hill at St John's to start the first TT. As there were no specified standards for riding gear, they turned out in a selection of leather, tweed and oilskins. Wearing additional belts and pouches for spare parts and sometimes a spare inner tube over the shoulder, they probably looked a motley crew, but they were courageous pioneers, for few would have ridden a race that was anything like the one that faced them on 28 May 1907. Dispatched in pairs at one minute intervals, all had to ride with fuel consumption in mind; the amount remaining in each rider's tank at the end was measured and publicized.

Fastest rider on a twin-cylinder machine in 1907 was Rem Fowler on a Norton. Suitably braced with 'a glassful of neat brandy tempered with a little milk' before starting, he returned a race average speed of 36.22mph, set the fastest lap of the day at 42.91mph, and had a petrol consumption

figure of 87mpg. Fastest overall and winner of the newly created Tourist Trophy was first man home on a single-cylinder machine, Charlie Collier. On his family-built Matchless, he rode to a race average speed of 38.22mph, with a fastest lap of 41.81mph at 94.5mpg.

Fowler had an eventful race, with delays to progress caused by falling off twice, repairing a front-wheel puncture, changing several sparking plugs, tightening his drive belt twice and fixing a loose mudguard. Such problems were quite usual in early TT races, meaning that competitors needed to have mechanical skills as well as riding ones. In contrast to the many difficulties experienced by Fowler, overall winner Collier had a relatively trouble-free run during the 4 hours, 8 minutes and 8 seconds it took him to complete the first race for the magnificent silver Tourist Trophy, a gift to the organizers from the Marquis de Mouzilly St Mars.

The motorcycles used in 1907 were still recognizably derived from pedal cycles but they were not easy to control. While trying to race at speed over poor road surfaces, riders had to juggle levers to achieve the right balance between mixture strength, spark timing and throttle opening, whilst also remembering to top up the drip-fed total-loss lubrication system by operating a manual oil pump at regular intervals. The bikes were tall with wide handlebars, had virtually no springing and possessed only poor brakes. Tyres were of a narrow 2¼-inch beaded-edge section and were inflated to high pressures to help them grip the rims. Most lacked any form of clutch or gearbox, so the single gear chosen had to be a compromise between

Ready for the fray prior to the 1908 TT, Captain Sir Robert Keith Arbuthnot, Bt, shows off his Triumph, a typical machine of the day.

gaining the best speed on the flat while retaining the ability to climb hills and negotiate sharp bends. The direct drive from engine to rear wheel was usually by leather belt. As races ran over roads littered with horseshoe nails and sharp stones, punctures were frequent. Top speed was said to be about 65mph.

Confirming that speed was important to all who took part in the first TT, the Triumph Engineering Company Ltd's post-race advertising claimed that 'The Triumph made faster time than any machine in the race after deducting time lost for repairing punctures'. However, the Norton Manufacturing Company Ltd countered with an advertisement saying 'The fastest machine in the Tourist Trophy was the Norton twin, in spite of misleading statements to the contrary'.

GETTING FASTER

Pedals, previously used for starting and to aid hill-climbing, were banned for 1908. That had little effect on race speeds, but the elimination in 1909 of the fixed petrol allowance and the freedom given to run without silencers certainly did, because it allowed for full throttle all the way, where machine and road conditions allowed. This meant that as well as meeting the need for speed, riders could satisfy another aspect of human nature – trying to defeat their fel-

low riders. As a result, Harry Collier (brother of 1907 winner Charlie) brought his Matchless home in a time almost 25 per cent faster than previous winners, pushing the race average speed up to 49.01mph and setting the fastest lap of 52.27mph. That was a huge increase from the previous fastest lap of 42.91mph and provided an early example of how rule changes can impact on race speeds.

The speeds achieved in 1909 may not sound fast to current TT fans, but they would have impressed those who saw and read about them. The maximum speed allowed on the roads of Britain at the time was 20mph (14mph on the Isle of Man), and with a low level of vehicle ownership, few people had any experience of what it was like to travel at 60-plus mph. They would have been in justifiable awe of those early racers.

A force to be reckoned with in the early years of TT racing, past winners Charlie and Harry Collier took their Matchless machines to first and second places at the 1910 TT, although it was Harry Bowen on his BAT who set the fastest lap at 53.15mph, in what turned out to be the last TT to be run over the St John's Course.

1911: THE MOUNTAIN COURSE

The Isle of Man Tourist Trophy races were organized by the Auto Cycle Union (ACU), who governed motorcycle sport in most of Britain. In a deliberate attempt to hasten motorcycle development, in particular to advance the adoption of variable gears, it moved the races from the St John's Course to the far more demanding Mountain Course in 1911. No one could have realized what a profound effect that move would have on motorcycle development over the next 100 years, for the Mountain Course became a test-bed for almost every new design feature, with manufacturers confident that if a new development could withstand the rigours of a TT race, then it was fit to market to the general public.

Early TT meetings comprised just a single race, with classes for single- and multi-cylinder machines. But in 1911 two separate races were run, carrying the titles of Senior and Junior, in which singles and multis raced each other. The multis (almost exclusively twins) were permitted to run with a greater engine capacity; for the Senior they had an upper limit of 585cc with singles limited to 500cc, while in the Junior, twins could be up to 340cc and singles 300cc. Race distances were five laps and 187½ miles for Seniors and four laps covering 150 miles for Juniors.

Machines entered for the smaller class were considered 'Lightweights' of the day and some manufacturers wanted to retain pedals for the race. However, determined to spur on the development of smaller machines, the ACU refused

Ballacraine was approached from the opposite direction in the early TT races. In 1910 the organizers ramped the outside of the corner to help the single-speed machines maintain momentum for the climb that followed up to Ballaspur. Not everyone got it right and there were spills. However, a doctor from Peel was on hand and his car can be seen here, parked on the course and with the handles of a stretcher sticking out of the window.

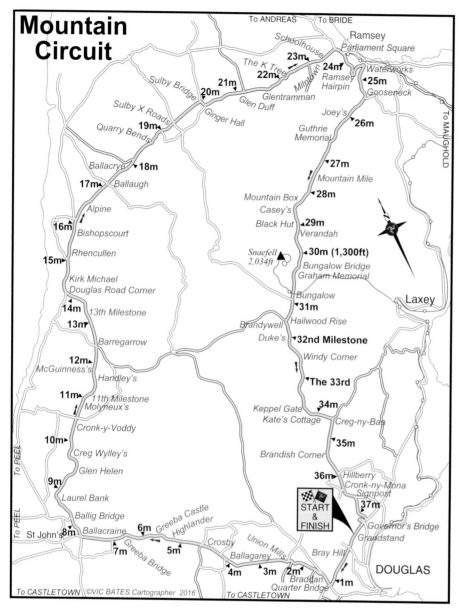

The route of the TT Mountain Course.

descent from Snaefell would be dangerous, even though the real concern for most was the 1,400ft (430m) ascent of 'the Mountain', particularly as the iron engines of the day were known to lose power when hot.

When first used for motorcycles in 1911, the Mountain Course over Snaefell (Snow Mountain) was 37½ miles long and its route was almost the same as today's, except that on the outskirts of Douglas at Cronk ny Mona, riders turned right and rode through Willaston to reach the top of Bray Hill, rather than going via Signpost Corner, Governor's Bridge and the Glencrutchery Road as they do today. The start and finish were located on a flat stretch of road after the bottom of Bray Hill before it commenced its descent to the Quarter Bridge.

On the approach to that first 1911 Mountain Course TT it became clear that most manufacturers had accepted the need for variable gears and examples of most of the available types could be seen. A report of the time told of 'compound and epicyclic gears in the back hub and on the engine-shaft, counter-shaft gears, and direct gears by means of expanding engine pulleys with and without the rear wheel moving in unison to maintain the correct tension of the belt'.

Among manufacturers taking on the challenge of the new course were Triumph, Rex, Scott, Indian, Matchless, Humber, Forward, Norton, Zenith, Premier, Singer and Rudge-Whitworth. Most claimed they were running standard catalogue models, but there was already a recognition of the benefit to sales from winning a TT, with much time and effort put into the preparation of the machines entered. Those who saw the insides of factory-prepared motorcycles told of components polished to a mirror finish while, to cope with the bumpy, potholed course, there was additional brazing, much use of split pins and binding with insulating tape.

their request. Meanwhile, as has always been the case with the Tourist Trophy meeting, other people had ideas on how the event should be run, with the motorcycle press floating the notion of a minimum weight limit for riders because they believed that those of small stature would gain an unfair advantage on the climb of the Mountain. Indeed, their proposal was that any rider weighing less than 140–150lb (63–68kg) in full riding gear should be barred from the event. There were dissenting voices on other aspects, too; for example, not everyone agreed with moving the TT to the Mountain Course. There were claims that the

SPEEDS

No one really knew what race speeds would be achieved over the new course in 1911. There were pre-race reports that the fancied Oliver Godfrey had been timed at 80mph on an Indian at Brooklands, but he was probably riding a bike that was larger than the 585cc limit set for twin-cylinder machines at the TT. In addition, the poor road surfaces on the island would certainly reduce maximum speed from that achieved at Brooklands' concrete bowl. Another report told how past winners the Collier brothers had their TT machines ready in good time, and Charlie was said to have reached 68mph on the road, with his new expanding and contracting engine pulley giving ratios of between 3:1 to 5:1. Of the 'Lightweights' in the Junior race, it was predicted that a few would reach 55mph and many 50mph, perhaps faster downhill. Meanwhile, the Isle of Man authorities had been debating whether to increase the island's overall speed limit from 14 to 20mph, but faced with difficulties of enforcing either figure, it voted to abolish the limit instead.

Pre-practice reports on the condition of the roads were not encouraging but have to be judged by standards of the time, for the surfaces were still 'unmade', being of rolled macadam with no tar binding. It was clear from the first lap of practice that the section from Ginger Hall to Ramsey was in very poor condition, as was the Mountain Road, which was strewn with loose stones and was described by *The Isle of Man Weekly Times* as 'dreadful'. The same newspaper urged that Bray Hill be swept before riders tackled it at what it said would be 70mph.

Practice sessions were all early morning and started from the Quarter Bridge on the outskirts of Douglas. Perhaps seeking to minimize disturbance to local inhabitants around the course, the ACU decreed that practice would be allowed for just one week prior to racing in 1911. However, after representations from the traders and hoteliers of Douglas, who sought to maximize income from the TT, this was extended to two weeks of practice, all of which

Bray Hill in Douglas, just a few years before use in the first Mountain Course TT in 1911.

Winner of the 1911 Junior TT, Percy Evans (Humber), takes a tight line at the tricky Ramsey Hairpin.

took place over open roads. That decision to extend the practice period was an early example of peripheral commercial interests influencing the running of the TT, as they do to this day.

Given the conditions in the first year of using the Mountain Course, it is not surprising that there were accidents to riders during practice and, regrettably, the TT saw its first fatality when Victor Surridge fell from his Rudge at Glen Helen.

Both the Junior and Senior TT races of 1911 were held in dry weather, with the former run on Friday, 30 June with thirty-seven entries over four laps, and the latter on Monday, 3 July with sixty-seven entries over five laps. The man who rode to victory in the 150-mile Junior TT was Percy Evans on a twin-cylinder Humber with belt drive and three-speed hub gear. He averaged 41.45mph and set the fastest lap of 42.00mph, finishing well ahead of Harry Collier (Matchless) in second place.

Racing bikes of the day generally ran with small-bore, straight-through exhausts, which gave them a crackling note. Riders would also have been able to hear a regular slap-slap from their belt drives, sundry clickings from the exposed valve gear and usually a loud knocking from the engine when it was put under load at low revs.

DISQUALIFICATION

In the 1911 Senior race, the two most fancied runners, Charlie Collier and French-Canadian ace Jake de Rosier, battled closely for the lead on the first few laps, until de Rosier fell at Kerromoar. Limping in to what was then named the Ramsey Depot (what we now call the Pits, of which there was another at Braddan Church), de Rosier borrowed tools to fix his Indian and, although he rode on to the finish, he was disqualified for what the organizers classed as 'receiving outside assistance'.

Jake de Rosier urges his Indian through Stella Maris as he leaves Ramsey to commence the Mountain climb in 1911.

The intrepid Charlie Collier speeds over Ballig Bridge on his Matchless.

Meanwhile, Collier and his twin-cylinder JAP-engined Matchless were eventually beaten into second place by Oliver Godfrey on his two-speed, chain-driven, twin-cylinder Indian. The latter's average race speed was 47.63mph, while the fastest lap went to Frank Philipp (Scott) at 50.11mph. Thus the 1911 event established the first race average speeds and fastest lap speeds for the Mountain Course, so offering a target for future years and causing one publication to speculate 'is a 60mph or even a 70mph TT possible in the future?'.

Mention has been made of Jake de Rosier's disqualification and, although Charlie Collier was initially credited with second place, he too was disqualified. In his case it was for taking on fuel at other than the authorized depots at Ramsey and Braddan.

De Rosier was probably the top racer in North America at the time while Collier held a similar position in Britain, so the serious penalties incurred by those star riders showed how important it was to be fully prepared for a TT race – in all respects. De Rosier's Indian would undoubtedly have received the most careful mechanical preparation, but failure to secure his tool-bag properly meant that he lost tools during the race and thus had to borrow some when he stopped at Ramsey, so leading to his disqualification. Quite how past-winner Collier managed to miscalculate on fuel and thus be forced to borrow some at Ballacraine is not known, for he was such an experienced racer. However, it is worth mentioning that the TT was still the only race of its kind run in Britain. Collier had taken part in point-to-point road races on the Continent, but in Britain his only opportunities to race were on some of the larger boarded cycle-tracks, in relatively short hill-climbs, at the concrete speed bowl of Brooklands, or, if he had chosen to, in the occasional sand race.

Both of the 1911 races provided victories for twin-cylin-

der machines, and the fact that they were fitted with variable speed gearing was no doubt to the satisfaction of the organizing ACU. Yet while the event as a whole was considered a success, and manufacturers learned valuable lessons from it, many of them were far from happy with the still young Isle of Man Tourist Trophy meeting.

The Continental Tyre and Rubber Co. (GB) Ltd advertised the successful use of its products by Junior and Senior winners of 1911.

1912: DISCONTENT

Soon after the 1911 TT, manufacturers voiced their displeasure with the event. Many and varied complaints were aired: that the Mountain Course was dangerous, that they did not like twin- and single-cylinder machines competing in the same race, that the original concept of using touring machines was being lost, that it was expensive to take part in, that it interrupted production at their factories, to name but a few. Given the concerted nature of these complaints, it seems that these were not just the usual gripes from bad losers but real concerns. Such was the strength of their feelings that the majority signed a bond not to take part in 1912, with a financial penalty falling on anyone who broke its terms.

Not all manufacturers were party to that bond, The Scott Motorcycle Company and H. Collier & Sons Ltd (makers of Matchless machines) being amongst those who refused to sign, but it left the ACU to run an event that would be mostly made up of private runners. Having previously relied on the entry fees and voluntary contributions from manufacturers to help fund the running of the event, this was a real blow to the ACU and could easily have finished the TT after just one year's running on the Mountain Course. To its credit, the ACU decided to take the financial risk and go ahead with the 1912 races.

Sales of motorcycles were booming and in a crowded market, with little other than the views expressed in the few motorcycling magazines of the day to go on, the buying public still looked for honest pointers as to which machines to buy. TT results could help provide those pointers.

A FRENCH TT?

Even today the Isle of Man TT races cannot be run without the annual approval of Tynwald, the Manx government, and the ACU were kept waiting for that approval for the 1912 races. Perhaps in an attempt to provoke a decision, the motorcycle press wrote about how easy it was to get permission to run road races in France and that, for many, it would actually be simpler to get there rather than to the Isle of Man! This notion began to build momentum and even found support in the French motorcycle press. In January 1912 the ACU decided to write to the Manx authorities and press for a decision. If an early response was not forthcoming, it resolved 'to communicate with one of the principal French motorcycle clubs with a view to holding this important event in France'. Tynwald's approval was received before the end of the month.

REDUCED ENTRIES

Come the closing date for entries to the 1912 TT and those for the Senior totalled forty-nine, while for the Junior it was twenty-six. Comparative figures from 1911 were sixty-seven and thirty-seven, showing the effect of the manufacturers' boycott. Sadly, racing had taken its toll on some of the previous year's top Indian riders, for Jake de Rosier was lying badly injured in a Los Angeles hospital, while Moorhouse (third in 1911) had been killed at Brooklands. The danger of practising on open roads, as all TT sessions were, was brought home to riders after John Gibson, 'travelling down Bray Hill at a good speed', collided with a car that backed out of a side road into his path. Gibson survived the crash, but was injured.

There was nothing radically new in design-wise for the machines entered for 1912, but one important change to the regulations saw the upper capacity limit for the Senior race set at 500cc and for the Junior 350cc. This meant that, for the first time, single- and twin-cylinder engines would compete on level terms in each race. Entrants in the Senior were chasing a first prize of £40 and for the Junior it was £30. In addition, gold medals were awarded to the winners and to any other rider finishing within 30 minutes of the winner's overall race time.

Course conditions in 1912 were much the same as in previous years, although the island had gained its first stretch of tar-sprayed macadam on the short straight between Quarter Bridge and Braddan Bridge on the outskirts of Douglas. Quarter Bridge itself had been widened considerably, as had the Hall Caine bends, which were now described as 'all out'. Hall Caine was a renowned author who lived some 6 miles from the start at Greeba Castle, which is how those bends are known today.

WET

It was difficult to gain real pointers to riders' form during practice in 1912, for several of the sessions were affected by rain, making the roads muddy and riding conditions difficult. Come race day, riders in the Junior faced torrential rain at the start of their race, which eased and then stopped on the second lap.

Very wet conditions at Quarter Bridge for Harry Bashall (Douglas) in the Junior TT of 1912.

This was the first TT to be held under really wet conditions, and as well as affecting the course, it offered a challenge to the waterproofing of magnetos and plug leads. Unfortunately, some machines were found wanting in those areas, leading to early retirements. To add to rider difficulties, the exposed belt drives used by most machines were prone to slip when coated with road mud and this had the effect of reducing speed, particularly on hills.

Fastest man proved to be Harry Bashall on his Douglas; as an indication of the difficult conditions, he stopped eight times during the race to give attention to his machine. Bashall's race average speed was 39.65mph, which was a commendable figure when compared with the previous year's winning average speed of 41.45mph in the dry. Fastest lap was by second-placed man Eric Kickham, also on a Douglas, at 41.76mph. There were just eleven finishers out of twenty-one starters.

SINGLES OR TWINS

At the previous year's TT, twin-cylinder machines had a capacity advantage over the singles and were victorious in both races. The question for 1912 was how would twins fare against singles now that they were on equal capacity terms. By taking the first two places in the Junior race, the Douglas concern showed that twins were still front runners, but how would the big bikes do?

Conditions for the Senior TT held on Monday, 1 July were better than for the previous Friday's Junior race, although there was rain before the start, the wind was strong and there was some mist over the Mountain, where wandering sheep were said to be troublesome. Riders were despatched singly at one-minute intervals. Pace-setters in the

early stages of the Senior were team mates Frank Philipp and Frank Applebee on their twin-cylinder, two-stroke, water-cooled, two-speed, chain-driven Scotts. They were hoping to keep an assortment of single- and twin-cylinder machines at bay over the five laps and 187½ miles of race distance. The pair maintained their lead positions until the fourth lap, when Philipp suffered tyre troubles, leaving Applebee to take victory and be followed home by James Haswell on his single-cylinder Triumph, with Harry and Charlie Collier third and fourth on their Matchless twins. So two cylinders were again victorious over one, but with the first six places in the Senior TT evenly distributed between singles and twins, it appeared that the ACU had got it right by equalizing capacities for 1912.

The 1912 Senior race did not create any records, but given the conditions, Frank Applebee's race average speed of 48.69mph and fastest lap of the race at 49.44mph were to be admired.

Summarizing a TT race in a couple of paragraphs gives no real hint of the thrills, spills and endeavour involved. The picture here shows how Frank Applebee had to ride to achieve victory and most others would also have been on their personal limits. Not everyone made the finish and the post-race reports tell of falls, valve troubles, fuel difficulties, fires, punctures and failure of other components.

DRIVE BELTS

These were mostly of leather, one reason being that it had plenty of 'give' and was thus able to cushion some of the shocks imposed by each firing stroke. Prone to slip in wet and muddy conditions, belts also had a tendency to stretch and to snap their fastening links. Riders carried repair kits to deal with such problems.

While chain drives tended to stretch less than belts, most riders liked to subject new chains to a lap of the course before using them in a race, thus taking out some of the stretch. Once stretched, a metal chain stayed stretched. Users of leather belts also liked to stretch them before a race and having done so they would remove them from the machine and hang them up with a substantial weight attached. This was to preserve the stretch, for leather would gradually shrink back towards its original length when not loaded.

BRAKING

Earlier mention was made of drive belts slipping under muddy conditions. This was mostly due to mud getting on the dummy rim of the rear wheel, which the belt was trying to drive, and on the engine pulley. That dummy rim, sometimes called the belt rim, was also used for the basic slowing process, a block of friction material being pressed

Frank Applebee and his Scott trying hard at Kate's Cottage during his winning ride in the 1912 Senior TT.

Typical rear-wheel arrangement showing the dummy rim and multi-link leather drive belt. The basic rear brake is also visible.

against it by operation of a brake pedal. Again, mud on the dummy rim reduced braking effect, just adding to the difficulty of racing in the wet. With the same tyres used in all weathers, poor conditions also increased the danger of losing adhesion and creating what riders of the day called 'sideslip'.

Machines were fitted with two brakes, the second usually being of the horseshoe or stirrup shape that utilized two brake blocks bearing against the wheel rim – like the pedal cycles of the time – and could be on either the front or back wheel. It was a time when riders were cautious about using the front brake, but even when used together, the brakes offered limited stopping power to reduce speed for corners, or to control the descent to Creg ny Baa, which was described as 'the sharpest pull-up on the course'. Brakes of the time were not progressive in action, having a tendency to 'grab' and induce skidding, but some must have been better than others, for a report from the 1912 Senior race observed: 'the Triumph riders approached the bends much faster than the majority, relying absolutely on the efficiency of their brakes in the last 50 yards to steady their breakneck speed'.

In addition to using their brakes, riders sought to aid the slowing process by making use of the valve-lifter on the approach to corners. By pulling a lever they lifted the exhaust valve off its seat and broke the seal to the combustion chamber. This largely negated the effect of the firing stroke and thus reduced drive. As they rounded the corner, the lever would be released and the exhaust-valve would revert to normal operation.

1913: ENDURANCE

Early TT races were a test of endurance and Frank Applebee had to ride for almost 4 hours to take victory in the five-lap Senior TT of 1912, with lesser riders in the saddle for much longer; some had to be helped from their machines at the finish. In a continuing quest to push motorcycle development and reliability, the TT organizers shocked everyone when they announced that the Senior TT of 1913 would be over seven laps and the Junior over six. Fortunately, they recognized the extreme demands this would put on riders and so split each race into two sessions. Two laps of the Junior were run on the Wednesday morning, after which

the machines were locked away under ACU control and the Senior runners did three laps. After a day's rest, the riders then rode their remaining four laps on Friday. The event had recovered its popularity with manufacturers by 1913 and those that were left from a combined original entry of 148 rode together on the Friday, with Seniors identified by red waistcoats and Juniors wearing blue.

Overall victory in the 1913 Junior TT went to Hugh Mason (NUT-JAP), who despite spending most of the previous week in hospital after a practice crash, lifted the average race speed to 43.75mph and set the fastest lap of 45.42mph. As in 1912, Senior victory went to a two-stroke Scott, this time with 'Tim' (H.O.) Wood aboard. His race

W.F. Newsome took second place in the 1913 Junior TT on his Douglas, after racing for 5 hours, 9 minutes and 20 seconds. He rode a Rover in the Senior race and *Bicycling News and Motor Review* wrote: 'He sustained a badly-gashed tyre two miles from the depot; he walked and ran there, obtained a new cover, and ran and walked back, fitted the tyre, and finished – enabling the Rover team to win the team prize'.

average was fractionally less than Applebee's in 1912, but he broke Godfrey's lap record from 1911, increasing it from 50.11mph to 52.12mph, in noticeably better riding weather. Spectators, and most of those who read about the races, were pleased to see the lap record broken by a handsome 4 per cent, but it induced a magazine of the day to publish an article titled 'Slowing Down the Senior Tourist Trophy'. Interestingly, a read of the article revealed that while the title was a recognition of some peoples' views, the writer was of the opinion that, 'figures seem to show that the limits of speed fixed by the roads and by the engine dimensions have already been reached in the Senior event'.

1914: NEW FACES

For the 1914 races, the start was moved to the top of Bray Hill, where temporary pits, grandstand and scoreboards were erected. It was a year when crash helmets became compulsory for the record entry of 159 and one where two new marques joined the list of TT winners, as Eric Williams took an AJS to race and lap records in the Junior and Cyril Pullin piloted a Rudge to record-breaking victory in the Senior. Tim Wood (Scott) was credited with the fastest lap in the Senior, breaking his own record from 1913, with a speed of 53.50mph and, in an unusual occurrence, past winner Oliver Godfrey (Indian) tied for second place with newcomer Howard Davies (Sunbeam). TT watchers noted that both victories in 1914 went to single-cylinder machines. This was a contrast to previous years, when twin-cylinder machines had prevailed, although the fastest lap and second places by Wood and Godfrey on twins showed they were still a force to be reckoned with.

HANDLING

A recurring theme at the TT during the years running up to the outbreak of the First World War in 1914 was that although manufacturers were increasing engine outputs and thus, in theory, speeds, the poor road conditions meant that riders were unable to use the full 10–12bhp available to them. Those who studied the handling of machines over the potholed and loose surfaced roads met with in TT racing could see that some makes handled better than others. This resulted in greater attention being given to frame and fork design, to improve handling and allow riders to travel marginally faster over the poor roads. It was an early lesson for manufacturers – which would be repeated many times over the next century – that engine power over the TT Mountain Course counted for little without comparable road-holding.

SPEED SELLS

Whether the phrase 'Speed Sells' was in use in the early days is not clear, but manufacturers were certainly aware that speed was a plus factor and used it in their advertising. Many of them added a 'TT Model' to their catalogues, aimed at buyers who desired a machine resembling a racer, with slightly downturned handlebars, sometimes a little engine tuning and usually a premium on the purchase price. Not all such machines would have been from manufacturers who had actually contested the TT, but a report told that by 1914: 'It is the exception to peruse a catalogue which does not list a TT model'. However, another report described most manufacturers' TT models as: 'merely his standard mount masquerading under false colours'.

Despite the general wish to go faster, the poor road conditions over the Mountain Course limited the growth in TT lap speed in the period 1911–1914 to just over 3mph, going from 50.11mph to 53.50mph.

Soon after the 1914 TT the development of racing motorcycles was put on hold, as major nations spent four years fighting the First World War. Indeed, it was to be six years before racing for a Tourist Trophy returned to the Isle of Man.

In 1914 the start was moved to the top of Bray Hill, where Eric Williams (AJS) is shown finishing the Junior race.

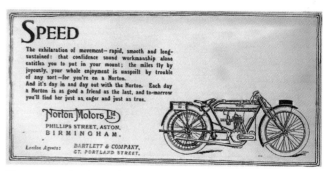

Norton pushed the Speed theme in this advertisement for its 'TT Model'.

CHAPTER TWO

A SPEEDY DECADE

When the First World War ended in November 1918, manufacturers gave priority to the production of motorcycles for road use, so racing had to wait its turn. It was the summer of 1920 before the sound of racing motorcycles once again reverberated around the Mountain Course.

DEVELOPMENT

The concentrated efforts put into war usually accelerate development in specific areas and 1914–18 saw considerable advances in aero-engine design, often on a no-expense-spared basis. With similarities in the performance needs of aero and motorcycle engines, such as light weight combined with low fuel consumption, high output, reliability, accessibility and so on, there was speculation on how post-war motorcycles might benefit from wartime advances in aero-engineering. Surprisingly, the answer given by some well-regarded names was along the lines of 'not a lot'. James Norton, of Norton Motorcycles Ltd, explained that 'aero production methods could not be applied profitably to the motorcycle industry', while George Stevens of A.J. Stevens & Co. Ltd, makers of AJS, opined: 'I cannot say that the experience gained during the war has helped manufactur-ers in the matter of improved general design, but it will undoubtedly result in better and improved methods of construction.'

A strike of moulders in early 1920 threatened both normal production and the racing plans of many firms. As early as February, some realized that they would not be able to compete at the TT due to the effects of the strike, while firms like Triumph and Zenith – with full order-books – continued to concentrate on production of roadsters, rather than divert efforts to the preparation of machines for racing. BSA, Ariel, Scott and Rudge were among others not making works entries, but there were whispers that some of those non-contenders lobbied for the TT not to be run in 1920, perhaps because they realized that their actions would lose them the chance of a prestigious TT win. Fortunately their efforts failed and the good news was that there were several new companies who intended to enter. In addition, there were private runners ready to challenge the Mountain Course, even though some would surely have been put off by the £21 entry fee – a substantial sum, equivalent to some £850 today.

The Model 9 Norton of 1920 shown above is very similar to those supplied prior to the First World War, while the advertisement from 1919 reminded potential buyers of AJS's earlier Tourist Trophy success and racing pedigree.

An early shot of Ballig Bridge. TT riders tackled it on the diagonal, from left to right, and were airborne over the hump.

1920: THE TT COURSE

With many Manxmen away fighting, the Mountain Course received only basic maintenance during the war, but an optimistic report from February 1920 told that 'hundreds of men – mostly discharged soldiers – are now employed getting the Isle of Man roads in good condition'. Reporting on an inspection lap a month later, *The Motor Cycle* claimed that, 'with the exception of a few short stretches, it is in a safe and satisfactory condition for the forthcoming race'. However, when ACU Secretary, Tom Loughborough, visited the Island in late April, he was not so impressed with course conditions. He felt that while much of the going was just about acceptable for racing, the stretch from Ginger Hall to Ramsey was in such a deplorable state that, as he informed the Manx authorities, if it was not put into good repair the 1920 races would have to be abandoned.

There was a change to the route of the TT course in 1920: as riders neared the end of a lap, they no longer turned right at Cronk ny Mona but carried on to Signpost Corner, then went via The Nook and Governor's Bridge to join the Glencrutchery Road, where a new start, finish and pits area had been created just before St Ninian's crossroads. In round figures, the new lap distance became slightly longer at 37¾ miles.

There was also a small diversion after leaving Parliament Square in Ramsey, due to a dispute over the use of what was a private stretch of road on the approach to Cruickshanks and May Hill.

WELCOME THE LIGHTWEIGHTS

After the on/off scenario of the previous few months, the Island welcomed the first post-war TT in 1920. It came with some sixty entries, almost evenly distributed between Senior and Junior races, which were scheduled for Tuesday 15 and Thursday 17 June. Early morning practising was available for two weeks before, with riders warned: 'Competitors should note that the roads are not closed to other traffic during the times allotted to practising, and carts and other traffic may then be encountered'.

In another slightly difficult-to-believe scenario, an appeal was made early in practice for anyone with a spare ACU-approved crash helmet to offer it to the organizers, for some competitors arrived on the island without one!

It was mentioned in Chapter 1 how in the early days of the TT, 350cc machines were informally known as Lightweights. For 1920, machines up to 250cc were invited to race in a class of their own within the Junior (350cc) TT race and those 250s were given the formal title of Lightweights.

To qualify to race, each competitor had to complete a minimum of six laps in practice, with at least one being covered within 1 hour by Seniors, within one hour and 10 minutes by Juniors and 1 hour 30 minutes by Lightweights.

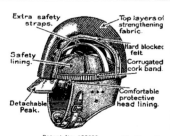

An ACU-approved helmet from 1920.

Riders competing in the TT in 1920 knew they were taking on a challenge of man versus mountain.

Cyril Pullin rounds the loose-surfaced Gooseneck on the early part of the Mountain climb.

The TT was still a unique event in Britain. Post-war motorcycle competition had recommenced with events like hill-climbs, long-distance trials, sand racing and so on, but with Brooklands not having reopened until April 1920 and a dearth of other venues, real speed events were largely absent, and speed and spectacle was what both riders and spectators sought. Many pre-1914 TT riders had been to war and some had not returned. Who would take a win in the 1920 TT was difficult to forecast, for those pre-war riders with course knowledge were now six years older, while for some of the newcomers it would be their first attempt at genuine road racing.

PROGRESS?

For all the talk of war-time developments not being of much aid to motorcycle design, everyone expected racing motorcycles at the 1920 TT to be faster than those of 1914. Chain drive and variable gears had become almost universal, while advances in metallurgy allowed the use of components that did not suffer the same degree of performance-robbing heat distortion as in previous years. Also, better production machinery permitted manufacture to closer tolerances. Aluminium alloy pistons were to be used by several makes, overhead valves were being introduced, steel flywheels lightened and bikes given a lower overall build. All were considered to be improvements that could enhance performance.

So while those manufacturers with TT entries in 1920 like Norton, Sunbeam, ABC, Duzmo, Indian, AJS, Blackburne, Wooler, Douglas, Diamond, Levis, Ivy, among others, had done their bit for progress, what about that other vital constituent of racing, the Mountain Course itself? As

indicated above, it was in no better condition than in 1914, with an often loose and stony surface littered with multiple potholes and ruts that could not be dodged, together with particularly rutted and rocky going along parts of the narrow Mountain Road. That meant, once again, that in spite of manufacturers' best efforts to boost machine performance, course conditions would restrict speed in many locations.

There had been pre-TT talk of 1920 race bikes with 80mph performance, but hard information was difficult to come by. In the secrecy of their own testing facilities, manufacturers may have measured output in units of brake horse power (bhp) as we do today, perhaps seeing figures around the 15bhp mark, but the most commonly published ratings were generic ones. All 500cc machines were classed as 3½HP and 350 models as 2¾HP, with no distinction between stages of engine tune or any attempt to portray true output. It was said that 500cc Sunbeam side-valve engines were showing 5,000rpm on the bench, but limitations in valve gear performance would see their peak power being produced at nearer 4,000rpm, or less. Norton's entries were under the care of Brooklands record-breaker D.R. O'Donovan, and while the company maintained that its bikes were close to standard, he calculated that they were achieving revs of 4,300 in top down the Mountain, which equated to a speed of 76mph. It was a time when any bike with a compression ratio approaching 6:1 was regarded as highly tuned.

RACING RETURNS

Six years after the last TT and following two weeks of practising to hone riding skills and prepare machinery, the combined field of Junior and Lightweight competitors lined up on the Glencrutchery road, ready to be despatched on five laps and 187½ miles of racing over the Mountain Course.

AJS brought what was the nearest to a new engine to the race. Of 350cc, it had a hemispherical combustion chamber, exposed pushrods and valve springs operating overhead valve gear, plus lightened piston and flywheels. Their riders had four gears available to them and Roy Bacon tells how that was achieved with 'a two-speed countershaft gearbox, the choice of ratios being doubled up by fitting two primary chains with a selector at the engine sprockets'. Overall machine weight was claimed to be just 217lb (99kg) and output rated as 10bhp. The AJS offered a lively package, which allowed 1914 Junior winner, Eric Williams, to leap into the lead of the Junior race, with similarly mounted Howard Davies and 'Harry' Harris second and third. The pace was hot at the front, but became too hot – approaching the mid-point those first three dropped out, each with serious mechanical issues. Fortunately for AJS, they had been able to call up second-place man in the 1914 Junior, Cyril Williams, as a late replacement for a rider injured in practice and he took over and built a substantial lead.

As he began his descent of the Mountain on the last lap, Cyril Williams must have felt that victory was his. But nothing is certain in TT racing and at Keppel Gate he suddenly lost all drive. The remaining 4 miles to the finish must have been a nightmare, as he coasted downhill, struggled uphill and shoved manfully on the long stretch from Governor's Bridge to the finishing line. Aware that his lead was being eroded at every step, he staggered over the line exhausted and only just able to take in that he had held on and taken victory from Jack Watson-Bourne on his Blackburne.

The race and lap speeds told the story of this dramatic race, for Cyril Williams' average race speed of 40.74mph was much slower than Eric Williams' race speed of 45.58mph back in 1914. It was Eric who set the fastest lap in 1920 before his forced retirement, boosting his 1914 lap record from 47.57mph to 51.36mph.

Levis two-strokes dominated the new Lightweight class and took the first three places. First of them was Ronald Clark, who survived a spill near the Thirty-third milestone and whose fastest lap time was 43.00mph. This was an excellent effort for a 250, for they were severely taxed by the Mountain climb, with some of their riders talking of 'foot-slogging' around the Gooseneck.

Two days later twenty-seven riders lined up for the six-lap Senior TT. It was pace-setter in practice, George Dance, on his Sunbeam who led for the first two laps, until forced to retire. Manxman Dougie Brown then led for the next two on his Norton, before being reeled in by Sunbeam-mounted Tommy de la Hay, who held the lead to the finish. This time records were set in both race average speed and lap speed, the former being lifted from 49.49mph to 51.48mph, while lap speed went up from 53.50mph to 55.62mph, a figure set by George Dance on his second lap.

It was a year when single-cylinder machines were victorious in all three races, despite the presence of V-twins and flat-twins in the Senior and Junior classes.

TOO FAST?

Even with the less than fulsome support received from manufacturers in 1920, the races were rated a success, although one item that attracted post-race discussion was whether the 500cc machines were too fast for course conditions. *The Motor Cycle* was strident on the issue, writing 'engine capacity must be reduced for future races. Machines of 500cc are too fast for the course'. It went on to advocate a maximum capacity of 350cc for TT race bikes.

While people recognized that riders of 500cc machines were not always able to use full power in 1920, what they could not know was that the Isle of Man would accelerate its road-surfacing programme through the early years of the 1920s and thus offer much improved conditions for racing.

1921: THE 'TRADE' RETURNS

Manufacturers and their associated component suppliers were often referred to in motorcycling circles as 'the Trade'. Some had abstained from supporting the 1920 TT, but they were back in force for the 1921 event. This resulted in entries of sixty-five for the Junior race and sixty-eight in the Senior, with ten manufacturer's teams nominated for the Junior and eight for the Senior – a healthy situation.

With opportunities for true road racing limited to the Isle of Man, British manufacturers knew that the TT, with its long lap of varied going, offered them test and develop-

Ronald Clark (Levis) leaves Sulby Bridge in a cloud of dust.

ment opportunities that could not be achieved elsewhere. Also, in its own words, the organizing ACU considered it to be 'the duty of the Competition Committee of the ACU so to frame their conditions as to provide such a spur to progress that the most lethargic of manufacturers must realize that a reputation made needs keeping'. The motorcycle press plugged a similar theme with, 'the technical value of the Isle of Man races is enormous to any manufacturer who is genuinely on the lookout for weak places in his production and their possible cure'.

The aim of the TT was still to aid the development of 'the ideal touring motorcycle'. Stripped-out racers were not wanted and the race regulations specified minimum weight limits for each class. In 1920 it was 132¼lb (60kg) for 500cc machines and 110¼lb (50kg) for 350cc.

While the 1920 TT had come too soon after the war for some manufacturers to get organized to race, a year later many of them had their TT machinery out and about early, with reports of several teams visiting the Isle of Man for unofficial testing in March and April 1921.

COURSE CONDITIONS

The Manx Highway Board was tar-spraying more of the Island's roads, although most of its activities were confined to the towns and larger villages, with little done on the roads that linked them. The 37¾ miles of the Mountain Course were still largely of rolled macadam with its customary potholes, ruts and loose material, meaning that in dry weather riders trailed dust clouds that rose to hedge height and lingered for minutes. Not only was this unpleasant for all concerned, but it created a real danger for riders attempting to pass. In the wet the potholes filled with water

At an early 1920s TT, Bert Le Vack applies too much throttle too soon, on the loose surface of Ramsey Hairpin.

that could not be avoided by anyone travelling at speed, so machine and rider got covered in mud.

In 1921 the Mountain Road was not the principal route between Ramsey and Douglas that it is today, as most travellers took the coast road. Little use meant little maintenance and it showed – so much so, that on the descent of the Mountain there were places where the road surface was the natural bedrock, which was a highly dangerous and uneven surface to race over. Fortunately the Highways Board offered to blast the rock away and create a better surface before racing commenced. As an illustration of the relatively poor wearing qualities of the ordinary unbound macadam road surfaces, a report from early May said, 'the Mountain Road is rather bad, but will not be repaired too early in case of rain rendering further repair necessary'.

THE MACHINERY

Manufacturers approached the 1921 TT with real enthusiasm and there was a 'buzz' on the approach to the event that enveloped everyone concerned, leading to claims that they were to witness 'the finest motorcycle races in history'.

The previous year's Senior TT winners, Sunbeam, were back with both side-valve (sv) and overhead-valve (ohv) models, but decided to use their tried and tested sv versions in the race. Norton again claimed to be running near-standard models, which came with a shortened wheelbase and lower build, aimed at improving handling. They also had a couple of experimental ohv models, while advertising their 16H sv model as 'undoubtedly the fastest countershaft-geared 3½HP machine extant'. Triumph brought 4-valve ohv engines and 2-valve side-by-side versions, but decided to stick to their older sv design for the race. Scotts were back with their two-stroke twins and were the only maker with water-cooled engines.

It was a TT debut in works form for the sizeable BSA concern, who entered six riders on new models in the Senior. These were fitted with an inclined ohv engine incorporating new design elements in the valve gear, mechanical lubrication and a distinct low overall build. They received plenty of pre-race publicity and, after setting fast times in testing at Brooklands, much was expected of them.

Amongst the entries for the Junior race, 1920 winners AJS returned with 350cc machines that were similar to the ones they used in 1920. They had their cylinder heads and barrels copper-plated to aid heat dispersion, before receiving a customary coat of black. Pistons of the day were full-skirted and often heavily perforated below the rings. The overall trend was for three-speed countershaft gearboxes, increased use of small internal-expanding brakes, plus a mixture of manual and mechanical oil pumps.

THE RACING

There was the customary fortnight of practice to sort riders and machinery in 1921 and then the Junior race, where it was no surprise to see past winner Eric Williams ride to victory on his AJS, 4 minutes ahead of similarly mounted Howard Davies and Manxman Tom Sheard. The little 'Ajays' were in a class of their own and Williams set a new race record of 52.11mph, while Davies took the fastest lap at 55.15mph, claiming his top speed was just 73mph.

While the AJS men were the heroes of the hour after the Junior, they were not without challengers during the race. Jim Whalley on his Massey Arran was in the running for most of the time, but on the last lap suffered a front-wheel puncture at Windy Corner and took a heavy fall. Battered and bleeding, he remounted and rode in on the rim to a gallant fifth place, with the bike stuck in second gear and the exhaust pipe scraping the ground.

In the race for Lightweights, run concurrently with the Junior, winner Doug Prentice (New Imperial) upped the average race speed to 44.61mph, while Bert Kershaw (New Imperial) set a new lap record at 46.11mph. Levis and Velocette two-strokes chased home the winning four-stroke.

With speeds advancing in the smaller classes, two days later it was down to the Seniors to show what they could do. Again there was talk of 80mph potential from some Senior bikes, with Freddie Dixon claiming 85mph from his Indian, which was a single-cylinder model with a rear-inclined cylinder. Destined to ruffle a few feathers, however, was Howard Davies, who was down to ride his '73 miles-an-hour' 350cc AJS in the Senior race against all the others mounted on 500s.

The Senior got under way in good conditions and spectators were treated to the usual variations in riding styles, particularly when cornering. Most leant in, while some, including Freddie Dixon, often leant out, although earlier foot-down styles had now been dropped. But it was the sit-up and neat cornering style of Howard Davies and his little 350cc AJS that won the day after six laps and 226½ miles of racing, adding over 3mph to the average race speed to make it 54.50mph and leading home the Indians of Freddie Dixon and Bert le Vack. Fastest lap went to Freddie Edmond (Triumph) at 56.40mph.

Not all of the new ideas and machinery that manufacturers bring to the TT are successful, but few fail on the scale of BSA in 1921. The Birmingham concern's TT debut was a disaster, for none of its six machines finished the race.

With speeds advancing, there were ever more people who maintained that the 500cc Senior machines were too fast for the Mountain Course, and with his lower-powered, neat-handling 350 taking a Senior victory in 1921, Howard Davies probably added fuel to their argument. Perhaps reflecting the discontent around the topic, one magazine picked up on post-race gossip and wrote, 'there was talk in the Island of arranging next year's TT on French soil, and there is much to be said in support of the suggestion'. Others talked of the races going to Ireland.

BOMBSHELL!

What had been gossip about moving the TT from the Isle of Man took on a far more serious tone in August 1921, when the ACU Competitions Committee publicized its recommendation that the 1922 TT races be held on a 30-mile road circuit at Spa in Belgium. Much discussion followed in which many claims and counter-claims were made. The balance of opinion seemed to favour the move to Belgium, but at its meeting in October, the ACU General Committee meeting rejected the recommendation of its Competitions Committee. This was a surprise, for it really looked as though the TT had been lost to the Island.

Lodge clearly felt that speed sold sparking plugs.

Belgium had offered a financial inducement to the ACU to move the TT, which was not available from the Isle of Man. Indeed, some felt that the Island was less than welcoming to an event that boosted its economy. But then, not every resident of the Isle of Man was a fan of motorcycle racing and its followers.

1922: RETURN TO THE ISLAND

Harsh words had been spoken about the Isle of Man by elements of the ACU during negotiations for moving the event to Belgium and no doubt bridges had to be rebuilt with the Manx authorities on the run-up to the 1922 TT.

Over in Manxland, tar-spraying of roads was being extended out of the towns and the place was described in late April as, 'literally buzzing with steamrollers'. As far as the TT course was concerned, it was good news for riders to hear that the new surfacing now reached over 4 miles out from Douglas to Crosby.

In a small change of route, riders returned to using the original private stretch of road leading from Parliament Square to Cruickshanks Corner in Ramsey, which they had used up to 1914. It was a change that must have saved time, for it was slightly shorter and eliminated a couple of slow corners. Also, what were described as 'big changes for the better' had been made on sections of the Mountain Road, amongst them being substantial widening at Windy Corner and Keppel Gate. Everyone expected those improvements would contribute to faster lap speeds.

Entries were slightly up in 1922, with thirty-two Lightweights, thirty-eight Juniors and sixty-seven Seniors, for which experienced top riders like Davies, Dance, Dixon and Bennett were joined by three newcomers who were destined to go on to make TT history: Stanley Woods, Walter Handley and Jimmy Simpson. The last admitted in *Racing*

Just eighteen years old when this photograph was taken at the end of the 1922 Junior TT, Stanley Woods looks a little dazed. That is hardly surprising, for with virtually no racing experience and in his first TT, he had just completed five mishap-strewn laps and 187 miles of the Mountain Course, finishing in fifth place at an average speed of 50mph.

Reminiscences that his debut in 1922, 'was the very first time I had ridden in a long-distance road race of any description'. This was not unusual, for apart from a few races held over somewhat shorter courses in Ireland, there was nothing in Britain that offered riders the type of road-racing experience that would be helpful in contesting the Isle of Man TT. Despite his lack of experience, Jimmy Simpson managed to persuade the Scott concern to provide him with a machine to race, while Stanley Woods talked the Cotton Motorcycle Company into supplying him with a machine. Woods had done a lap when visiting the TT as a spectator in 1921, but neither Simpson nor Handley had been around the course before setting out on their first lap of official practice. With Simpson it showed when he fell off near Governor's Bridge, then ignored signals to stop. Handley made TT history by starting off in the wrong direction on his first lap. Both found themselves in trouble with the race organizers.

Stanley Woods had a most eventful ride on his 350cc Cotton, for he struck the kerb at Governor's Bridge just before his refuelling stop, dislodging his exhaust pipe from the engine and coming in for petrol with naked flames flickering from the exhaust port. There was no requirement to stop the engine while refuelling in those days and with his eager pit attendant a little careless, Woods and the Cotton were suddenly engulfed in flames. Swift action from

The sweeping left-hand bend at Union Mills, some 2½ miles from the start.

bystanders prevented a disaster, but Woods' cord breeches were badly scorched, as were the upper parts of his legs. Tying the errant exhaust pipe to the frame with a bit of cloth, he rejoined the race, only to have a pushrod break at Braddan Bridge. Hastily fitting a spare, he continued, but later lost the use of his back brake. This meant he had to rely on the minuscule front brake visible in the photo. This was not enough to slow him on the approach to Ramsey Hairpin, where he took a heavy fall. Picking himself up, he once more rejoined the race and was glad to see the chequered flag, after an exhausting 3 hours 50 minutes and 33 seconds riding, in a creditable fifth place. No one could have forecast that his raw young racer would go on to win ten TT races, finishing his career with a best race average speed of 89mph.

By 1922 the Lightweight race was in its third year of running and was awarded its own Tourist Trophy, while the previous practice of awarding gold medals to winners and top finishers in each race was dropped and silver replicas of the Tourist Trophy given instead.

There was a good feeling running up to the 1922 event, for factory competition departments had been busy and were keen to put their ideas to the test of TT racing. Grumbles could still be heard about the course not being able to handle 500s at top speed, but most riders of 500cc machines aimed to ride the TT course at less than full throttle, because those who went flat out from the start with what were still fairly fragile engines rarely made the finish. Almost every winner's post-race comments indicated how they started carefully, nursed the engine until mid-race, assessed their positions and then, only if necessary, finished at full throttle.

RECORD SPEEDS

Race week in 1922 was blessed with good weather throughout, and riders responded to a year's development of machines and improvements to the course with record speeds in all classes. How much of that increased speed could be attributed to the hard work put into machine development and how much to course improvement, no one could say for certain. This combination of machine development, course improvements and, often, a star rider's efforts, was to be the pattern of future TT speed increases.

What was noticeable in 1922 was how the top places were distributed over a wide number of manufacturers, with five different makes among the first seven finishers in the Senior (won by Alec Bennett on a Sunbeam), eight different makes among the first nine finishers in the Junior (won by Manxman Tom Sheard on an AJS), and the first six finishers all riding different makes in the Lightweight

Geoff Davison refuels his Levis at the Pits. The job of the Boy Scouts was to clean the rider's side number plates.

(won by Geoff Davison on a Levis). Those results would have been pleasing to manufacturers, for it allowed more of them to obtain publicity for their products.

The increase in race speeds achieved in 1922 ranged from around 8 per cent in the Senior to over 10 per cent in the Lightweight, but what really grabbed public attention was Alec Bennett's new lap record in the Senior at 59.99mph. It meant that a 60mph lap was within touching distance at a time when most ordinary people, including many motorcyclists, still had no idea what it was like to travel at a mile a minute, let alone to average it for 226 miles while riding through towns, villages and over mountain and moorland.

MACHINE DEVELOPMENT

Race machines were providing increased performance year on year at the TT and from the purely mechanical side, this arose from both engine development and improved general construction. However, Alec Bennett's Senior race victory in 1922 came on a bike with an established single-cylinder, side-valve, long-stroke engine measuring 77 × 105.5mm, at a time when there was a trend to use a shorter stroke. It turned out to be the last side-valve to win a TT. It had been recognized for some years that there were performance gains from the adoption of overhead valves, but it was only in the early 1920s that improved valve material did away with the snapped valves and subsequent wrecked engines so often experienced by pioneers of the ohv layout. Most valves, springs, pushrods and tappets were exposed, making effective lubrication difficult, although there would be sufficient oil and grease around to attract dirt and grit. This unpleasant mixture could even be enough to accelerate tappet wear during a long race, so affecting valve clearances and engine tune.

The 1922 Senior TT-winning Sunbeam still utilized rim brakes front and rear at a time when there was a definite move to small internal expanding brakes. The latter allowed riders to make greater use of the front brake and so reduce their lap times, whereas they often did not bother to use the stirrup type due to its ineffectiveness. A few makes continued to use a contracting band brake on the rear.

As manufacturers moved to planning their machinery for the 1923 TT, more were using aluminium alloy pistons, while two-strokes were leading the way with aluminium cylinder heads. Some perhaps considered following the example of the 1922 Sun Vitesse, which had an aluminium head and an aluminium barrel surrounding a cast iron liner. It also had basic crankcase rotary-valve induction.

There was a move to mechanical lubrication of four-strokes, although some retained a 'manually' pumped drip-feed as back-up. This was sometimes foot-operated. That sort of caution also extended to those running ohv engines, with riders known to carry spare pushrods during a race.

Gearboxes were almost all three-speed with hand-change, but the two-speed Scotts utilized foot-change, while some Nortons were fitted with a form of foot-change that lacked any positive-stop mechanism. Primary drive was by exposed chain, and most clutches were exposed to counter the build-up of heat in use.

Component suppliers continued to develop their products for increased performance and reliability. This extended to chains, carburettors, tyres, sparking plugs and magnetos. In respect of the latter, ignition was universally by way of high-tension magneto. Suppliers were keen to get top riders using their products so that they could advertise successes, while riders were happy to have their names associated with components in return for retainers and performance-related bonus payments from the trade.

Elements such as frames showed much variation between makes, and the TT course often revealed shortcomings in their designs, both in terms of handling characteristics and in strength. Fractured frames were common. Front suspension was by girder forks and links, incorporating a simple coil-spring allowing limited movement. Although rear suspension was occasionally tried, it had never been seen on any of the front runners.

Race machines still ran with single touring-type saddles. If riders tried to adopt more of a crouched style to lessen wind resistance, this was usually achieved by sliding rearwards onto the back mudguard.

Lubrication was generally by vegetable-based castor oils. Perhaps as a result of the high speeds being obtained

Pratt's Motor Spirit – one of several fuel suppliers of the 1920s.

at Brooklands on the stripped-for-speed machines used there, some TT competitors followed their example and used alcohol-based fuels in the search for more power.

In their search for more speed, manufacturers often copied the performance-enhancing modifications of others and, when combined with their own improvements, this served to accelerate the year-on-year gains in performance of racing motorcycles.

RACERS

Since the TT's inception it had been commonplace for manufacturers to try out their newest development during the races. If successful, then the modification or improvement would usually be incorporated in the following year's road-going models. However, by 1923 there was a feeling that the machines produced to challenge for a Tourist Trophy had lost their previous connection to 'the ideal touring motorcycle' for which the event was originally created. They had, instead, become close to out-and-out racing motorcycles. Writing some fifty years later in his book *Racing Round the Island*, Bob Holliday attributed a change of emphasis at the event to the impact of Alec Bennett's 59.99mph lap in 1922, saying, 'Dramatically, from being a happy-go-lucky, free-for-all sporting adventure, the TT had become serious, professional business. And there was money in it!'

Use of specialized race machinery widened the performance gap between the top men and ordinary runners and also took manufacturers down the expensive road of having to establish race departments to be in with a chance of

Harry Harris and his AJS speed towards Tower Bends above Ramsey to take second place in the 1923 Junior TT.

success. Of the increased speeds that followed, Bob Holliday wrote, 'it was the speed aspect which gave the TT a new life, transforming it into a spectacle irresistible to millions who have fallen under the spell of its unique, magical attraction'.

ADVENTURE

The TT has always been a great adventure for both riders and spectators. Even getting to the island was exciting for those with everyday working lives. Racers would mostly take their bikes by train to Liverpool and push them from the ferry terminal to the landing stage, for support vans were a rarity. Spectators would ride their bikes to the ferry from all over Britain. One persuasive advertisement of the time rather underestimated the problems associated with effecting passage by telling them:

> There is no difficulty whatsoever in getting the motorcycle aboard at Liverpool, and plenty of porters are available should no pals be present to assist up the gangway at high tide. It is less easy to get it ashore at Douglas, but here again there are porters in plenty, though it is wise to fix a fee with them before giving the order.

There was no mention of how steep those gangplanks could be at certain states of the tide, nor of how slippery they could become.

Once aboard, passengers hoped for a smooth crossing. Unfortunately, a lot of the sailings were anything but, and

with many of the bikes making the trip on the open decks, most riders were glad when that part of their TT adventure was over.

TUNERS

Manufacturing concerns who supported the TT varied greatly in size and this often dictated how they went about their racing. Some would set aside a small area at their works and divert a few of their most skilled workers to preparing bikes for the TT in the weeks leading up to the event, while a select few could afford a permanent race department. There were even some small businesses who took production bikes to the island and used the two weeks of practice to turn them into race-ready machines.

When it comes to speed, there have always been individuals who have been able to take a motorcycle and make it go faster than identical machines from the same maker. Sometimes those men were to be found working for a particular manufacturer, but often they worked on a freelance basis. In the 1920s, many based themselves at Brooklands, which was a hive of racing, development, testing and record-breaking. Previous mention has been made of Norton's ace tuner, Dan O'Donovan, and among others who achieved fame as tuners in the 1920s were Bert Le Vack, Bill Lacey, Dougal Marchant, 'Woolly' Worters and Nigel Spring. Men like Le Vack, who worked for several companies during the decade, had been top racers. All had their tuning secrets, which might relate to carburation, ignition, valve gear, fly-wheels or other components. They would even have pistons, valves, springs and the like specially made out of the newest metals of the day. It was all part of their never-ending search for the speed and reliability that would bring their machines home at the head of the field and thus earn the retainers and bonus payments from the trade that gave them a living.

1923: IMPROVEMENTS AND DEVELOPMENTS

Every TT brings new mechanical developments, and in 1923 Douglas had redesigned their flat-twin engine, while Matchless returned to the event with a 350cc overhead camshaft (ohc) model. Long-time supporters of the event, Indian, also brought a new model, which the book *Franklin's Indians* described as 'a purpose designed TT machine'. The man behind it was former TT competitor

Charles Franklin, an Irishman who had been chief designer at Indian's Springfield factory for several years. It sported an upright single-cylinder sv engine and, maybe, this was the 500cc Indian that would deliver the 85mph top speed that rider Freddie Dixon had been claiming from his American mount for several years previously.

As well as mechanical developments, most TTs feel the benefit of course improvements. For 1923, the approach to Braddan Bridge had been widened, while the notorious Sulby Bridge had been widened, flattened and tar-sprayed. So, come the racing and everyone expected the 60mph barrier to be smashed, but it was not to be. Adverse weather for the Senior race saw local man Tom Sheard use his course knowledge to cope with thick mist on the Mountain and ride his Douglas to victory at 55.55mph from fellow Douglas rider Jim Whalley. Freddie Dixon managed third on his new Indian racer, in what was the Indian factory's last appearance at the TT. In better weather, new records were set in the Junior won by nineteen-year-old Stanley Woods on a Cotton; and in the Lightweight, where Jock Porter was victorious on his New Gerrard. Setting the fastest laps in those two races were two very quick riders of the day – Jimmy Simpson (AJS), who pushed the Junior record up to 59.59mph, but fell off on Bray Hill after tangling with a slower rider, and Wal Handley (OK) who managed 53.95mph in the Lightweight. Those three debutantes of the 1922 races, Woods, Handley and Simpson, put in quality performances to finish the 1923 TT with a win and two fastest laps between them.

SIDECARS

New in 1923 was a race for sidecars of up to 600cc, run over three laps. Victory went to the versatile Freddie Dixon (Douglas) at a race average speed of 53.15mph. Norton at last adopted overhead valves and Graham Walker rode one to a close second place, while Harold Langman (Scott) set the fastest lap at 54.69mph. All three were also accomplished solo competitors.

A sidecar outfit enters the dip at Governor's Bridge.

In his role as a solo rider, Graham Walker, while welcoming the increased use of tar-surfacing on the island's roads, expressed reservations about racing over it in the wet, saying of 1923, 'the newly tarred sections of road, which we had blessed in the fair-weather practising, became death traps'. Presumably this was because they became polished and slippery. Ironically, he had previously told how the extreme demands of racing over the unmade Sulby Straight had made him physically sick.

THE 'AMATEUR' RACES

The Manx Motor Cycle Club had sought to run a one-lap race for amateur riders at the TT in the early 1920s, but the ACU would not agree to it. However, the idea of a locally

The sort of young rider keen to contest an early 'Amateur' race.

organized race did not go away and it gained support when the ACU threatened to take the TT races to Belgium for 1922. That did not happen, but the Manx MCC pressed ahead and organized the first Manx Amateur Road Race Championship over the Mountain Course in September 1923. It was an event that was completely separate from the TT and one that sought to distance itself from the growing commercialization, professionalism and specialization of the TT. With a change of title to the Manx Grand Prix in 1930, it runs to this day.

COMMERCIALIZATION

In contrast to the ideals of the Amateur races run by the Manx MCC – which itself had difficulties with defining and enforcing the term 'amateur' – The Isle of Man Times wrote in 1924, 'Let us rid our minds, once and for all, that the TT races are sport. They are not. That idea was exploded years ago, when the present regime of the ACU came into power. The whole series of races is purely and simply a business or commercial proposition.' That local newspaper was merely stating what was obvious to the motorcycle manufacturers, hoteliers, the motorcycle press, the Steam Packet Company, local charabanc owners, publicans, Isle of Man Government and the many other concerns who experienced financial gain from the TT. And it was nothing new, for as far back as 1913, when the races seemed in jeopardy following the manufacturers' boycott of the 1912 event, columnist 'Ixion' of The Motor Cycle wrote, 'The future of the TT is primarily a financial question'.

Concentration on the commercial aspects by some elements involved in the TT has not prevented generations of road racing enthusiasts from looking upon the event as a great sporting occasion. They learned to love the course, the top racers became their heroes, the winning makes of machine went to the top of their wish lists and they were happy to part with their hard-earned cash to support the event. The TT was an annual adventure in speed for them, as it was for those who competed. That is the way it was in the 1920s and, fortunately, that is the way it is today.

1924: SMOOTHER TIMES

The relationship between the TT organizers and the Isle of Man authorities was still a precarious one, with the ACU making it known that they would like to move the event to England, where it would make them money – although parliamentary approval would be necessary to close public roads – while the Manx authorities showed their dislike of the ACU by giving minimum support in the many areas where their cooperation was required. Fortunately, there were people on the island prepared to work for the benefit of the TT, including elements of the press. They acted as intermediaries and in April came a report, 'Manx authorities drop their hostile policy and intend to give every assistance to the ACU'. This was followed by an article in The Isle of Man Times saying, 'The value of these events is now realized. They are the Island's best advertising medium…'.

A race for 175cc machines was introduced in 1924 and they were classed as Ultra Lightweights. One novel feature was that the sixteen entries were despatched via a massed start for their three-lap race. The Lightweight race had nineteen entries, Junior fifty-six, Senior thirty-three and Sidecar nine. The low figures for some of those races meant there were hardly enough machines to retain spectator interest over a 37¾-mile lap, although the acrobat antics of sidecar passengers while cornering certainly served to entertain. Due to the introduction of the extra class, the first rider away in practice left at 4.15am if it was light enough.

Much money had been spent on the course and it was almost all tar-sprayed. Riders were loud in their praise for its condition, but still spoke of some 'looseness' in places on the Mountain, which was also affected by long, shallow ruts, which they called 'tramlines'.

On the run-up to the TT there were the customary claims of new and exotic racing engines under construction, but their manufacturers sometimes deemed it prudent not to subject them to this most demanding of events. Instead, they brought modified versions of the ones used in 1923. Press reports of the day told of 'engine efficiency having reached a high pitch', although it was a time when a compression ratio of 7:1 was still considered too high for a 500 on ordinary petrol.

While larger firms built and developed their own engines, smaller concerns used proprietary power units from the likes of JAP, Blackburne and Bradshaw, who produced special versions for competition use. It was not unusual for seven or eight different makes of motorcycle to be using JAP engines in a TT race.

HANDLING AND BRAKING

It was mentioned in Chapter 1 how in the early years of Mountain Course use, manufacturers recognized the need to develop the handling qualities of their frames and forks to cope with the poor condition of the course and with increasing power outputs. That need was just as important in the post-1920 period, when improving road conditions allowed the use of greater power and so put more demands on road-holding. Development in such areas then required brakes to be uprated to cope with the higher speeds. Stopping was a hot topic in 1924, for it was realized that after power and handling, better braking could win a race. Internal expanding brakes were now the norm, and not only were drums getting larger – although still only averaging about 6in in diameter – but firms like Matador and DOT were fitting two to the front wheel and one to the rear. Again it was an area for experimentation, particularly in the search for suitable brake lining material. Most attached this to the shoes, which then bore onto the inside of the metal drums, but Webb produced fabric-lined drums and plain cast iron shoes, while Douglas continued with their experimental disc brake from 1923, which had the friction material fixed to the disc, with a v-shaped metal 'pad' bearing upon it.

RECORD-BREAKING

Riders of the day seemed to agree that, with its 80mph approach speed, Hillberry was the fastest corner on the TT course. Taking this sweeping uphill right-hander as fast as they dared, they would seek to ride a classic line from the left on the approach to clip the apex on the right and then run out to the left, avoiding running too far because of the adverse camber, loose material and substantial earth bank on the exit. With its long approach, it was a bend that gave them time to build-up the necessary 'bottle' to take it on their personal limits. Apart from riding ability, speed was also governed by the solid bank on the apex, which jutted further into the road then than it does today. Some of the top riders were asked to estimate their speed through Hillberry and responded as follows: Alec Bennett 60mph, Freddie Dixon 55–60mph, Graham Walker 55mph, George Dance 54–55mph, Tom Sheard 50–55mph.

Only the previous year, when the bend had still to be properly surfaced, a very impressed onlooker had described

Tommy de la Hay tackles a loose-surfaced Hillberry on his Sunbeam.

Stanley Woods drifting through during his winning ride in the Junior race and 'throwing up a bow-wave of dirt and stone from his wheels. All through this giant slide at perhaps 60mph he was rock steady, master of his machine and himself.'

That described the fastest corner, but what about the racing in 1924? Well, that too was the fastest, so much so that it is no exaggeration to describe race and lap records as having been 'smashed'. Edwin Twemlow (New Imperial) lifted the Lightweight lap record from 53.95mph to 58.28mph, while in the Junior race his brother Kenneth brought another New Imperial into first place and Jimmy Simpson lifted the lap record from 59.59mph to an incredible 64.54mph. So fast was Simpson's best Junior lap that it exceeded the new lap record of 63.75mph set by Freddie Dixon during his ride to third place in the Senior race. That was won by Alec Bennett on a Norton, which, while still largely based on their standard Model 18, had been revitalized by the newly appointed Walter Moore. It was the company's first solo TT win since 1907. The new Ultra Lightweights did their best to join this festival of speed, with Jock Porter taking victory on his New Gerrard and setting the fastest lap at 52.61mph. Only in the Sidecar race was the previous record not broken, Freddie Dixon's fastest lap falling slightly short of the 1923 figure and George Tucker taking another victory for Norton, using a four-speed gearbox of their own design.

IN CONTROL

In what was his third year at the TT, Jimmy Simpson was developing a reputation for being a fast rider capable of setting lap records, but unable to bring his machine to the finish. It was an unwanted reputation that was to grow through the rest of the 1920s and into the 1930s. By contrast, in winning his second Senior TT, Alec Bennett showed signs of why he would end the decade as one of the most successful and respected TT riders. Of his Senior ride in 1924, Bennett told how he took absolutely no chances during the race and how he did not use more than three-quarter throttle for the first four laps. Thereafter he slightly increased his pace in order to keep second-placed man Harold Langman (Scott) at bay and finally triumphed by a margin of 1½ minutes.

To speedy Jimmy Simpson went the glory of being the fastest over one lap, but to Alec Bennett went victory, the right to hold aloft the magnificent Senior Tourist Trophy in front of cheering crowds and the substantial winning bonuses from his entrant and the trade. Norton were justifiably pleased with the result and with the subsequent increase in demand for the Model 18 roadsters, priced at £80.

Racing through Laurel Bank in the early 1920s, over narrow, loosely surfaced roads with overhanging hedges.

A catalogue illustration of the Norton Model 18 of the mid-1920s.

This was the expression used to describe the increased dynamism of the decade's social, artistic and cultural activities and it was also applicable to the racing of motorcycles at the TT, particularly in the middle years.

Things were moving on apace in several directions at the Island races, with the whole of the Mountain Course finally tar-sprayed and qualifying times in the Lightweight, Junior and Senior classes reduced to 55, 50 and 45 minutes. AJS came with a 500cc engine, firms like Velocette, Norton and New Hudson adopted dry sump lubrication, and more responsive engines encouraged the occasional use of twist-grip throttles. Wired-on tyres fitted to well-base rims were in general use and ever more technical advances were incorporated in the twenty-seven makes of machine entered for the five TT races of 1925.

The man who came roaring back to form in 1925 was Howard Davies, abetted by record-breaking performances from Wal Handley, Jimmy Simpson, Edwin Twemlow and, on three-wheels, Len Parker. Davies' previous TT performances included second place in his first TT of 1914, plus first and second places in 1921. However, the six races in which he rode between 1922 and 1924 brought six retirements. Tired of this, he set to after the 1924 event to build his own idea of what a motorcycle should be, giving the finished product his initials, HRD. Aimed at the higher end of the roadster market and priced accordingly, it was no surprise when he brought racing versions to the island, for himself and employee 'Harry' Harris to tackle the Junior and Senior races.

Regarded by the press as 'a dark horse' with his brand new black-and-gold racers, Davies had the advantage of being chosen by tuner Bert Le Vack to use his specially prepared pushrod JAP racing engines, and he proved a shrewd choice. Taking a fine second place to Wal Handley

It was difficult for a rider to control a race from the front in the 1920s, for he only received information on his position during pit stops. It was the New Imperial team that introduced a basic flag-signalling system for its riders as they passed the pits on a non-stop lap. In essence, if a red flag was shown from the 'New Imp' pit the rider was being told to go faster, while if a yellow was displayed, things were OK and he was to maintain the same pace.

Amongst the newcomers to the 1924 TT races was Irishman Joe Craig. He was a man who was to exercise considerable control over the racing activities of the Norton marque in later years.

Howard Davies is carried shoulder-high after his victory in the 1925 TT. Howard's left hand is resting on the shoulder of tuner Bert Le Vack.

in the Junior, where Handley lifted the race average speed by almost 10mph to 65.02mph and raised the lap record to 65.89mph, Davies shocked the established opposition in the Blue Riband Senior TT by riding his new machine to victory at a race average speed of 66.13mph, leaving the speedy Jimmy Simpson to take the lap record at 68.97mph but again fail to record a finish.

Howard Davies raced in some style, for a report of the time told how at his pit stop he 'had a hurried drink of champagne and went off again feeling quite refreshed'.

The 1925 TT was run in front of record crowds and proved a triumph for single-cylinder proprietary engines, with only Len Parker's sidecar-winning Douglas twin being fitted with the maker's own power unit. The HRD was typical of the small concerns of the time, having a JAP engine, Burman gearbox, Binks carburettor, Webb forks and with hubs, rims, magneto, mudguards, chains, tyres, plugs and so on also supplied by others. In the case of the HRD, this assembly of components was backed by a sound basic design, resulting in a motorcycle that was also attractive to the eye, with its early use of the saddle-type petrol tank rather than the customary flat-tank mounted under the top frame rail.

1926: EVER FASTER

Come 1926, the Sidecar TT was dropped from the programme of races due, some say, to manufacturers' opposition to the gymnastics performed by passengers while cornering, which was totally out of step with how they wished sidecar outfits to be portrayed to the buying public. The

Ultra Lightweights were also dropped, in their case due to lack of entries and thus lack of spectacle. This left a three-race TT meeting, for 500cc Senior, 350cc Junior and 250cc Lightweight machines.

Since the TT restarted after the First World War, it had taken just five years for the Senior lap record to climb from 55.62mph in 1920 to 68.97mph in 1925, an increase of some 25 per cent. The Junior lap record had increased by nearly 30 per cent over the same period, and the Lightweights' by 40 per cent. One effect of those improved race and lap times was to narrow the differential between classes, with times set by the Juniors not far behind the Seniors. As people were no longer protesting about 500s being too fast for the course, it seemed clear that the speed of the 350s had been increasing at a greater rate than the 500s', for which estimated maximum speeds of 90mph were now being quoted.

Many would conclude from these figures that motorcycles were growing increasingly successful in challenging the TT course, but that would not be the view of half, and sometimes two-thirds, of the entry, who customarily failed to finish a race. The 1926 Senior TT saw twenty-two finishers out of fifty-seven starters, which indicated that while there may have been progress in many directions, the Mountain Course was still a formidable adversary. So much so, that there was opposition to the decision to increase the race distance from six to seven laps for all classes in 1926 – which amounted to 264½ racing miles. As well as taxing the machines, the extra lap meant another 30-plus minutes in the saddle for riders; on the eve of the 1926 TT the fastest lap time stood to Jimmy Simpson in 32 minutes 50 seconds, at a speed of 68.97mph.

NO ALCOHOL

In the mid-1920s the world was already beginning to question where future supplies of petrol were to come from, and alcohol was being spoken of as a potential substitute. Indeed, several countries of the British Commonwealth were identified as able to grow crops on the scale needed to allow alcohol to be derived from them in large quantities. Despite that, a decision was taken to ban the use of alcohol-based fuels at the 1926 TT, meaning that only petrol and petrol/benzole mixtures were permitted. This meant using lower compression ratios than with alcohol, and works Nortons were running at 6.4:1.

The effect of the ban was mixed. JAP engines were probably affected more than most, for much of their development was done at Brooklands, where the use of alcohol was common. Certainly, the JAP name was not so often seen among the top finishers in subsequent TTs, although the closing of their race department at the end of 1925 on economic grounds and the consequent loss of Bert Le Vack may have been contributory factors. They continued to supply engines for racing.

FOREIGN ENTRIES

There had been a few foreign machines contesting the TT in the early 1920s, such as a team of Peugeots from France in 1924, but in 1926 the Italian concerns Garelli, Bianchi and Moto Guzzi were present with entries spread across the three classes. Bianchi ohc models gained a praiseworthy three finishes in the Junior race, but Garelli, with what was said to be a 350cc twin-piston, single-cylinder, two-stroke machine, did not finish the race. Moto Guzzi's Pietro Ghersi was entered in the Senior and Lightweight races. He failed to complete the Senior but came home in second place in the Lightweight, only to be controversially 'excluded from the results'.

The Bianchi team that contested the 1926 TT.

BONUS PAYMENTS

The reason for Ghersi's exclusion was that he used an Italian Fert sparking plug rather than the Lodge make that he had specified at the weigh-in. Full details are lost in the mists of time, but one assumes that, before he weighed in, Lodge offered him a bonus payment based on results, but were then disappointed to find that he had not raced with their plug.

The whole business of bonus payments to riders from the trade was fraught with difficulties and accompanied by a fair amount of underhand tactics. Prize money at the time was modest but bonus payments were generous. Top riders

Stanley Woods' personal record of his earnings from winning the 1926 Senior TT.

would already be guaranteed financial retainers paid by the factory for whom they were racing and from the principal members of the trade like petrol, tyre, chain, carburettor and spark plug companies. For them, bonuses were the icing on the cake.

Reproduced here is Stanley Woods' summary of the income he received after winning the 1926 Senior TT, courtesy of David Crawford, author of *Stanley Woods – The World's First Motorcycle Superstar*. Everybody loves a winner and these various suppliers did to the tune of £1,631, a figure that amounts to some £88,500 at today's values.

The issue of bonus payments was a problem to the trade. At regular intervals they would come to agreement amongst themselves to limit payments, then someone would break ranks and the spiral would start again. Such monies certainly oiled the wheels of racing in the 1920s.

Spectators could watch the 1926 races from the new permanent TT Grandstand, set about 200 yards further back along the Glencrutchery Road from St Ninian's Crossroads. New pits and start areas were also provided in front of the Grandstand.

It was a year in which British manufacturers brought their latest developments to the island – Rudge 4-valve heads, Triumph with new engines, Sunbeam double-hairpin valve springs and Blackburne a V-twin engine for Rex-Acme. In addition, entry numbers were good, racing was excellent and records were broken in all classes. Stanley Woods set a new race average speed with his first win on a Norton in the Senior, but it was that man Jimmy Simpson who set the fastest lap, becoming the first to break the 70mph barrier at 70.43mph, although, yet again, he failed to finish the race on his AJS. Although Jimmy Simpson did not finish many of his races, manufacturers did put value on one of their riders setting the fastest lap, so he would usually be forgiven for failing to finish. However, AJS were not too pleased that he put the con rod through the crankcases in that 1926 Senior.

The reliable Alec Bennett took race and lap records in the Junior on a Velocette, the first TT victory for an ohc engine. The 'Velo' engine was in its second year at the TT and was said by factory employee and rider Fred Povey to produce 20bhp on a compression ratio of 7:1. It was also an important moment in the history of Veloce Ltd, which built both future sales and competition activity on the reputation gained from that first TT win.

'Paddy' Johnston led home a Cotton one, two and three in the Lightweight. Strangely, although having been 'excluded from the results' of the Lightweight race, which is not the same as being disqualified, Pietro Ghersi received official recognition of his new lap record of 63.12mph, a fine achievement for a newcomer to the course.

Senior winner, Stanley Woods, later told Mick Woollett of his Norton, 'I'd say that the top speed was about 90mph … the output was 30 horsepower or so'. Indications of Norton power

A rider passes through Crosby in 1926 in the upright riding position used by most at the time.

output in later years suggest that Stanley was over-optimistic on output in 1926 but about right on speed.

CONDITIONS

Given the high race speeds achieved in 1926, it is perhaps surprising to hear that riders were critical of the state of the course when practice started. Specifically, they were concerned that loose chippings were nullifying the benefits of earlier work to surface roads and ease bends. Such chippings, which were substantially larger than the ones used

This 1927 photo at the Bungalow shows the extent of loose chippings at the roadsides.

in today's surface dressing, were spread after the roads had been tar-sprayed and their incorporation into the wearing surface was a bit hit and miss. It also sounds as though the Highway Board may have been a bit late with its course preparation on the run-up to the 1926 races, but 37¾ miles of road is a lot of road to sweep – and, of course, much of it did not get swept.

In most places, the roads were still not as wide as they are today and what we would see as lack of maintenance resulted in vegetation overhanging road edges. In addition, the outer margins of the road would get covered in the loose chippings thrown there by the passage of vehicles. The result was to narrow the effective riding line, making it particularly dangerous to be carried out wide on bends and also restricting opportunities for overtaking. Mechanical road-sweepers and verge trimmers were still something for the future.

THE REWARDS OF VICTORY

Proving the benefit of a TT win, the HRD concern experienced healthy sales of its road machines after taking victory

in the 1925 Senior and returned in 1926 with eight entries on new duplex cradle-framed models. The factory actually brought eleven machines to the island and announced that after the racing they would all be offered for sale at full list price. As an indication of the way that speeds were increasing on road and track, HRD's HD 90 model was marketed as a 90mph roadster.

During the mid-1920s, several manufacturers found that the combination of increased speeds and use of larger brakes created front fork and brake problems. This was typical of the lessons learnt from going TT racing with ever faster motorcycles.

1927: COMMUNICATION

The world of the late 1920s was very different from today when it came to publicizing and reporting on the TT. Radio was in its infancy, telephones were for the privileged and most relied on the printed word, principally those in the weekly magazines *The Motor Cycle* and *Motor Cycling*. New at the 1927 event was the newspaper *The TT Special*. Containing full race reports and edited by 1922 Lightweight TT winner Geoff Davison, it appeared for sale on the island immediately after each race and could be posted anywhere in the world. Later to include editions covering each practice session, it went on to become a TT institution.

The mainstream national press largely ignored the TT unless they wished to criticize it, and in 1927 occurred a tragedy that they seized on. Practice sessions were still early morning and run over roads that were not closed to normal traffic. During one of those sessions, 22-year-old Archie Birkin met a fish van heading towards him near Rhencullen and, swerving to avoid it, he crashed and was killed. The Birkin family was well known and his death was widely reported.

The ACU had been asking for roads to be closed during practice for many years, but the island had resisted it. How-

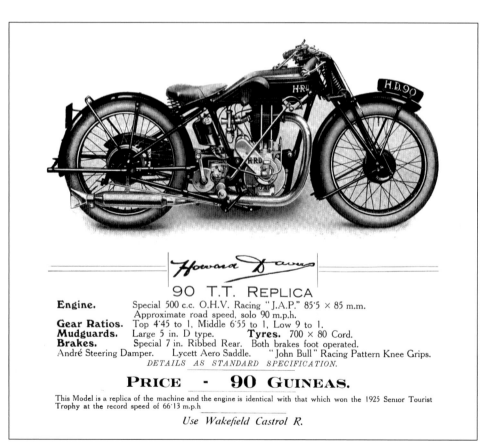

90 T.T. REPLICA

Engine. Special 500 c.c. O.H.V. Racing "J.A.P." 85·5 × 85 m.m.
Approximate road speed, solo 90 m.p.h.
Gear Ratios. Top 4·45 to 1, Middle 6·55 to 1, Low 9 to 1.
Mudguards. Large 5 in. D type. **Tyres.** 700 × 80 Cord.
Brakes. Special 7 in. Ribbed Rear. Both brakes foot operated.
André Steering Damper. Lycett Aero Saddle. "John Bull" Racing Pattern Knee Grips.
DETAILS AS STANDARD SPECIFICATION.

PRICE - 90 GUINEAS.

This Model is a replica of the machine and the engine is identical with that which won the 1925 Senior Tourist Trophy at the record speed of 66·13 m.p.h.

Use Wakefield Castrol R.

Claiming to be a replica of the machine that won the 1925 Senior TT, this is the Howard Davies 90 TT Replica of 1926.

ever, Archie Birkin's death changed opinions and the annual Road Closing Orders for the races were extended to cover practice periods from the following year – 1928. The bend where he fell is now known to TT followers as Birkins.

TOO EASY?

Further course improvements in 1927 included substantial widening of Braddan Bridge, allowing it to be taken at approaching 50mph and, according to Wal Handley, saving several seconds on lap times.

Perhaps while sitting comfortably at his desk, a staff member of *The Motor Cycle* wrote in 1927, 'if more road improvements are carried out the value of the races will be seriously decreased'. He was entitled to his view, but it was not shared by riders who had to race for seven laps. Top runners on 500cc machines were in the saddle for just under four strenuous hours. Lesser 500 riders took much longer and riders of 250s took longer still.

The roads of the TT course may have been tar-sprayed in their entirety, but in many cases this was done over existing surfaces with very basic foundations. While they were certainly an improvement over the earlier unmade roads, the wear caused by growth in ordinary traffic and increase in race speeds accentuated bumps, of which there were plenty. Oliver Langton rode to seventh place in the 1927 Senior race and told how course conditions were such that he had to summon all his courage on the very bumpy Cronk y Voddy straight, before taking a hand off the handlebar to operate the hand gearchange of his New Hudson. On such rigid-framed machines with basic girder front forks, it was still a physical challenge to ride ever faster over roads that were nowhere near today's standard in width, finish and smoothness.

EASING THE PACE

There was an influx of ohc motors to the 1927 TT to join the forerunners of previous years, including examples from Blackburne, AJS and Norton. The new Walter Moore-designed 500cc CS1 engine from Norton was allocated to previous Senior TT winners Alec Bennett and Stanley Woods to race, while two ohv engines were used by the other Norton works entries, Joe Craig and Jimmy Shaw. The 1927 Nortons also came with a new cradle frame, 8in-diameter brake drums front and rear and a new saddle tank. The new ohc engine was said to be capable of 95mph and, when timed on Sulby Straight, Stanley Woods clocked 93.7mph.

The customary setting of new record race and lap speeds continued across all classes in 1927, but in the Junior and Senior races the pace of increase eased to about 1mph,

Alec Bennett rode his new CS1-engined Norton to victory in the 1927 Senior TT. The other rider in leathers (standing) is his Norton team mate Jimmy Shaw.

rather than the 5mph lifts of the major road-surfacing years of the early to mid-1920s. The new ohc Norton delivered a win in the Senior, where Stanley Woods looked as though he was going to walk away with victory on the new model until, with a lead of several minutes, he struck clutch trouble and saw first place go to team mate Alec Bennett. This made Bennett the only man to win Senior TT races with sv, ohv and ohc engines. To Woods went the fastest lap of 70.90mph, while second place went to rising star Jimmy Guthrie on a New Hudson.

Freddie Dixon took victory in the Junior on a JAP-powered HRD. Working for JAP at the time, there was no doubt that Dixon hand-picked and prepared his engine to ensure that it was the best available. Lightweight victory went to Wal Handley (Rex-Acme), and here the increase in race average speed was greater, rising by some 5 per cent from 60.20 to 63.30mph, with Luigi Archangeli (Moto Guzzi) finishing second.

Racing motorcycles of this era were not fitted with rev counters and riders had to estimate when to change gear, or wait for valve-float, something which the increasingly common ohc design helped to reduce with its better control of opening and closing of valves.

1928: ROADS CLOSED

Come the 1928 TT, riders welcomed the new closing of roads to other traffic during practice periods, which were spread over twelve days. Such an extended period could be hard on race machinery and some riders used 'hack' machines in the early stages – Stanley Woods told of using a Model 18, on which he said, 'I got a lot of laps in at quite high speed … later in practising I switched to my race machine' – while factories would sometimes use last year's race models. Unusually, the island was blessed with good weather for the entire practice period. Not everything was perfect, however, with riders reporting the roads to be bumpy.

Experienced onlookers detected improved road-holding as a feature of practice, particularly on corners. No doubt further attention had been given to frame design and by now there was a general adoption of saddle-tanks and low seat height. Velocette experimented with rear-springing, said to be 'built under Draper patents' and involving exposed, inclined springs under the seat giving some 3 inches of movement. They increased rear tyre size from 2.75 to 3.00 and also introduced a positive-stop foot gearchange, for their four-speed gearbox. Similar positive-stop change mechanisms were adopted by most manufacturers in following years. As well as doing away with the need for a rider to take his hand off the handle-bars while changing gear, they allowed a quicker change and thus saved the rider more seconds a lap. It really was difficult to keep track of the many gradual machine improvements, each one contributing to the chipping away of lap times.

A WET SENIOR RACE

In the late 1920s TT races were always run to their scheduled times, whatever the weather. There was no question of delaying the start by an hour to allow mist to clear from the Mountain or to let the roads dry. When the customary maroon was discharged at the start, no. 1 pushed off for some four hours of racing, followed by the remainder of the field at specified intervals.

There had been relatively few wet TT races, but the 1928 Senior was a shocker, with rain for most of the time. Victory went to Charlie Dodson (Sunbeam), even though he had a major fall at Keppel Gate on lap six and split his crash helmet from top to bottom. That spill lost him the lead to Graham Walker (Rudge), but the Rudge failed with less than half a lap to go. Dodson came home the winner, trailing the rear stand broken in his crash. Two other new names amongst the placemen were George Rowley (AJS) in second and Tommy Hatch (Scott) in third. Almost inevitably, the fastest lap went to Jimmy Simpson (AJS), but race and lap speeds were well down from those set in dry conditions. The Junior was won by Alec Bennett on a Velocette and he broke both race average and lap records by a small amount, his new race record being faster than that set in the previous year's Senior and the lap record going over 70mph, for the first time for a 350. It was his fifth TT victory – another

record for the time. Frank Longman won the Lightweight on an OK-Supreme at slightly less than the previous year's record-breaking speeds.

STRIP-DOWN

After each race, it was a requirement for the engines of the first three finishers to be stripped and measured in the presence of race officials. The press were also given an opportunity to view the dismantled engines and they published the results of what they saw, making comment on valve springs, piston rings, carbon deposits and piston colour, plus further observations about the state of chains, brakes, tyres, oil tightness and so on. After the 1928 Senior, both the first and second place Sunbeams were seen to have broken piston rings.

The experienced AJS concern did not have to submit their engines after the Junior race, for, having made a late decision to change the make of valve springs, five AJS machines retired from the race with broken springs.

SPEED OR TIME?

While year on year changes and improvements to the Mountain Course continued to help reduce the time taken to complete a lap, after the major road-surfacing programme of 1923–5 it was the better engines, improved handling, stronger braking and general machine improvements that contributed most to the speed increases of the late 1920s.

There was no doubt that the primary TT interest of the press, spectators and post-race advertising was in the speeds achieved. During the 1920s this information was conveyed by the published lap speeds and race average speeds and it was from those that the public deduced what happened in a race, using the figures to fuel their imaginations as to the skill and daring shown on track. For all the concentration on speed, there was little hard information as to actual speed achieved at specific locations, and when speeds were mentioned, they were usually estimated. As an example, most people recognized that the drop from the Fifth Milestone to The Highlander was one of the fastest parts of the course, although in 1929 it was neither as straight nor as smooth as it is today. A report in *Motor Cycling* at the time concluded, 'generally speaking, of the faster machines – and many were doing about 95 to 100mph – the Nortons seemed to be the steadiest'. It went on to describe Stanley Woods' and Jimmy Simpson's treatment of the bumps there, telling how they 'executed prodigal aerial feats'. There were still plenty of locations on the course where machines became airborne and, over seven laps, each landing gave a severe test to the rigid-frames of the day.

Race and lap speeds were still climbing, but the really important information for riders came not from quoted speeds, but from their lap times. What they wanted to know after every practice lap or race was whether machine improvements and their riding skills had reduced the time taken to cover the 37¾ miles of the Mountain Course. For them, lap time was the benchmark, not lap speed. At the approach to the 1929 TT, the fastest lap times stood to Stanley Woods in the Senior class at 31 minutes 54 seconds (70.90mph) and to Alec Bennett in the Junior at 32 minutes 13 seconds (70.28mph). In the Lightweight it was shared by Frank Longman and Alec Bennett at 35 minutes and 8 seconds (64.45mph).

S. Jackson races through the narrow main street of Kirk Michael in 1929.

1929: END OF A DECADE

As practice opened for the 1929 TT, road conditions were said to be very good. Among the machine developments was a general stiffening of construction, which, as well as applying to frames and cycle parts, extended to things like webbing to crankcases and bulking-up of engine components. Such alterations were said to be required to cope with increased power and speed, although it was acknowledged that they increased overall machine weight.

As practice progressed, the road-holding of the works Norton, Sunbeam and Velocettes received praise, recorded lap speeds were high and accidents were few. It was not just increases in maximum speeds that were bringing faster lap speeds, for positive-stop foot-change mechanisms were spreading and were reckoned to save many seconds a lap. Also, Norton had at last moved from lever to twist-grip throttles and also claimed to have improved their engine pick-up, which saved further seconds when pulling away from tricky spots like Ramsey Hairpin and the Gooseneck.

On race day Charlie Dodson (Sunbeam) took his second Senior TT win in far better weather than his first win in 1928 and at a race average speed 10mph faster. While that provided a very real indication of how the weather can play havoc with race speeds, there must have been other factors involved; Dodson lopped 1 minute 7 seconds off the previous best lap time, which had also been set in the dry in 1927, raising the speed to 73.55mph. Sunbeam also took the team prize, for the third year in succession.

In only his second year at the TT, Freddie Hicks brought his Velocette home first in the Junior, reducing the lap time by 18 seconds and increasing the lap speed to 70.95mph. The 350s had narrowed the speed margin between themselves and the 500s in the second half of the 1920s, but it now looked as though the 500s were holding them at bay, with machines like the Norton CS1 reputed to give 28bhp and almost 100mph.

After a TT apprenticeship that started back in 1922, Syd Crabtree provided the Excelsior marque with its first TT victory in the 1929 Lightweight race. Still fitted with hand gearchange, the Excelsior did have four speeds and 8in-diameter brake drums, which were noticeably large for a 250. Pietro Ghersi led the race for five laps on his rapid Moto Guzzi before retiring, and he knocked 1 minute 10 seconds off the previous fastest lap time, setting a new figure of 66.63mph.

SPEEDS

Before leaving the 1920s, a look at the growth in speeds achieved between 1920 and 1929 shows that it really justified the title of a speedy decade, for lap times increased every year in all classes except when affected by wet weather. Fastest lap speeds in the Senior class went from 55.62mph to 73.55mph, representing growth of 32 per cent. That was to be the highest percentage rate of growth in TT history for the class, much of it deriving from the vast improvement to road surfaces in the first half of the decade.

Henry Tyrell-Smith fell from his Rudge at Glen Helen when leading the 1929 Senior TT. After a delay, he remounted and carried on with three cracked ribs to take third place.

claimed that not all was well with the event and in the aftermath of the 1929 races, the respected and influential magazine *The Motor Cycle* questioned the future of the TT, using headlines like 'A Crisis in the History of the Sport' and even asking 'Will there be another TT?'

Looking back, it seems that *The Motor Cycle* could not come to terms with the fact that the nature of the TT had changed. No longer was the primary aim of competing manufacturers to develop their 'ideal touring motorcycles' from the machines they raced – which is what the TT was originally created for. Instead, they knew that the TT was by now a sporting spectacle of speed, for which they had to develop specialized racing models. Through the 1920s it had been seen that success in TT racing enhanced a manufacturer's name and brought increased sales of his road-going machines. Such a spin-off extended to more than just the winning marque, for a top ten placing was held in high regard and even entering the TT brought benefits to a manufacturer's image.

There was still knowledge to be gained from racing that could be used to the benefit of roadsters, but that was now seen as a bonus, rather than the primary purpose of competing. However, racing was an expensive business, and at the end of the 1920s the world was feeling the effect of an economic recession, which even a TT win could not overcome with increased sales. Some manufacturers could no longer afford to develop special race machines and perhaps it was those that *The Motor Cycle* had in mind when it advocated that the event be remodelled.

In the Junior and Lightweight classes, growth in speed over the decade was even greater at 38 and 55 per cent, respectively.

CRISIS?

Despite the limited opportunities available to publicize the TT in its early years, the Isle of Man was gradually becoming known as an island of speed and a TT win was held in high regard, even outside the world of motorcycling. Through the 1920s many of the manufacturers who achieved a Senior TT victory received a civic welcome and celebration when they returned to their home towns. There the Tourist Trophy, together with the race-winning machines and riders, were publicly fêted in recognition of the glory brought to the area by the win. However, despite its prestige, some

CHAPTER THREE

FAST FOREIGNERS

1930: BUSINESS AS USUAL

The Isle of Man regarded the Tourist Trophy races mainly as an enhancement to its tourist industry, as something to publicize the island's name to the wider world. To this end, in 1930 it belatedly offered financial support to the event, allocating a sum of £5,000, of which £3,500 went to attracting and paying the expenses of foreign riders and £1,500 to supplement prize money. The latter was set at £200 to the winning entrant and £50 to the winning rider, with entry fees of £33.

There were eleven 'foreign' entries, plus thirteen 'colonials' in 1930. They were part of the total entry of around 135 across the three races, to be run on Monday, Wednesday and Friday of race week. Almost all were riding British-built machines, with many on KTT Velocettes, which Bob Holliday described as the first 'over-the-counter' replicas of race-winning motorcycles to be marketed. The 'Velo' was an honest 350cc race bike of which Titch Allen wrote 'nothing was added for effect or for sales appeal and nothing was omitted for price cutting'.

Despite the previous year's suggestions by *The Motor Cycle* that radical change was required for the event, demand for rides in 1930 suggested that contestants were content with the existing arrangements. There were a few changes, however, the principal one being that practice was reduced from two weeks to nine days, with the first session being on a Thursday. All were early morning, even though the organizers had been asking to run evening sessions for several years.

There had been more road improvements, which would help to reduce lap times. Particularly beneficial was the substantial widening on the approach to Glen Helen, plus widening at Kirk Michael and through to Ballaugh. As well as making those stretches faster, it also created improved opportunities for overtaking, an important factor for top riders seeking to set good times. However, some of the time gain was probably lost by the reported poor road conditions at Bray Hill and Windy Corner. Also, riders told how there was a tendency for the tarred surfaces to soften on the racing line during the latter stages of a race, even at normal

Works to widen the approach to Glen Helen before the 1930 TT.

The 500cc JAP 500 twin-cylinder engine for 1930. Twin-cylinder entries were rare at the time.

temperatures. Road finishes were not so well developed as today and in hot weather exposed tar would melt, creating hazardous conditions to race over.

The Wolverhampton-built Sunbeam marque finished the 1920s with two consecutive Senior TT wins for Charlie Dodson, and he was back with his George Dance-tuned machine in 1930, looking for a hat trick. Norton had been absent from the podium places since Alec Bennett's Senior win in 1927, but with a much-modified ohc engine from Arthur Carroll and Joe Craig, they were hoping to get back to winning ways. Velocette had a longer-stroke engine, AJS returned with its chain-driven ohc models in both Senior and Junior classes, while, in addition to its single-cylinder engines, JAP had a 500cc twin available, which was used by the Excelsior, Cotton and OK Supreme concerns.

Magnesium alloy was starting to be used to save weight. There was also a trend for brake-drums to be ribbed to aid cooling, while the customary copper pipes that conducted oil and petrol around the outside of the engine were being replaced by armoured rubber versions to aid reliability. All contributed to the step-by-step improvements to racing motorcycles of the time; if they survived practice, such improvements would then be given the ultimate test of seven racing laps over the Mountain Course.

A RUDGE YEAR

Rudge had achieved an encouraging third place finish in the 1929 Senior race, their first time on the podium since Cyril Pullin's Senior TT win of 1914. For 1930 they came with their tried-and-tested 4-valve heads on Senior machines and an advanced radial 4-valve layout on Junior machines, which their designer and competition chief George Hack considered to be still experimental.

Practice gave an indication of what was to come and race time proved highly successful for Rudge. With his forceful riding style, Wal Handley stormed to victory in the Senior on one of the Coventry-built machines, setting new race and lap records, even though the weather deteriorated during the race. He was backed by Graham Walker, who took second place, with Jimmy Simpson (Norton) in third. In taking just 29 minutes 41 seconds to set the new outright lap record at 76.28mph, Handley became the first man to lap at under 30 minutes.

Using its experimental 350, Rudge went even better in the Junior race, taking the first three places with Henry Tyrell-Smith, Ernie Nott and Graham Walker, again with record race average and lap speeds, the former going to Tyrell-Smith and the latter to Ernie Nott at 72.20mph.

As ever in TT racing, most interest was generated by the Senior race, followed by the Junior, with the Lightweight bringing up the rear. The 1930 Lightweight completed a record-breaking year on the Island, with Jimmy Guthrie riding an AJS to first place and reducing the race time by 3¼ minutes, while Wal Handley took the fastest lap on his Rex-Acme, just beating Ghersi's record of 1929 with a new figure of 66.86mph.

After the success of Sunbeam racing motorcycles in the 1920s, which included four Senior TT wins, the company's best showing in 1930 was fourth place in the Senior for Charlie Dodson. In the words of Sunbeam expert Gordon Champ, 'this was to be the end of serious racing' by Sunbeam, who by then were owned by the industrial conglomerate ICI.

There is an old saying that 'racing improves the breed', and while the race machines of 1930 were moving away from models produced for the road, those manufacturers at the top of the racing tree, like Sunbeam, Rudge,

Wal Handley taking victory in the 1930 Senior TT in the wet. That road surface looks slippery!

Norton and AJS, were also producing very competent road-going motorcycles, whose performance, handling and reliability must have benefited from their TT racing experiences.

1931: MORE SPEED

The top manufacturers of 1930 returned for the 1931 TT, along with makes like OK-Supreme, Raleigh, Montgomery, Douglas, New Imperial and others, while among entries from abroad came FN, NSU, Moto Guzzi and Motosacoche. The fifty-eight entries for the Senior race, fifty-one for the Junior and forty-four for the Lightweight gave a total entry of 153, almost twenty more than in 1930.

Charlie Dodson takes Hillberry at speed in 1932.

Increased knowledge of combustion chamber shape and port design was yielding engines with more power, some of which were fitted with downdraught carburettors. The wider adoption of four-speed gearboxes helped make the best use of this power. The business of stopping was also subject to improvement, with larger-diameter ribbed drums and experiments with linked brakes. JAP engine development had been spurred in part by their participation in the new sport of dirt-track/speedway racing and their highly tuned singles were running 8:1 compression ratios and offering peak power at 6,000rpm.

To enable riders to 'get down to it', reduce wind resistance and take advantage of the increased power on offer, more machines were fitted with rear mudguard pads, and the occasional one with one-piece rearward saddle extensions. Pre-TT rumours of the appearance of supercharged engines in 1931 proved mostly unfounded, although Harold Willis did take a supercharged Velocette out for a lap during practice.

The general growth in speeds meant that mid-race mending of punctures and other roadside repairs were largely a thing of the past, particularly for potential winners. Race bikes no longer carried tool boxes, although some riders still thrust a couple of spare sparking plugs in a pocket and a plug spanner down a riding boot.

WHERE'S THAT?

The naming of parts of the course was not as clear as it is today and reports of the time saying that 'Glen Helen had been eased off at the top' and 'Creg Willey's Corner much widened', were both probably referring to works at

what today is known as Sarah's Cottage. One ACU official thought that particular 'easing' would save riders two or three seconds a lap, for it also included widening of Creg Wyllies. The stretch between Ballaugh and Sulby was said to have been relaid, while that from the Black Hut to Creg ny Baa had been resurfaced. At Brandish, the ditch on the outside had been filled and the road widened, and riders claimed they could now take it 8–10mph faster than before.

The last improvement contributed to riders achieving increased speed on the approach to Hillberry, which Graham Walker and Alec Bennett said was now 100mph, while Hillberry itself was taken at 70mph. Their opinions of speeds at other locations in 1931 were: Bray Hill 100mph, Quarter Bridge 35mph, Braddan Bridge 45–50mph, Ballacraine 40mph, Ballaugh Bridge 50mph, Sulby Bridge 45mph, the Bungalow 40mph, Windy Corner 50mph, Kate's Cottage (they still called it Keppel Gate) 80mph and Creg ny Baa 40mph.

PRACTICE

Riders used the early morning practice periods to work up to race speed, but attitudes to practice varied. Casual competitors would put in one lap and then retire to one of the refreshment tents in the Paddock, provided courtesy of Dunlop and Cadbury. There they would exchange gossip before returning to their hotels for breakfast. Stanley Woods tells a story from 1934 that, after making an involuntary stop at the Sulby Glen Hotel, he wheeled his bike round the back and found several others parked. Going into the hotel he saw that the other competitors had stopped from choice and were taking cups of tea before setting off again. Those with a more serious approach would put in as many as three laps each morning, perhaps four, often stopping at the pits between laps to make adjustments.

Races were still run over seven laps and riders customarily made two pit stops, meaning that one of their riding sessions during a race would be a non-stop three laps. During one practice session in 1931 Jimmy Simpson claimed to have put in four laps without stopping. This would have been of concern to others, for Norton were already showing good form in practice and if they were able to get away with only one pit-stop during the race, they would save another 40–45 seconds.

RACING

Joe Craig had been working as competitions manager of Norton for almost two years, and his efforts with much-modified ohc engines finally met with success at the 1931 TT. And what success! Rudge had all but swept the board in the Senior and Junior events of 1930 and Norton copied their winning ways in 1931, leaving Rudge to take one third place in the Junior, although their 250s did take first and second places in the Lightweight, with Graham Walker achieving his first TT win. But it was young Percy 'Tim' Hunt who rode his Model 30 (500cc) and Model 40 (350cc) Nortons to record-breaking victories in the Senior and Junior TTs, the first time such a double had been achieved.

Riders had to contend with the vagaries of the Manx weather during racing in 1931, for in the Junior race a gale blew down the Mountain and in the Senior it blew them up. This played havoc with their choice of gearing, but those with four-speed gearboxes were likely to have fared better than the three-speeders. Norton, having previously relied on three speeds, now reaped the benefit of having a new four-speeder.

It was another year of substantial advancement in both race average and lap speeds, with machine development making the major contribution to the setting of new records in all classes. Jimmy Simpson (Norton) became the first to break the 80mph barrier, when he went round on his 500 at 80.82mph. 'Tim' Hunt lifted the Junior record to 75.27mph and Graham Walker put almost 5mph onto the Lightweight lap record, lifting it from 66.86 to 71.73mph – an astonishing achievement. It was also another year when the leader board was monopolized by British machines and riders, with names like Guthrie, Woods, Nott, Mellors, Tyrell-Smith and Handley taking the podium places. The last-named rider failed to complete the Senior, however, after falling at the bend some half a mile past the Eleventh Milestone, which now carries his name. While foreign machines and riders were present, they made relatively little impression on race results.

The BBC made time to broadcast a limited account of the Senior TT in 1931, which provided good publicity for manufacturers and the event. It was something the corporation allocated more time to in the years that followed, eventually transmitting TT reports worldwide and helping develop what was becoming a global fan base.

1932: TECHNICAL ADVANCES

The island welcomed the TT back in 1932 and works teams set up their temporary workshops in local premises belonging to hotels, garages, engineers and even undertakers. Others with business at the TT, like trade representatives, would base themselves in hotels, where their contact details would be publicized in local newspapers and the motorcycle magazines. *The TT Special* advised, for example, that Reuben Harveyson was at the Castle Mona Hotel on behalf of Ferodo, while Sid Burns, of the

Norton riders like Stanley Woods became frequent visitors to the winners enclosure during the 1930s. Joe Craig is standing second from the left.

Velocette proudly advertised their TT victories with this transfer on the petrol tank of their machines.

competing Fibrax brand of stopping material, was at the Carlton Hotel.

Norton had not only impressed with their speed and reliability when they swept the board in 1931, but also with the handling of their Senior and Junior machines. This spurred other makers to work on improving handling over the ensuing winter but, as ever in the racing game, Norton also worked to stay ahead of the opposition on the road-holding front, coming to the 1932 TT with front forks fitted with extended links and new damper springs to aid the previous single spring. They also made use of new magnesium alloy (elektron) crankcases and other weight-saving measures, which resulted in the 500 weighing in at 312lb (142kg), while the 350 was said to be 298lb (135kg). Both came with larger-capacity petrol tanks and, like virtually everyone else, now used 14mm sparking plugs instead of the earlier 18mm type.

Burman, Albion and Sturmey-Archer could supply four-speed gearboxes, while Velocette redesigned their own box. Some firms were said to be experimenting with the use of plain bearing big-ends, others were modifying their lubrication systems, and Rudge decided to stick with its use of coupled brakes. Almost every rider now used a twist-grip-type throttle; returning Alec Bennett still preferred the old lever type, but set to self-return.

There had been a considerable fall in sales of new motorcycles in the early 1930s and manufacturers who went to the expense of TT racing were all hoping for good results. These would bring favourable publicity and

boost sales, for motorcyclists of the time were impressed by Isle of Man performances and enjoyed having the name of a TT-winning bike on the tank. There were over twenty makes competing, including a first entry of Jawas in the Senior, which were described as workmanlike jobs in red and gold, but on the heavy side.

SULBY SPEED TRAP

The TT Special newspaper made a point of timing riders during practice. Sometimes it would be from point to point, such as Ramsey to the Bungalow, or even over the short length involved in rounding and exiting the dip at Governor's Bridge. They also timed riders over a 1-mile stretch of the Sulby Straight and quoted the speeds attained. While the resultant figures were keenly awaited by readers, they tended to ignore a number of factors that affected the quoted speeds. For example, due to riders tackling the preceding Quarry Bends with varying degrees of skill, not everyone was at maximum speed when they entered the mile. Also, some 500s were applying their brakes for Sulby Bridge before the end of the timed stretch. Clearly, it was not a totally accurate affair, particularly as there was no guarantee that timed riders were always at full throttle. Top riders were also sometimes missing from the published figures, perhaps because they had missed that particular practice session. In addition, the reports seldom mentioned if there were favourable or adverse wind conditions that could have affected the speeds achieved. During one timing session in 1932, fastest 500 was Henry Tyrell-Smith on a Rudge at exactly 100mph, a similar speed being reached by the fastest 350, Harold Willis on a Velocette, while Wal Handley was the quickest Lightweight on a Rudge at 88.6mph.

Riders acquainted themselves with the latest road improvements during practice in 1932, the most beneficial of which was widening at Laurel Bank. Come the racing, it proved to be another successful year for Norton, with Stanley Woods riding to victory in both the Senior and

Approaching Sulby Crossroads, part-way down the Sulby Straight, in the 1930s.

Junior events at record race average speeds. Stanley also set a new lap record in the Junior of 78.62mph, with Jimmy Simpson (Norton) recording a new fastest lap in the Senior of 81.50mph. As in 1931, Norton took first, second and third in the Senior with Stanley Woods, Jimmy Guthrie and Jimmy Simpson; while in the Junior, it was Rudge who filled second and third places with Wal Handley and Henry Tyrell-Smith. In the Lightweight race, Leo Davenport took first place at record-breaking speed on a New Imperial, and Rudge were second and third with Graham Walker and Wal Handley, the latter setting a new record fastest lap of 74.08mph. To put the rapidly increasing speeds in the Lightweight in context, Handley's lap record in 1932 was faster than the lap record of 73.55mph set by Charlie Dodson when winning the 1929 Senior TT.

Motorcycle racing was yet to have its own World Championship, but by now there was an established circuit of Continental Grand Prix and other major races. Norton carried their TT form into such events, taking victory in eleven of the twelve major races they contested in 1932 and proudly advertising, 'The machine that can successfully stand up to the terrific strain of racing, is the machine that will offer best service to the ordinary tourist'.

EVER FASTER

Everyone had become used to TT lap and race speeds increasing year on year, but why was this? The topic was considered in the previous chapter and the main reasons identified. They were course improvements, increased engine power and improved braking and handling, along with input from star riders. Other contributory factors have been mentioned: the move from hand to foot change, four-speed gearboxes, use of lighter materials, more responsive engines, wider tyres, changes to race regulations and so on, but a growing contribution was being made by the increase in mechanical reliability, which meant that machines could be ridden harder for longer. Speaking of the situation that existed when he started TT racing some ten years before, 1932 double winner Stanley Woods told how race machines of the earlier time were relatively fragile, saying, in effect, that anyone who went off fast into the lead at a TT would not be expected to win, or even finish, for despite being racing bikes, they had to be treated with care and 'nursed' through such a long race.

In 1932 riders still started with cold engines, so they may have gone easy on the throttle for the first few miles, but thereafter it was flat out, if necessary, although they still preferred to ride with something in hand. Not that the reliability problem had been completely solved, for Norton had two works machines break down in the 1932 Junior; they were probably being ridden to their limits, for when riders like Woods, Guthrie, Simpson and Hunt were striving for victory, the competition was intense.

Norton did introduce a system of riding to team orders, aimed at preventing riders breaking their machines in competition with each other. At the TT the agreement was that they would race for the first three laps and thereafter maintain their positions to the end. It was not popular amongst such a competitive group of riders and led to Stanley Woods setting up his own signalling system at Sulby to supplement the information passed to him by Norton at the pits.

While increased reliability would have come mainly from the efforts of individual manufacturers, the long-term participation in racing of suppliers of items like carburettors, tyres, chains, sparking plugs, petrol, oil and so on had seen them improve the quality of their products and make a material contribution to overall reliability. Having said that, after a post-race inspection of the top-finishing machines in 1932, *The Motor Cycle* told its readers that 'many of the chains were in a disgraceful state ... including broken rollers'. But 264 racing miles was a long way for an exposed chain to go without attention, for there was no lubrication, nor was there easy facility to adjust them at pit stops.

THRILLS AND SPILLS

Mention has been made of intense competition between riders, and Jimmy Simpson recalled the times with the words, 'the race of the moment was the one thing that mattered – there was no thought for the future, no count of the risk'. Most riders got swept along by the competitive atmosphere that prevailed, but some were found out by the demanding nature of the Mountain Course. Spills were frequent in the early days, when riders would usually pick themselves up, kick the bike into shape and carry on racing. But as speeds increased, what were previously spills turned into what were more appropriately called crashes. The consequences of such incidents on such an unforgiving course could be serious and fatalities became more frequent. That was a high price to pay for what was primarily a sporting event.

1933: REDUCED ENTRY NUMBERS

From a total entry of 153 across the three races in 1931, the figure fell to ninety-five in 1932, then picked up slightly to ninety-eight in 1933, which included foreign machines such as Jawa, Moto Guzzi and Eysink. Manufacturers come and go at the TT for various reasons, and in 1933 Rudge, who had hit trading difficulties, did not submit works entries. Fortunately, they did make their race bikes available to their previous team riders, Graham Walker, Henry Tyrell-

Smith and Ernie Nott, but perhaps lacking the competitive edge that comes from a true works effort, the only podium place for a Rudge in 1933 was a third for privateer Charlie Manders in the Lightweight race.

The position of Rudge was a reflection of the difficult economic conditions in Britain at the time, where the sales of new motorcycles plunged from 146,700 in 1929 to 52,200 in 1933. The TT organizers could do nothing but soldier on, although the reduced entries in each race meant riders were well spaced out around the 37¾ miles of the Mountain Course, particularly as ninety-eight entries did not guarantee ninety-eight starters, for major mechanical faults and injuries to riders usually resulted in a proportion of non-starters.

THE MOUNTAIN COURSE

By now well established in its fully tarmacadamed state, the course was subject to regular wear and tear from ordinary traffic, meaning that periodic resurfacing was necessary – and, given its length, this was carried out in stages. The result was that conditions varied from year to year and riders were always keen to know the state of the roads before setting out to practise. After the Highways Board had finished its preparations for the 1933 TT, which included widening and easing at the Thirty-third Milestone, one journal reported 'there is now a surface on the roads that will gladden the hearts of the riders'.

Mention has already been made of the hazard created for riders by molten tar and it was something they just had to face up to. Efforts were sometimes made to lessen its effect by sprinkling the worst areas with sand or cement dust but that really was a mixed blessing for racers to cope with at speed.

There has been a long-held view amongst some of those who visit the Isle of Man just for the racing that any altera-tion carried out to the Mountain Course is done primarily for the benefit of the TT races. That is not so. Outside the four weeks of the TT and MGP periods they are ordinary roads traversed by the cars, lorries, buses and motorcycles of the island's residents. As traffic demands increase, safety measures like the easing of blind bends, the need for road widening and other highway engineering requirements, all bring about change. This has been going on for over a century, for the benefit of Manx road users. Those improvements have undoubtedly played a major part in making the course faster for riders and thus have increased race speeds, but a truer description of the official attitude to highway improvements is that the authorities have regard to the impact of their works on the racing and try to avoid any adverse effects.

By 1933 the Highways Board was talking proudly of its 'non-skid' road surfacing, but it was still a hand-spread tarmacadam mix, finished by rolling and, after a year or so, surface dressed with tar and chippings to extend its life.

One good thing about improved surfacing and course improvements was that it did allow riders to make the most of the extra power and speed that manufacturers were building into their race machines. As ever, it was top riders who could extract the greatest benefit and their services were in high demand. With the natural tendency of such top riders to be offered the fastest machines, it increased the performance gap between them and ordinary riders on lesser machinery.

Top riders also sought to maximize their earnings by moving between manufacturers and sometimes riding for more than one make. In 1933, fast man Wal Handley was entered on an OK-Supreme in the Senior, Velocette in the Junior and Excelsior in the Lightweight. Messrs Burney and Blackburne provided a new 250cc engine for the Excelsior, which became known as the Mechanical Marvel. It had a radial 4-valve head, two splayed inlet ports and twin exhaust ports.

WEIGHT SAVING

As mentioned earlier, growth in performance brought the requirement for racing motorcycles to be strengthened in all areas, with bulked-up components in engines, plus sturdier frames and associated parts, wider tyres and larger fuel tanks. The result of this was to increase machine weights through the late 1920s and early 1930s. While the need to retain overall strength remained, manufacturers attempted to compensate for increased weight by making more use of light alloys in areas like crankcases, gearbox shells, cylinder heads, cylinder finning, hubs, mudguards, engine plates, brake plates, handlebars and anywhere else where

Braking hard but with care on the approach to Creg ny Baa.

they could reduce the load to be carried for 264 racing miles. There were also experimental light-alloy wheel rims available.

CHANGES

Among some obvious changes to machinery in 1933 was heel and toe form of gearchange lever, commonly seen on Continental machines and now adopted by a few British riders. Sunbeam had used hairpin valve springs for some time, and they could now also be seen on Velocettes and Jawas, for most valve gear was still partially exposed. Norton used aluminium-bronze cylinder heads, and the use of bronze to aid thermal conductivity was adopted by other manufacturers over the next few years, sometimes just as a 'skull' for the combustion chamber. The only two-stroke entry was that of a Scott going under the name of the Reynolds Special, entered by Liverpool motorcycle dealer A.E. Reynolds.

Race regulations had previously required exhaust pipes to extend back as far as the centre of the rear wheel spindle, but growing knowledge of the important effect of exhaust pipe length on performance saw that requirement dropped.

Foreign machines were still trying to make an impression and Jawa brought a 350cc single to join its 500, which had gained a little speed to go with its reliability. The 500 had a sheet metal frame, unit construction of engine and gearbox, and coupled brakes. Husqvarna also made an appearance, with a motorcycle that was rated as fast but heavy and with poor handling. In 1933 foreign machines and riders had yet to make an impact on Island racing, while all the winning was being done by single-cylinder machines.

NORTON DOMINATE

The history books show that Norton swept the board at the 1933 TT. In the Senior, Stanley Woods led home Jimmy Simpson and Tim Hunt at record-breaking race average and lap speeds and he did the same in the Junior from Hunt and Jimmy Guthrie. It was a comprehensive demolition of the opposition, on a scale not previously seen, with reports of the time claiming that Norton's 500 gave just over 30bhp at 5,500rpm, on a compression ratio of 7.1:1.

With his double victory in 1933 following his similar double in 1932, Stanley Woods now had six TT wins and, at just over thirty years of age, stood at the pinnacle of motorcycle racing. Importantly, he had reached the top with the reputation of invariably bringing his machine to the finish. Woods gave a few insights into his riding style, telling that achieving the greatest possible speeds on the fastest bends was of prime importance, rather than trying too hard on the slower ones; and that taking a line that missed the

worst bumps was often better than using what looked like the obvious but bumpy one. It was still a little before the use of rev counters, so he drove the engine by ear, always closing the throttle on upward changes and easing it over jumps, in both instances aiming to avoid over-revving. He indulged in minimal slipping of the clutch and used both brakes together, the front harder than the rear. He stopped only once for fuel in the seven-lap Senior race, when he took on the petrol/benzole mix used by most teams.

With such a commanding performance in the Senior and Junior races, Norton rather took the attention away from Syd Gleave's record-breaking ride to victory on his new Excelsior 'Mechanical Marvel' in the Lightweight. But while Norton received much praise for their performance, they also came in for criticism, with some suggesting that such total dominance was bad for the future of the TT. The chance to complain about the event also brought to the fore the old chestnut about it not aiding the development of road machines. This seemed to be the excuse to start talking about its future, with ideas ranging from having a massed start to having a standard touring TT or running it on a short circuit. It was understandable that manufacturers putting money into the event looked to get something positive out of it, but most people saw the TT as a sporting spectacle of speed, and that is all they wanted of the event.

1934: MOUNTAIN ROAD

The long-standing problem of sheep wandering onto the Mountain Road and into the path of racing motorcyclists, was largely cured for the 1934 TT after the whole length was fenced. The new fencing also allowed for the removal

Riders were still wearing body-belts in post-war years, as seen in this photo of Denis Parkinson from 1948.

of the gates across the road, which previously had to be opened by marshals prior to each practice and race session. However, the fencing required concrete support posts, which created an unyielding barrier to anyone who rode wide on a bend. It was a time when the outside of those bends would also be crowded with spectators leaning on the fence, in a manner that is not acceptable today.

While the course was reasonably well surfaced, it was very bumpy at racing speeds and many riders wore a body-belt of the type more associated with off-road scrambling. This would be worn over their two-piece horsehide leathers, along with a tie-on waistcoat carrying their race number.

ENTRIES

In 1934 the world was gradually coming out of economic recession and motorcycle sales were increasing, although the benefits of that had yet to be felt at the TT, where overall entries were only slightly up, at 101. New to the event was the Vincent HRD Company with three entries on JAP-powered 500s. It was a brave venture by a small concern, whose total production in 1933 had been just under one hundred road-going motorcycles. Unusually for race bikes of the time, they came fitted with rear suspension, something which Philip Vincent had utilized on all his motorcycles after taking over the double TT-winning HRD name in 1928.

FOREIGN CHALLENGE

The early 1930s had seen British machines taking all the podium places in the Senior, Junior and Lightweight TTs and having little trouble in repelling the challenge of the few foreign makes entered. However, top man in Island racing, Stanley Woods, a professional motorcycle racer out to make the best possible living, decided that he had had enough of Norton's financially constricting team orders and looked elsewhere for a source of racing bikes for the 1934 season. Bankrolled by a substantial retainer of £1,500 from the parent company of Mobiloil, he came to the 1934 TT with entries on a Husqvarna for the Senior, AJS for the Junior and Moto Guzzi for the Lightweight.

Woods was an astute man who left nothing to chance. Making early visits to the three supplying factories, he worked with them to improve the bikes he was planning to race. Pre-TT testing left him optimistic of putting up a good showing with the twin-cylinder Husqvarna and single-cylinder Moto Guzzi, but he rejected the AJS as not good enough. On the run-up to the TT, his plans generated premature headlines like 'British road racing supremacy in jeopardy'. Husqvarna also brought 500s for Ernie Nott and Gunar Kalen, plus a 350 for Nott to ride in the Junior race.

Jimmy Simpson copes with the bumps of the railway bridge at Union Mills in 1934.

NORTON AGAIN

After all the pre-event talk of the foreign challenge, when it came to the 1934 TT, Norton continued their winning ways. With much modified, lightened and faster bikes, they showed good form in practice, with Jimmy Simpson recorded on the Sulby Straight at 106.5mph. They took the first two places in the Senior race with Jimmy Guthrie and Jimmy Simpson, while Walter Rusk came third on a Velocette. It was a similar situation in the Junior, with Guthrie again winning from Simpson after a neck-and-neck duel, and Ernie Nott bringing his Husqvarna home in third.

Following a troublesome practice period, the relatively new to the TT 'Husky' of Stanley Woods held second place in the wet Senior race until running out of fuel on the last lap, just 10 miles from the finish. It was a good showing, and consolation for Woods came in the form of the fastest lap at 80.49mph, somewhat down on the lap record due to the poor conditions.

The Husqvarna performance was considered a promising one, for having shed much weight and improved the handling from 1933, the bikes carried the requisite speed and looked a threat for the future. In addition they showed that twin-cylinder machines could once again mount a serious challenge to the singles, something that had not happened at the TT for many years.

In the Lightweight class it was another convincing victory for the speedy little Rudge singles, which were said to develop 24bhp and were fast enough to claim the first three places with Jimmy Simpson, Ernie Nott and Graham Walker. It gave a long-awaited TT win to Jimmy at record-breaking speed.

Rudge had fully expected to be challenged by Moto Guzzi in the Lightweight race, for Stanley Woods unofficially broke the lap record by a big margin on his first lap of practice. However, a mistake during preparation in the Guzzi camp saw Woods' bike seize its engine on the first lap of the race, and although he was able to continue, the edge had gone off its performance and he finished fourth. As in the Senior race, he had done enough, however, to show that the 250 Italian Moto Guzzi could be a threat to British manufacturers in future years.

That 1934 Lightweight race was blighted by the death of previous winner, the experienced Syd Crabtree, who fell from his Excelsior on the Mountain. No one saw Crabtree's accident in the misty conditions that prevailed and it was sometime before the organizers realized he was missing and organized a search party. It drew attention to the paucity of marshals on the Mountain section of the course and led to the creation of the travelling marshals service the following year.

1935: DEVELOPMENTS

The TT was a year-long topic of discussion for the sporting motorcyclist and the motorcycle press. Early in 1935 came a rumour that the 4-cylinder, water-cooled and super-charged Italian Rondine would come to the Island in June, but that did not happen. Mention of such multi-cylinder foreign exotica had commentators on the racing scene writing that 'British manufacturers are literally clinging to the single although by rights its day has passed'. The Norton singles had been further developed, with compression ratios lifted, power output of the 500 up to 34bhp, larger petrol and oil tanks, a 'new' gearbox, a degree of enclosure to the rocker box and a claimed maximum speed of 110mph.

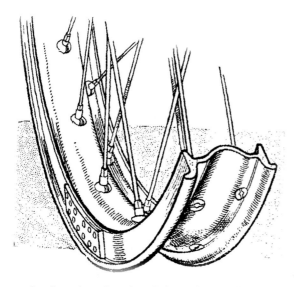

An early alloy rim, plated and riveted at the join.

Moto Guzzi, OEC and Vincent HRD were the only entries with rear suspension in 1935, a feature many considered was long overdue for general use in racing. Meanwhile, ever more firms were using light alloys, with increasing use in wheel rims, even though some felt it necessary to rivet a plate at the join in construction.

Firms were beginning to experiment with megaphone exhausts to boost top-end performance, Velocette and Norton among them, and JAP offered a twin-carburettor arrangement on their single-cylinder engines, via two induction pipes to a single inlet port. Cross rotary-valve engines were tried by Cotton and Rudge, while Excelsior appeared with a new 250 ohc engine. Rev counters also made an appearance. They were a help in gaining optimum performance and an aid to reliability, and would come to be universally adopted in the next few years.

Joining the foreign entries from NSU, Jawa and Terrot was the German firm of DKW, with its technically interesting 250cc split-single two-strokes, which were said to give some 25bhp at approaching 5,000rpm. They were water-cooled, with a piston-pump form of supercharging, and used rubber to control movement of the front forks rather than springs. Particularly noisy, with a high fuel consumption, they needed large petrol tanks. With the prestige of a TT victory well recognized abroad, foreign machines amounted to some 20 per cent of the total 107 entries.

Stanley Woods returned in 1935 with Moto Guzzi rides in the Lightweight and Senior races, accompanied by Omobono Tenni. The 250 was a development of the model he had used in 1934 and the 500 was a 120 degree V-twin that had been campaigned on the Continent, but which came to the island with a new sprung frame, the action of which was controlled by friction adjusters. Top speed was said to be 112mph.

On the organizational side, the requirement that machines start a race with cold engines was dropped and a warming-up period was given, in which machines were ridden up and down the Glencrutchery Road, with a line of metal dustbins keeping them apart. It was a characteristic of the Velocette racers that they did not deliver their full performance until thoroughly warm. Seemingly that could take a full lap, perhaps due to them carrying a gallon of engine oil.

Jimmy Simpson had retired from racing at the end of 1934 and was employed in the competition department of Shell Oils. He was present at the 1935 races and, having assessed the latest road improvements and resurfacing, expressed the view that they were worth 10 seconds a lap to top riders.

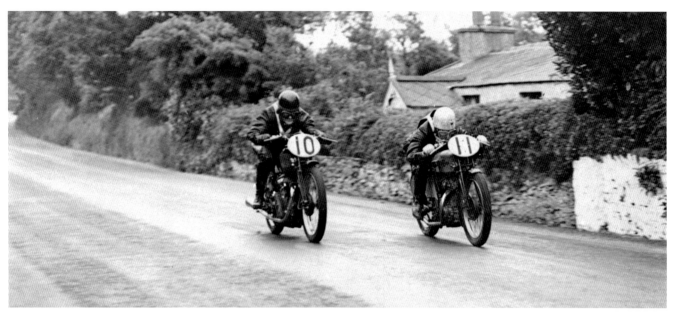

Battling it out in 1935. Number 11 looks a little more determined than number 10.

ESCAPISM

Enthusiasm for TT racing could offer a way of escaping the burden of wordly affairs. *The Motor Cycle* put it nicely in 1935, writing 'Who cares what Hitler says, or whether there has been another coup in the Balkans? This week we don't read the national papers – we live, dream and read motorcycles.'

PROGRAMME

The programme of racing for 1935 opened with the Junior on Monday of race week. In less than perfect conditions, the stylish Jimmy Guthrie led team mates Walter Rusk and John 'Crasher' White to victory at a new record race average speed of 79.14mph, with the fastest lap going to Rusk, who was just 3 seconds short of the lap record. It was Norton's fifth consecutive Junior victory.

Weather conditions were poor for Wednesday's Lightweight race, where, nevertheless, Stanley Woods (Moto Guzzi) rode to an emphatic 3-minute victory over the Rudges of Henry Tyrell-Smith and Ernie Nott, setting new race average and lap records for the 264½-mile race. That was a long way for a 250 that was revved to over 7,500rpm and the little Moto Guzzi's engine suffered valve gear failure just as Stanley shut off at the finishing line.

Celebrations of victory in the Lightweight were overshadowed by the death in the race of Doug Pirie in a crash at the Thirty-third Milestone. The inquest into Pirie's death was held the following day and the coroner recommended to the ACU's representative that the organizers

should stop any race in which bad weather prevailed. The next day was scheduled for the Senior race, but with travelling marshals reporting that visibility on the Mountain was down to 20 yards and with the Coroner's recommendation ringing in their ears, the organizers postponed the race until Saturday. A degree of chaos ensued for riders, organizers, marshals and those spectators who were booked to leave the island on the Saturday – and for the 12,000 spectators who had been shipped in overnight just to see Friday's Senior.

A RACE TO REMEMBER

There had been many close-fought duels in the almost twenty-five years' use of the Mountain Course, but with this book's concentration on detailing the ever-increasing speed aspect of the TT, it has not been possible to give full accounts of earlier races. However, the record-breaking 1935 Senior TT merits a proper description.

A TT race is a form of time trial where riders set off at intervals. In the 1930s the previous year's winner was always offered number 1 in the following year's race, but the remaining start numbers were determined by ballot. This meant that principal rivals might not see each other during a race, so they rode against the clock. Each rider had his own strategy, some going fast from the outset, while others held something in reserve. Their riding could well be affected by the in-race information they received about how their rivals were doing, and the need to stop for fuel could often change the shape of a race.

Practice for the 1935 Senior had shown that it would be a contest between the combined strength of the Norton team of Guthrie, Rusk and White and the lone effort of Stanley Woods on his Moto Guzzi, though nothing could be taken for granted over a race distance of 264½ miles and there were certainly others capable of challenging for a win. Come the race, it soon turned into a two-man duel between Jimmy Guthrie, who started at number 1, and Stanley Woods, who started 14½ minutes later at number 30. Almost half a minute behind Guthrie on corrected time at the end of the first lap, Woods was a concerned man, for his 500cc bike shared the same valve gear components as those that had failed as he crossed the finishing line on his 250 a few days before. Falling further behind, it was not until his stop for fuel at the end of the third lap that the Guzzi rider began to claw back some of Jimmy's lead.

Norton were convinced that the thirsty twin-cylinder Moto Guzzi would have to make two stops for fuel and planned their race accordingly. However, they had failed to notice in the final practice session that, in a classic act of TT subterfuge, Woods had used a slightly bigger petrol tank, which he retained for the race. Activity in the Moto Guzzi pit as Woods neared the end of his sixth lap led Norton to believe their assumption about refuelling to be correct, for the Guzzi mechanics gave every indication of preparing for another stop. But Woods went straight through, albeit a substantial 26 seconds behind Guthrie, who had already been given signals telling him he was comfortably in the lead.

Putting aside concerns about the durability of his valve gear, Woods brought all his racing skills to that last lap. He used the Moto Guzzi's sprung-frame handling to its full, and in the final stages his new-for-1935 rev counter showed that he was taking the engine to well over 8,000rpm on the drop from the Mountain. But would it last and would it be enough to snatch victory?

It was clear at the finish that the race organizers, the public address announcers and the Norton camp did not think so, for Jimmy Guthrie sat on his Norton and received celebratory handshakes, pictures were taken and he was generally fêted as the winner. Then, some quarter of an hour after Guthrie had taken the chequered flag, came the unexpected announcement that Stanley Woods had clawed back the time deficit on the last lap and stolen victory by 4 seconds. In doing so he set a new lap record of 86.53mph, taking 1 minute and 12 seconds off his own previous fastest lap from 1933 in the process and thus lifting it by almost 4mph. It was a truly outstanding performance, which made him an eight-times TT winner.

Moto Guzzi had been contesting the TT since 1926 and by taking the coveted Blue Riband Senior and the Light-weight race in 1935, the Italian firm showed that the foreign challenge was now truly a force to be reckoned with in Island racing. Rusk and Duncan had followed Guthrie home on Nortons, but in fifth and sixth places there was more foreign machinery, with Oskar Steinbach and Ted Mellors on German NSUs.

1936: RUMBLINGS

The interruptions to racing caused by the poor weather in 1935 led some to question the suitability of the Mountain Course for such an important race as the TT, particularly as machines were getting ever faster. Suggestions were made about finding an alternative course on the Island that kept to the low ground and would thus be less affected by mist. There was no immediate action, but the topic continued to rumble in the background for the next few years.

Increased speeds put ever more demands on riders. At 100mph plus, racing bikes were an uncomfortable ride, with their vibration, noise and lack of suspension. Add to this the need to fight the wind in bulky two-piece leathers, topped by a draughty pudding-basin helmet and goggles, and it meant that spending well over 3 hours in the saddle for the 264 miles of a TT race was a wearing business.

A total entry of only eighty-six across the three races in 1936 was cause for concern, but firms like Norton and Velocette, who openly stated that they went racing for the worldwide publicity it could earn them, were there. Indeed, the small Velocette company attributed its survival in the difficult trading days of the early 1930s to the fact that 50 per cent of its production went for export, the orders for which had largely been gained through the publicity achieved from racing.

The Moto Guzzi marque was absent, as Italy was at war in Abyssinia.

COURSE IMPROVEMENTS

Bray Hill had been resurfaced and was now rated as faster, although the humps where side roads joined the hill still caused the fastest riders to leap considerable distances.

Five miles further on, at an improved Greeba Castle, the easing of bends helped increase speeds, because, as Graham Walker explained, riders now took it in third gear and 'you didn't drop below ninety'. Just after the Eighth Milestone at Ballig Bridge, the notorious hump had been levelled and the reconstructed bridge was widened and realigned to give a straighter run. In the opinion of leading riders, the works there saved them 3–5 seconds a lap, while other changes for 1936 were estimated to contribute to an overall reduction in lap time of 10–15 seconds.

Jock Leyden's sketch shows Ginger Wood coping with the humps on Bray Hill.

This photograph shows ordinary traffic using Ballig Bridge in the days before it was realigned, flattened and widened.

Speeds were recorded on Sulby Straight in just one practice session and the highest were: Senior – Oskar Steinbach (NSU), 107.1mph; Junior – Noel Christmas (Velocette), 96.8mph; Lightweight – Henry Tyrell-Smith (Excelsior), 84.9mph. All figures were slightly down on the previous year's fastest, under similar damp conditions.

Riders were also timed over a half-mile stretch from the top of Bray Hill and through the bottom. The best class times were set by Stanley Woods (Velocette), Noel Pope (Velocette) and Arthur Geiss (DKW).

FUEL

Topic of the moment at the 1936 TT was the fuel used, with concerns about perceived anomalies in what was permitted. Most ran a 50/50 petrol/benzole mix, but there was much technical discussion about the place of tetra-ethyl lead – included in pump fuel, but not allowed in race fuel – and the incorporation of alcohol, which Cleveland Discol pump fuel was claimed to contain. It was clearly an important issue, for it could affect engine tune and race performance.

MORE 'SPRINGERS'

With Moto Guzzi taking two TT victories in 1935 on machines fitted with rear suspension, and the similarly equipped Vincent HRD concern receiving favourable comment on their bikes' handling, it was no surprise to see other makes come to the 1936 TT fitted with rear springing, among them being Norton and Velocette. Moto Guzzi had used a system with scissor-action struts controlled by adjustable friction discs, whilst Vincent HRD used inclined under-saddle springs that were enclosed and fitted with friction band adjusters. Norton's effort was of simple vertical plunger style, incorporating springs but no damping, while Velocette's was of vertically mounted hydraulic units, with no springs, but assisted by compressed air. These varied approaches to the same problem offered a classic example of manufacturers pursuing the same development from different directions, or, as Kevin Cameron put it, 'When ideas are new, many competing expressions flourish'.

On the new machine front, AJS had introduced a V-four roadster at the end of 1935, and two supercharged versions were entered for the 1936 Senior TT. The engines were of double-V formation and riders were George Rowley and

Castrol oils were big supporters of the TT races.

Harold Daniell. Vincent HRD also brought a supercharged single for the Senior, but it proved temperamental in practice so was not raced.

Since their TT victories of the late 1920s, Velocette had been ever-present at the Island races. Sometimes only fractionally off race-winning pace and with their 350s usually more competitive than their 500s, they were always ready to snap up a podium position when the mighty Nortons failed. In 1936 they returned with modified frames, alterations to gearing and minor engine developments that kept their KTT models competitive. They also realized that to win they had to pay for a top rider, so they went right to the very top and hired Stanley Woods, who would also ride a DKW in the Lightweight race.

NORTON STILL DOMINATE

As well as benefiting from plunger rear suspension in 1936, back at the Bracebridge Street factory the Norton racers underwent their customary engine development over the winter and came with slightly revised bore and stroke, plus extra finning areas to heads and barrels. Every manufacturer who had ideas of TT glory would have gone down a similar road, for those who stood still were swiftly left behind.

Jimmy Guthrie went on to race his Norton to victory in the 1936 Senior at record-breaking speed, although second-placed Stanley Woods (Velocette) set the fastest and record lap at 86.98mph. Confirming the constant year-on-year progress made at the TT races, Stanley's 1936 record lap was even faster than his victory-grabbing last lap of 1935 on the Moto Guzzi. Walter Rusk (Norton) was a close third. In the Junior it was newcomer to the TT, former MGP winner Freddie Frith, who took first place on his Norton, breaking race and lap records and finishing ahead of 'Crasher' White (Norton) and Ted Mellors (Velocette).

Those who had ridden with rear suspension expressed themselves as generally satisfied with the new fitting, claiming it allowed higher corner speeds, reduced tyre wear, permitted harder rear-wheel braking and gave overall better control. In addition, increased comfort meant their bikes were less fatiguing to ride, a factor that could well be a time-saver towards the end of a long race.

In the Lightweight race, Bob Foster fended off the DKW challenge and rode his unit construction, pushrod-engined New Imperial to first place at a new race average record speed, with Henry Tyrell-Smith second on a 4-valve Excelsior and Arthur Geiss third on his two-stroke DKW. Stanley Woods (DKW) lost time to an early plug change. Thereafter he was challenging Foster for the lead and set a new record lap of 76.20mph, before retiring on lap six.

In tuning machines for TT racing, there is a tricky line to be maintained between performance and reliability. The temptation has always been to go for performance and so retirement rates ranged from 22 to 60 per cent in 1936. Such figures were not out of the ordinary, but there was little consistency and the percentage figures for each race varied year on year.

1937: MEGAPHONES

The benefit to top-end performance gained by the use of megaphone exhausts was increasingly recognized and they were being widely adopted. Norton competitions manager, Joe Craig, explained that his 500cc engine gained its greatest benefit from a 'megga' at 6,000rpm. Below 4,000rpm it was actually a disadvantage, for it upset the carburation, making the rounding of slow corners like Ramsey Hairpin and Governor's Bridge a stuttering affair. In fitting a megaphone, exhaust pipe length was critical and there was an impact on valve-timing and jetting of the carburettor. Another development for Norton was that the factory race engines were now fitted with double overhead camshafts (dohc), driven by a train of gears. They also had increased compression ratios and carried rev counters.

In 1937 almost every rider still rode his racing motorcycle from his garage/lodgings to the start area, prior to a practice or race. This was an extremely noisy and antisocial

A mute fitted in the end of Norton's megaphone exhaust.

business at 4.15am, and although riders were requested to travel as quietly as possible, most had to ride uphill to the start on open pipes, so it was an almost impossible task. In 1937 several riders were summonsed and fined for noise offences, and thereafter most rode with some form of mute in the end of the megaphone when not in race mode.

DKWs were so noisy that they took no chances with the law and towed their racers to the start. Once there, they needed to be warmed up for some 10 minutes prior to going out for practice.

The press published some speedy claims on the run-up to the 1937 event, writing that the 500cc Moto Guzzis would reach 126mph and the new entry 500cc BMW was good for 132mph. However, as will be seen, that did not happen at the TT. It was a year when there had been little change to the course, apart from some improvements over the Mountain.

MORE FOREIGN ENTRIES

Down to ride the sole BMW factory entry in 1937 was the experienced Jock West. His German mount was a 180-degree flat-twin, with supercharging, dohc, four-speed gearbox and single-plate clutch matched to shaft drive. Suspension was by plunger at the rear and hydraulically damped telescopic forks at the front. Much use was made of magnesium and the bike's overall lightness, combined with speed, suggested that it would be a formidable threat, particularly as it had already been raced with success on the Continent. The BMW represented an advance in motorcycle engineering and offered a distinct increase in performance, but could it deliver and use that higher performance over the roads of the Mountain Course at the level it did on race circuits abroad? Some pointed to the horizontal cylinders and shaft drive as being two factors that might make that difficult.

The talented Omobono Tenni was entered on Moto Guzzis in the Senior and Lightweight races, along with Stanley Woods in the Lightweight. Then there were NSUs present in the Senior and Junior races, DKW in the Lightweight and names like Terrot, Sarolea and Husqvarna adding spice to the entry of foreign machines and riders.

One new feature for the 1937 TT was the introduction of a single evening practice session. It was well received, for everyone knew that race engines were sensitive to atmospheric conditions and performed slightly differently during early-morning practice sessions from how they would during a race held later in the day.

A SPEEDY YEAR

Practice lap times and speed measurements on the Sulby Straight suggested that spectators were in for fast racing in 1937, and that is how it turned out. The Sulby figures taken in practice showed that speeds had increased from previous years, with Freddie Frith fastest Senior runner on his Norton at 120.60mph, followed by the Nortons of White and Guthrie at 116mph. It was a year in which *The TT Special* actually timed riders during the Senior race; the figures obtained showed Nortons out front, with Guthrie hitting 117.66mph, White 114.67mph, Frith 114.67mph, Tenni (Moto Guzzi) 113.94mph and Mellors (Velocette) 113.21mph. Given that the race turned into a titanic battle between Freddie Frith and Stanley Woods (Velocette), one wonders why no speed was quoted for Woods, for at the end of a race in which Frith lifted the lap record by over 3mph to record the first over-90mph lap at 90.27mph, Woods was just 15 seconds behind him at the finish. Both had been riding to their limit, with Woods experiencing a massive slide just after Ballig Bridge. White was third, while Jock West brought his BMW home in sixth place with a leaking fuel tank and Tenni retired his Moto Guzzi.

In the Junior race, Nortons swept the board with Guthrie, Frith and White taking the first three places. Again, records were smashed, with Frith and Guthrie setting an equal fastest lap of 85.18mph. As in the Senior, this was over 3mph faster than the previous year. Such an advancement, which in 1937 was largely down to machine development, was a huge compliment to the British manufacturers who had earlier been described as 'clinging on' with their single-cylinder racers. Speed trap figures showed the 350 Nortons reached just over 105mph.

The all-action style of Omobono Tenni (Moto Guzzi) at Windy Corner during practice for the 1937 Lightweight TT.

Continental machinery did make its mark in the Lightweight race, where Omobono Tenni came home first on his Moto Guzzi, with 'Ginger' Wood second on an Excelsior and Ernie Thomas third on a DKW. Tenni lifted the lap record from 76.20 to 77.72mph and became the first foreign rider to take TT victory on a foreign machine. Thomas recorded the fastest straight-line speed of 98.09mph, from Tenni at 95.34mph.

1938: STILL DEVELOPING

The search for improvements to increase speed and improve reliability was never ending. With the easing and widening of many bends and improvements in road-holding, TT machines now ran at wider throttle openings for longer and put ever more demands on their many components.

Renowned Australian engineer Phil Irving summarized the task of valves as 'admitting and liberating gas from the cylinder at appropriate moments'. It was a tough job at 7,000rpm and manufacturers experimented with various metals, usually using different ones for inlet and exhaust valves. The associated valve guides and springs were subject to similar experimentation. Aiding their efficient operation were developments in lubrication, with 1938 being the year of new, thinner oils. Advertisements from Castrol and Mobiloil claimed they would 'lubricate without oil-drag' and 'are necessary for high speed and maximum power'.

Clutches had a hard life and were usually of multi-plate design, using cork or woven asbestos lining material, with most still exposed to air to aid cooling. Carburettors were an important feature in maximizing performance and there was a move towards remote float chambers with flexible mountings to ensure a constant flow of fuel. More manufacturers were trying rear suspension, with some private runners grafting on their own systems.

While tyres were important, they were largely taken for granted. Troubles were few and durability was not a problem, most riders using one set for practising and a new, lightly scrubbed set, for the race. There were fewer tyre suppliers supporting the TT than in its early days, the principal ones of the 1930s being Dunlop, Avon and John Bull. Riders used ribbed front tyres and treaded rear, with sizes varying from 2.75 front and 3.00 rear on some Lightweights to 3.00/3.25 front and 3.25/3.50 rear on Junior and Senior models.

TT frontrunners, Norton, followed the example of BMW and came to the 1938 event with telescopic front forks, but they were merely spring-controlled with no hydraulic element and gave just 2in of travel. However, they did improve stability by reducing front wheel judder under braking. Meanwhile, manufacturers of traditional girder front forks, like Webbs, were still experimenting to improve their products. The Norton factory's attention was being diverted from racing by the need to fulfill contracts for the army, but Joe Craig knew they could not stand still and worked to achieve a little more power from changed engine bore and stroke dimensions, an increase in compression ratios to 8.3:1 (500cc) and 8.6:1 (350cc), plus increased finning to head and barrel. The company customarily used early-season Irish road races, like the Leinster 200 and North West 200, to try new ideas before the TT.

Velocette was another company running models with a long ancestry that received year-on-year development. By 1938 they had reached the KTT Mk VII versions, with their over-the-counter 350 giving 27bhp at 6,500rpm and the 500 yielding 34bhp at 7,000rpm. More was available from their works development models.

BMW returned in 1938 with a three-man team of Jock West, Georg Meier and Karl Gall, with 'Kompressor' machines that were said to have had engine heights raised to reduce the risk of grounding their projecting cylinder heads while cornering. As an indication of its serious approach, the BMW team spent two weeks on the Isle of Man in early April, learning the course on roadster machines. Team members were accompanied by a physical trainer, who also oversaw their diets with what was described as 'typical Teutonic thoroughness'. Much has been written about the political aspect of BMW's racing effort on Nazi Germany's behalf in the late 1930s, and at the 1938 TT the threat of war was in the air.

The course was described prior to the 1938 races as 'better than ever', with the biggest improvement being the reconstruction of about 1½ miles of the Mountain Road from just above The Cutting – now known as Guthrie's Memorial. Experts reckoned that improvement would be worth 5 seconds a lap. There was also road widening on the Lezayre stretch approaching Ramsey and further improvements at Greeba Castle.

GLAMOUR

During the 1930s the TT organizers worked to incorporate some glamour into the event, with the start area bedecked with flags and bunting, warming-up procedures held in sight of the crowded Grandstand, freshly painted scoreboards, public address system giving out information, advertising banners, and uniformed scouts bearing the flags of competing nations to the start line. The Island's Lieutenant Governor was driven along the Glencrutchery Road and took his seat in the Grandstand just before the start of each race and the starts were signalled by the firing of a maroon and the dropping of the timekeeper's flag.

Ewald Kluge and his DKW in 1938.

But there was a serious side to this sporting event, for one magazine wrote: 'Behind the glamour of TT week lies a battle for world business, watched by every potential purchasing country with the keenest interest', with another saying, 'Successes scored on the lengthy and demanding TT course have a value all of their own'. For all the potential monetary gains from TT success, some were still in it purely for the prestige of a win. In *Stanley Woods – The World's First Motorcycle Superstar*, David Crawford tells how Moto Guzzi had been contesting the TT since 1926, but 'As they were a small company with no business interests in Britain it was more a personal ambition of its directors than a sales effort.'

Another aspect of 'glamour' at the TT came from the high speeds recorded, and 1938 saw another lift. Fastest 500 on the Sulby Straight was Jock West at an impressive 130.4mph, followed by team mate Georg Meier at 121.6mph, a figure matched by the fastest single of 'Crasher' White (Norton), with his team mates Frith and Daniell very close behind. Of the 350s, Stanley Woods hit 112.5mph on his Velocette, well clear of his team mate Mellors at 107.1mph. Fastest 250s were the DKWs, with Ewald Kluge at 107.8mph and Siegfried Wunsche at 104mph. Those figures were set in practice, during which BMW teamster Karl Gall crashed and put himself out of the race.

NORTON'S RUN ENDS

Any thoughts that BMW's 'Teutonic thoroughness' in preparation would be carried over to the Senior race were dashed by mechanical problems, which brought about Meier's retirement at Quarter Bridge on the first lap, although Jock West did bring his BMW home in fifth place. It was the less powerful but better-handling Norton and Velocette machinery that contested the podium places, with victory going to Harold Daniell (Norton), who set new race average and lap records, with his fastest being in a time of 24 minutes 52.6 seconds, a speed of 91.00mph. It was the first time

that the 25-minute barrier had been broken. As in 1937, Stanley Woods (Velocette) was just 15 seconds behind the winner, with Freddie Frith (Norton) a close third.

Asked after the race to describe his record lap, Daniell gave a few insights into the bravery required to lap at over 90mph. Speaking of the sweeping downhill curves at the Eleventh Milestone, he told how he took them flat in top, using every inch of the road, adding 'the procedure is not recommended for beginners'. Of the series of bends at Birkins he said 'I have done it flat, but don't like to', while the Thirty-third Milestone was 'nearly flat out'.

In the Junior race, Stanley Woods and his Velocette ended Norton's seven years' winning run in the class. He was not unduly pressed and rode a controlled race at just under record speed, although he did set a new lap record of 85.30mph. Firms like Mobiloil, Dunlop, Ferodo and Amal were amongst those sponsoring Stanley and all were pleased to advertise his success. Mellors (Velocette) was second and Frith (Norton) third. One possible reason that Norton did not really challenge for the win was that Joe Craig is said to have geared all his bikes for totally calm conditions, while the race was run in blustery winds.

DKW at last matched speed to reliability with victory in the Lightweight, Ewald Kluge romping home some 11 minutes ahead of 'Ginger' Wood and his Excelsior. Kluge needed two pit stops on his thirsty two-stroke but lifted both race average and lap speeds, leaving the latter at 80.35mph. Although Kluge found reliability, his was the

Bill Beevers holds his Norton flat out through St Ninian's Crossroads, at the top of Bray Hill.

only one of the three works DKWs to finish the race, and the next six finishers were on Excelsiors.

In a sign of the times, the first three machines in each race were fitted with rear suspension.

1939: BUSINESS AS USUAL

With a total of 153 entries across three classes, the 1939 TT promised plenty of racing although, as usual, most of the interest and focus was on the works machinery. After many years of domination, Norton were not there with new works bikes, because pressure to meet military contracts at the factory meant that their riders had to make do with 1938 machinery. They had also lost their Competitions Manager, Joe Craig, who moved to BSA. By contrast, BMW were present with a three-man team on their latest supercharged models. Germany was also represented by works entries from NSU and DKW.

The ever-present Velocette factory had announced its KTT Mk VIII model at the 1938 Motorcycle Show and had works versions of the single-cylinder racer for Stanley Woods and Ted Mellors. It also brought its new supercharged twin-cylinder 'Roarer' to the Island, although it had only one exploratory run before being put to one side. AJS were present, having added water-cooling and weight to their supercharged fours to be ridden by Walter Rusk and Bob Foster, but Excelsior were absent. They issued an advertisement that explained that the fulfilment of military contracts took precedence over racing. They had no choice in the matter, having received government directives to switch production, although the former works bikes did appear at the 1939 TT as private entries, including an experimental 500.

War was looming and everyone knew it, but racing was due to go ahead, albeit in a strained atmosphere.

RACE WEEK

Practice now included three evening sessions and racing followed the customary TT programme: Monday was Junior race day, Wednesday was for the Lightweights and Friday for the Senior race. The weather for the opening 350cc Junior race was blighted by strong winds and showers, which slowed speeds. Nevertheless, the early laps turned into a close battle between Stanley Woods (Velocette), Freddie Frith (Norton) and Heiner Fleischmann (DKW), with Harold Daniell (Norton) and Les Archer (Velocette) not far behind. The lead chopped and changed, before Frith retired at Ballaugh and Daniell recovered from sliding off in Parliament Square to challenge Woods at the head of the field. At the finish it was Stanley Woods who took his tenth TT victory, followed closely by Harold Daniell, with Heiner Fleischmann third. In a not overly impressive showing by the German marques, Wunsche did bring another DKW home in sixth, but the entire NSU team retired.

Weather conditions were again poor for the Lightweight race, with heavy cloud and some rain. DKW had been speedy in practice, but on race day it was the Moto Guzzi of Omobono Tenni that led in the early stages, swapping

This plaque commemorates Karl Gall and is located on a course-side wall just after Ballaugh Bridge.

Georg Meier takes his BMW over St Ninian's Crossroads before plunging down Bray Hill.

the lead with Ted Mellors on a Benelli and with Stanley Woods (Moto Guzzi) third. Both Guzzis dropped out mid-race and the DKW of Ewald Kluge moved into second place, with Henry Tyrell-Smith (Excelsior) third. In deteriorating weather, those positions remained unchanged to the finish of what was the slowest Lightweight TT since 1935.

Come Senior race day on Friday, the weather was good for racing. Sadly, BMW teamster Karl Gall had lost his life in a crash during practice and it was left to Georg Meier and Jock West to challenge the semi-works Norton entries of Harold Daniell, Freddie Frith and 'Crasher' White, along with the works Velocettes of Stanley Woods and Ted Mellors.

The BMWs had been fastest in practice. Even though they looked bulky, they were 30lb (14kg) lighter than the works Nortons and Velocettes, and if their published power outputs were to be believed – it is possible to see later claims of 55, 60, 68 and 70bhp in print – not only would they 'walk' the race but records would be demolished. In the event, the day was made for Germany by Meier taking victory from West by just over 2 minutes, with Frith third, a further half a minute behind West. Had the Nortons been able even to match their speeds of 1938 things could have been closer, but they had lost the all-important edge that comes with full works support, as well as a year of development. Meier increased the race record marginally, from 89.11 to 89.38mph, while the lap record stayed intact.

The last observation is not intended to take anything away from 'Schorsch' Meier's victory, for it was a worthy performance in only his second year at the TT, but with their claimed power advantage the BMWs could have expected to be much further ahead. Maybe they rode a canny race, or perhaps the old adage that power on the TT course requires commensurate handling again held true during the 1939 Senior. Whatever, Germany snatched the Blue Riband of

motorcycle racing, the first time the Senior had gone to both a foreign rider and machine.

'Titch' Allen wrote some years later:

> *The 1939 Isle of Man TT marked the end of an era. Our one-time supremacy in all classes had been challenged by more advanced designs from Germany and Italy and toppled in the Senior and Lightweight races. Even in our traditional stronghold, the Junior, there was a German two-stroke knocking on the door and needing but a little more development and an Isle of Man star (rider) to win.*

SPEEDS

The growth in speeds during the 1930s was impressive. While improved road surfaces made a major contribution to their increasing speed in the 1920s, it was improvements to race machinery that had the biggest influence on speeds in the 1930s. The decade started with the fastest lap in the Senior class standing at 73.55mph and finished with it having climbed to 91.00mph. That represented a healthy 24 per cent growth, with increases in the Junior and Lightweight classes only slightly less.

All racing plans were put to one side in late 1939 upon the outbreak of the Second World War, bringing to a halt the year-on-year advances made in the 1930s in both machine development and speeds.

CHAPTER FOUR

POST-WAR PROGRESS

In the years immediately following the Second World War, Britain was a land of austerity, but even such major obstacles to motorcycle racing as petrol rationing and an absence of new machines could not hold back over six years of pent-up enthusiasm for the sport. Meetings started to be run on former airfields in 1946 and the MGP brought racing back to the Isle of Man later the same year. In 1947 the TT returned, bringing a mix of experienced pre-war riders and many who were new to the Mountain Course. It also came with an additional event called the Clubmans TT, which was open to those without international racing experience, riding standard production motorcycles.

1947: MACHINERY

The 1947 TT attracted 109 entries in the International races and sixty-four in the Clubmans. It was an excellent turn-out of riders, but where were all the bikes to come from? Most dug out pre-war models, including the Norton factory, which brought a four-man team to ride its 1938 race bikes. Former competitions manager Joe Craig had returned to Norton and he uprated the pre-war bikes with new hydraulically damped front forks and modified plung-

ers at the rear of its 'garden-gate' frame. The company also started production of a racer for sale to the general public. Called the Manx and priced at £298, it was based on the pre-war single ohc engine of c1936. Made in 350 and 500cc form, it was in short supply.

Velocette returned with a mixture of old and new for their riders, and of the works bikes it was said 'the majority of the bottom-end parts were pre-war stuff'. They were making new racers, but with only three men in their race shop, each taking several weeks to produce a KTT model from scratch, they had few bikes for sale.

Meanwhile, the enthusiastic Moto Guzzi concern supplied a retired-from-racing Stanley Woods with a new 250 and a 500, on which he entered Manliffe Barrington in the Lightweight and Freddie Frith in the Senior.

AJS had been busy and brought a brand-new model for experienced riders Les Graham and Jock West to ride. Built purely as a factory racer, it gained the nickname 'Porcupine' due to its spiked cooling fins. It was an air-cooled 500cc laid-down twin of unit construction, with geared primary drive and gear driven twin ohc. Housed in an all-welded frame and with telescopic front forks and swinging-arm rear suspension, its claimed dry weight was 310lb (141kg).

The Triumph name was represented by several private owners on twins. Perhaps they had been encouraged by Ernie Lyons' victory in the 1946 MGP, on a Triumph whose engine used components from a war-time generator.

Riders in the new Clubmans event faced similar difficulties in obtaining machines to race. Dealers had to be cajoled into supplying bikes from their limited allocations of new models and some were provided on condition that they went straight back to the supplying dealer after the race, for resale to a hungry retail market.

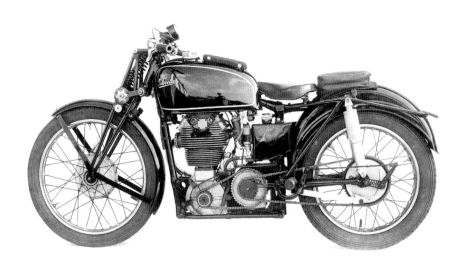

A factory-fresh Velocette 350cc KTT Mk VIII in 1947.

'POOL' PETROL

Hopes that the 1947 races would see race and lap speeds continue their upward climb were put on hold when the organizers found the only fuel available was 72 octane 'Pool'. This was an unbranded petrol derived from the pooled products of various suppliers. It was unreliable in quality and thus lacked the consistency that was so important to tuners setting up racing engines. It also necessitated lowering compression ratios from pre-war figures of close to 10:1 to something like 7.5:1, plus changes to carburation. The overall effect was said to reduce the output of a 500cc engine by some 8bhp.

At the end of 1946 the sport's ruling body banned supercharging, thus creating a level playing field on the induction front.

SPEEDS

The speed-starved spectators who thronged the roadside banks at the 1947 TT hardly noticed the difference in riders' performance from pre-war years, but the speed trap figures from Sulby Straight revealed the expected reduction in maximum figures. The very best pre-war speeds from 500 singles ridden by top riders were just over 120mph. Fastest in 1947 was Bob Foster on his works Velocette at 114.68mph, with the next fastest grouped at 109mph.

It was a similar story for the 350s, where the pre-war best was 112.5mph and post-war 107.81mph. There was a bigger differential among the Lightweights, with the pre-war fastest being 107.80mph and post-war 92.31mph. However, that was not a like-with-like comparison, for the fastest bikes pre-war were the particularly speedy two-stroke DKWs, while in 1947 it was the four-stroke Moto Guzzi of Manliffe Barrington. A better comparison was with Stanley Woods 1939 speed of just on 100mph, achieved on a similar Moto Guzzi.

In the new Clubmans classes, the highest speeds achieved at Sulby were:

Senior: Eric Briggs (Norton) – 98.92mph
Junior: Dennis Parkinson (Norton) – 93.28mph
Lightweight: Bill Jenness (Excelsior) – 74.09mph

Both Briggs and Parkinson rode 1939 International models with girder forks, and the Excelsior was also a pre-war machine.

There were no major changes to the course for 1947, but some easing of the Thirty-third Milestone did help rider progress, even if, as Ernie Lyons said, this had 'taken all the fun out of it'.

Come the racing in 1947, while it was keen and closely contested, both race average and fastest lap speeds were down in all classes. In the Senior it was by almost 7mph, in the Junior by about 4mph and in the Lightweight by 5mph. The three winners were Harold Daniell (Norton) in the Senior; Bob Foster (Velocette) in the Junior; and Manliffe Barrington (Moto Guzzi) in the Lightweight. All were experienced pre-war TT riders, so newcomer Artie Bell's second place in the Senior on a Norton was seen as a particularly good effort.

1948: STEADY PROGRESS

There were several course improvements over the winter that helped rider speed, including cutting back the bank on the apex at Hillberry – which was now taken at 90–100mph – widening at Cronk ny Mona and the eradication of several adverse cambers in Ramsey. However, the restraining effect of 'Pool' petrol continued to be felt, and while race speeds were slightly up on 1947, they were still well under record pace.

Manufacturers continued to make progress with machine development. Moto Guzzi fitted telescopic front forks to its 500 and the brave Omobono Tenni found these to his liking, being much the fastest man down Bray Hill in practice at 120mph, with other fast men around 112mph. Norton were still racing their modified 1938 TT models, while early in the year Triumph launched a 500cc twin-cylinder 'Grand Prix' model for racing. It came with components from the generator-based engine and with sprung-hub rear suspension. Seven were entered for the Senior race, but none finished. Velocette still used girder front forks, and although Freddie Frith did try a pair of Dowty telescopic ones during practice, his opinion was that just bolting on a pair of 'teles' was not enough and that the frame needed to be redesigned to suit.

It fell to AJS to introduce the only really new race machine in 1948. Designed as an over-the-counter racer for sale to the general public, the new model was called the 7R and was to remain in production for many years. It was a 350cc single with chain-driven ohc engine, 74mm bore and 81mm stroke, said to give 29bhp at 6,800rpm. Engine castings were in magnesium, finished in a distinctive corrosion-inhibiting gold paint. It had a cradle-type frame, front and rear suspension, the usual four-speed gearbox with exposed primary drive and, in a move being tried by others, a twin leading-shoe front brake.

The 7R came with narrow section tyres of 3.00 × 21 front and 3.25 × 20 rear. During practice the factory even tried a 3.00 rear in the quest for speed, for it was not quite as quick as the Velocette KTTs and Manx Nortons.

As an example of the supporting trade assisting with developments, Ferodo produced experimental brake lining materials for the several firms using twin leading-shoe set-ups.

WET AT SULBY

Riders were only timed once at Sulby during practice in 1948, under very wet conditions that offered no real basis for comparison. In better weather, they were clocked over an up-and-down 2-mile stretch from the top of the hill outside Union Mills to The Highlander pub; Ernie Lyons (Moto Guzzi) was fastest, averaging 116.1mph, followed by Freddie Frith (Triumph) at 110.7mph, a speed matched by

Ted Frend on a works Porcupine. The latter came with a strengthened frame, oil-cooler and other detailed modifications. Over the same stretch, Artie Bell (Norton) was the fastest 350 at 104.4mph.

There were twelve practice sessions, eight being for the International TT races and four for the Clubmans, with Moto Guzzi fastest overall.

NORTON AGAIN

After promising much in practice, the best Senior race finish on a Moto Guzzi was that of Omobono Tenni in seventh place, although he held third until the sixth lap. The first three places went to Norton men Artie Bell, Bill Doran and Jock Weddell, with Bell's race average speed being 84.97mph and Tenni setting the fastest lap at 88.06mph, almost 3mph below Harold Daniell's 1938 record of 91.00mph. Guzzi did get a victory in the massed-start Lightweight race, with Maurice Cann on his home-tuned machine. He also achieved the fastest lap at 76.72mph, finishing well clear of the string of pre-war British bikes that followed him home.

In the Junior, it was Velocette who showed their class with a win and fastest lap for Freddie Frith at 82.45mph, with similarly mounted Bob Foster some 4 minutes behind. The new AJS 7Rs put up a good showing, although no one could match the cheeky fourth place that Geoff Murdoch achieved when he rode one in the Senior race later in the week. It was a time when riders who had to watch the cost of racing often chose to buy a 350, as they could usually enter 500cc races on the same bike, so getting twice the number of rides.

The Senior Clubmans TT was for machines up to 1,000cc. John Daniels rode a Vincent HRD twin to first place at a race average speed of 80.51mph, while the Junior went to Ronnie Hazelhurst (Velocette) at 70.33mph and the Lightweight to Monty Lockwood (Excelsior) at 64.93mph, their speeds being slightly up on 1947.

An early AJS 7R racer.

Ernie Lyons on the 500cc Moto Guzzi at Quarter Bridge in 1948.

SPECTATORS

Post-war races drew big crowds to the TT, even though petrol was still on ration. This meant many came without their own transport, but fleets of coaches serving the Island's holiday trade were on hand to take race fans out to popular spots like Creg ny Baa or Ginger Hall. Such locations were served by a public address system, which provided commentaries from different points around the course. This helped spectators understand the progress of a race, for the leading riders would be scattered through the field and without help from the PA system, only those with stopwatches really knew what was going on.

1949: GETTING CLOSER

In 1949 the fuel supplied was still of 72 octane but was more consistent in quality. This allowed a slight upping of compression ratios and an advancement in recorded speeds and lap times, with the Junior race getting close to the best pre-war figures and the Lightweights slightly exceeding them. That Junior race had 100 entries, but on only three different makes: Norton, Velocette and AJS.

With regard to the Senior, Norton man Harold Daniell still held the race average speed record from 1938 at 89.11mph. He won the Senior again in 1949 after leader Les Graham (AJS) dropped out 2 miles from the finish, but was still over 2mph short of his 1938 figure. However, fastest lap setter in that 1949 Senior, Bob Foster, came close to Daniell's 1938 lap record of 91.00mph with a fine effort of 89.75mph on his Moto Guzzi, now fitted with leading-link front forks.

This was the first year of a new FIM-supported World Championship, and the TT was a scoring round. Freddie Frith finished the year as 350cc champion on his Velocette and Les Graham as 500cc champion on his AJS Porcupine. Speaking in later years, Frith said, 'The TT was the Blue Riband of racing then, worth more than a World Championship to people in the sport'.

In the Clubmans TT, the Junior, Senior and new 1,000cc races of 1949 were reduced from four laps to three and refuelling was banned. This turned the race for the thirstier 1,000cc machines into an economy run won by Dennis Lashmar (Vincent) at 76.30mph. The fastest 1,000cc lap –

The most exclusive Motorcycle in the World

ARIEL MOTORS LIMITED · SELLY OAK · BIRMINGHAM · 29

This is how Ariel advertising saw spectators on their way to the TT in the late 1940s.

85.57mph by Chris Horn – gave a much better indication of Vincent performance, but he, and other quick Vincent runners like George Brown, ran out of fuel. In just his second race over the TT course, Geoff Duke (Norton) recorded his first win by taking the Senior Clubmans. The Junior went to Harold Clark (BSA) and the Lightweight to Cyril Taft (Excelsior). Ignoring the fuel shortage fiasco of the 1,000cc race, the other three Clubmans races delivered increased race and lap speeds.

DOWN TO EARTH

During a TT meeting, riders spend much of their time living on a higher plane than lesser mortals. However, it can be a precarious existence and the high can easily change to a low. A good private runner of the late 1940s and early 1950s was Phil Heath. He told how when going well in a race, he hit oil at Quarry Bends and slid to earth. Standing up, his leather trousers slid down, as he had wiped off the buttons that connected them to his jacket – many riders still wore two-piece leathers.Having availed himself of a piece of string for a belt, Phil trudged to the nearest rail halt and took the local narrow-gauge steam train to Peel, sitting in a compartment with several ladies and their shopping baskets, off to do nothing more exciting than a bit of shopping. The railway line runs parallel to the TT course for some way here and to reinforce his 'return to earth', he sat watching fellow racers flashing by in the opposite direction, as the train chugged slowly along.

Many tales can be told by riders who have broken down out on the course. In the old days some returned to the start by horse and cart. Others were taken in and served tea and cakes by local homeowners, whilst many made it to the local pub and were generally plied with free drinks, so helping them overcome the disappointment of their breakdowns.

INTO A NEW DECADE

As the TT moved into the 1950s, the early years of the decade would later be seen as a period of transition. It was a time when the Norton marque extended its competitive racing life with a new frame, Velocette began to fade and AJS maintained a strong challenge, as did the enthusiastic Moto Guzzi concern. Other Italian manufacturers were also interested in the TT. Benelli already had provenance at the event, Mondial would mount a successful challenge with Lightweights, MV Agusta were on their way with Lightweights and 4-cylinder 500s, and they would be followed by the similarly equipped Gilera concern. Most of the Italian firms were already contesting and winning at Continental GP level and there was the likelihood of German marques such as BMW and NSU being readmitted to racing.

1950: THE 'FEATHERBED'

Harold Daniell had raced Norton motorcycles around the Mountain Course since 1930, using rigid, plunger and plunger/tele frames. He was in a good position to judge the new frame that Norton introduced in 1950 and was sufficiently impressed to call it the 'Featherbed'. As lap record holder on the Mountain Course, Daniell knew in those early post-war years that his basic plunger rear suspension was a limiting factor in determining how fast he could go. It was the old story of matching power to handling, for by now Norton had some 40-plus bhp on tap but without the road-holding to match.

Designed by Rex McCandless, Norton's new double-loop cradle frame was a brazed structure of thin-walled tube, which proved superior to the old garden-gate style in pre-season testing. Coming with a contoured petrol tank, rear-set footrests and lowered bars, it encouraged riders to adopt a more crouched style in the search for maximum speed.

The adoption of the featherbed frame extended the competitive life of Norton's ageing single when, although contemplating a new multi-cylinder engine, the Bracebridge Street concern did not proceed with it. However, they did continue to improve their single-cylinder engines. These came with new heads that dropped the bronze inner skull and were all aluminium. They also had the bevel housing for the ohc drive cast integrally, changes to finning, steel valve seats and so on. It was typical of the step-by-step modifications that had been a trademark of Joe Craig and Norton for so many years and which kept other firms busy trying to match them. There was a trend to smaller wheels, and a new Amal carburettor, later to become the GP, was in selective use by the Norton and AJS camps. Also on the topic of carburation, *Motor Cycling* wrote: 'methods of mounting remote float chambers with a view to stabilizing levels and insulation from heat, were, incidentally, as varied as the stars in the heavens'.

Pre-war sit-up riding styles were changing, aided by rear-set footrests, longer seats and fuel tanks styled to give some support to a rider adopting a leaning forward style.

EXPECTATIONS

Petrol rationing ended in Britain and this boosted TT crowds in 1950, when the well-subscribed International

At a time when the trend was to reduce wheel size, the older style 21in front and 20in rear of the Vincent Grey Flash are very apparent as Ken Bills tackles Cronk ny Mona.

races were permitted to run on 80 octane, although the Clubmans races were still limited to 'Pool'. British machines dominated the entry lists and included a surprise return of Vincent factory entries on new Grey Flash 500cc machines.

Expectations of home wins in the big classes were boosted by the first-time International TT appearance of Geoff Duke, who brought his special talents to the Norton team, along with Artie Bell, Johnny Locket and Harold Daniell. Duke also wore new, one-piece, close-fitting leathers, enabling him better to 'get down to it' and pare seconds off his lap times.

Speeds on Sulby Straight showed a noticeable increase over previous years, with Ted Frend on the AJS Porcupine hitting 126.80mph and Bob Foster (Moto Guzzi) close behind with 124.14mph. The latter was equalled by on-form AJS works runner Bill Doran, who later fell and put himself out of the races at the bend after Ballig Bridge that now carries his name. Juniors were also quicker, with Bob Foster (Velocette) recorded at 120.00mph, while Lightweights remained on a par with 1949 at 93.28mph. Subsequent performances in practice showed that, come race time, existing records would be under threat.

RECORDS BROKEN

Race week in 1950 started with the Junior 350cc machines. It was a race in which Artie Bell led a trio of Nortons to record-breaking victory, leaving the lap record at 86.33mph and beating Stanley Woods record of 85.30mph, set back in 1938. Norton had a repeat result in Friday's Senior, when Geoff Duke led home Artie Bell and Johnny Lockett, lifting Harold Daniell's 1938 lap record of 91.00mph to 93.33mph. Not only did the stopwatch show that Geoff Duke was faster than before, but he also looked the fastest, his neat riding style making him appear at one with the bike. Columnist

Geoff Duke crouched low over his 'Featherbed' Norton on Bray Hill.

Total commitment from Alex Phillip, as he speeds to victory on his Vincent HRD in the 1000cc class of the 1950 Clubmans TT.

'Ixion' of *The Motor Cycle* was moved to eloquence, describing him as 'a small, lithe, black figure nestling down along its backbone, with the engine disgorging thunder astern'.

It was a show of total dominance by Norton in 1950, Les Graham (AJS) being the best of the rest with fourth place in each race.

As had been the custom since 1948, the Lightweights were given a massed start, 2 minutes after the last Senior runner. A close tussle followed between Benelli-mounted Dario Ambrosini and Maurice Cann on a home-engineered Moto Guzzi. Cann led for most of the race, but Ambrosini snatched victory by one-fifth of a second, setting a new lap record of 80.91mph, some 12 seconds faster than Ewald Kluge's record from 1938 on a DKW.

Wednesday of race week was Clubmans day and races were back to four laps, with refuelling allowed. In another juggle with the regulations, riders had to perform the normal kick start but with cold engines. It was a change that was to cause problems, as did the slightly damp and misty conditions that kept speeds slightly below those set in 1949.

THE OBJECT?

Watching crowds had been thrilled by the high-speed racing of 1950, in both International and Clubmans events. But whatever they got from watching their chosen sport, *Motor Cycling* magazine was of the opinion that for British manufacturers 'the true object of the TT was to develop and demonstrate the high-performance motorcycle … in the hope that they will demonstrate the supremacy of British machines'. They did acknowledge, however, as thousands of spectators already knew, that the races were 'a great sporting event' and 'a magnificent spectacle'.

1951: A NEW CLASS

With the TT being part of the World Championships, the organizing ACU added a race for 125cc machines in 1951, later to be termed Ultra Lightweights. It ran over two laps, while the 250cc Lightweights had their race distance reduced from seven to four laps. Junior and Senior races continued to be run over seven laps, a distance of 264½ miles. That was a long way to maintain 100 per cent concentration and apply consistent riding skill. Indeed, one missed gearchange could ruin an engine and all the weeks of effort invested in a TT appearance.

Entry numbers continued to increase, with ninety-eight Seniors comprising nine makes, 100 Juniors and five makes, forty Lightweights with sixteen makes and thirty-one Ultra Lightweights with seventeen makes. In addition, although the Lightweight and 1000cc Clubmans classes had been dropped due to lack of entries, there were 169 Clubman entries across the remaining 350 and 500cc races.

The average British race fan was most interested in the Junior and Senior International classes, but was still keen to see what the four-stroke Italian Mondials and MV Agustas would do in the Ultra Lightweight class, along with the Spanish Montesa two-strokes. The latter ran on a 10:1 petrol/oil ratio and carried a reserve oil tank controlled by a tap, which the rider operated to provide an extra drip-feed of oil on the Mountain climb. Outputs of some 13bhp at 10,000rpm were spoken of for the Mondials, with 11½bhp at 9,500rpm for the Montesas. That was well above the power produced by the remainder of the field, made up by British DOTs, DMW, BSA, Sun and several home-brewed machines.

That the Mountain Course was going to be a stern challenge for contestants in the new 125cc TT was revealed early in practice, after only nine machines lapped within the 40-minute qualifying time. Following a meeting of the race stewards, the qualifying time was lifted to 45 minutes, but still only eighteen starters came to the line.

As ever, there was plenty to catch the interest in the larger classes. AJS had shorn the Porcupine of its spiked fins, worked on its carburation, shortened the wheelbase by an inch and reduced wheel sizes to 19in. Their 7R also had reduced wheelbase and wheel size, revised front forks and a compression ratio lifted to 9.4:1. Race teams were in their second year of working with 80 octane fuel, which was now to Air Ministry specification and consistent in quality.

After earlier experimentation by Velocette, Norton joined them in adding a reverse cone on the end of their megaphones. This was beneficial in aiding clean engine pick-up and acceleration in the lower rev range, more so on the 350 than the 500. In addition, Norton were now sell-

This is the 500cc MV Agusta with Les Graham (right), ready to weigh in at the 1953 TT. At its first Island appearance in 1951, it was fitted with telescopic front forks. The Earles forks fitted for 1953 did nothing to improve its appearance.

ing featherbed-framed Manx models to the public, although still with the single ohc engine. After experiencing tyre troubles during several of the Continental GP meetings in 1950, Norton changed supplier from Dunlop to Avon and also reduced rim size to 18in. Several makes showed slight enclosure of the rear of the seat and tail of the mudguard.

Velocette reduced their efforts in the larger classes, but did produce several works 250s, although gearbox problems put them out of contention.

One big attraction in the Senior entry list was Les Graham on a 4-cylinder MV Agusta. It proved fast and noisy in practice, but had questionable handling. It was not fancied for a win and was described by journalist Charlie Rous as 'an ugly brute which certainly did not look inviting to ride'.

NORTON YET AGAIN

The Norton effort at the 1951 TT was almost as good as in 1950, with Geoff Duke being a double winner of Junior and Senior classes, during which he set new race average and lap records. He left the Senior figure at 95.22mph and the Junior 91.38mph. Only AJS got a podium place amongst the Nortons, with Bill Doran finishing second on a Porcupine in the Senior. The MV Agusta retired without threatening the frontrunners.

Lightweights were also faster than before, as winner Tommy Wood (Moto Guzzi) put over 3mph on the race average speed and Fergus Anderson (Moto Guzzi) set the fastest lap at 83.70mph. The little Guzzis peaked at about

8,500rpm, ran on narrow 2.75 × 19 tyres and had a top speed of about 105mph.

It was the 10,000rpm Mondials that took the first four places in the new Ultra Lightweight race, with winner 'Cromie' McCandless setting a benchmark for future years at a race average speed of 74.85mph and fastest lap at 75.34mph. Top speed of his Mondial was about 90mph. The Mondials were followed by two Montesas, before Eric Hardy's DOT led home the rest of the field.

In the two Clubmans races, there were speed gains on the previous year but the overall lap record remained intact. Best times on the Sulby Straight for them were 109.77mph (Senior) and 104.07mph (Junior).

A Matchless G45 twin-cylinder racer in action.

1952: FURTHER DEVELOPMENTS

Riders and manufacturers left the Island in 1951 to spend the rest of the summer contesting the World Championships and the winter on machine development, the results of the latter being brought to the 1952 TT. Stories of winter activities always leaked out ahead of the races, one telling, 'From Monza … comes a report that ramps have been built there to enable an Anglo-Italian race team to test the reaction of their latest frame to high-speed hump-jumping'. It could only have been Les Graham and MV Agusta. Maybe it was an attempt to recreate Ballaugh Bridge. Handling had been a problem for the big MV in 1951 and would continue to be the subject of experimentation. The factory entered three 500s in 1952, but only Graham turned up to ride. He was also entered on one of the company's 125s, along with Cecil Sandford.

Norton had been busy and brought 'square' engines of 85.93 × 86.00mm for its 500s, which were said to permit higher revs and give a 5–7mph increase in speed. Their cylinder finning now enclosed the cam drive, they had new magnetos, rear suspension units had been given a slight forward lean, tyres were 3.50 × 18 rear for the 350 Junior machine and 'outsize' 4.00 × 16 versions for the 500 Senior.

AJS were still striving for a post-war TT victory and had much modified the Porcupine, now called the E95 model, with 45-degree cylinders and a new frame, while the works 7R was now the 3-valve 7R3, with two exhaust valves and ports. They had also built a twin-cylinder racer based on the 500cc Matchless Super Clubmans roadster engine in a 7R frame, which would go on sale to the public as the Matchless G45.

Velocette limited their works entries to 350 and 250 dohc models for Les Graham, which came with hydraulically damped girder front forks, five-speed gearboxes and twin leading-shoe front brake.

Moto Guzzi concentrated their efforts on the Lightweight class and, although they brought 4-valve head versions, they stuck to two valves for their three-man team at the TT. Meanwhile, there were private entries on Mondials in the Ultra Lightweight class.

COURSE CONDITIONS

The Mountain Course was reported to be in excellent condition, but it was still a very rough-textured surface compared to that ridden over today. Road maintenance was in the era of spread a layer of tar, apply granite chippings, usually by hand, run a steam roller over them and leave it to everyday traffic to do the rest. There was some attempt to mechanize the spreading of chippings, but it usually created a lined surface, which was not welcome when cranking over for a bend. Bare patches of tar soon appeared and the exposed tar would melt under hot conditions.

Journalist and racer Vic Willoughby was not happy with road conditions and wrote of 'ghastly undulations between Keppel Gate and Kate's Cottage', which upset the handling. The organizers took a positive step to improve safety by setting back the concrete fence posts on several of the Mountain bends.

NAMES

With its focus on speed, this book has to concentrate on the frontrunners, so it is not possible to plot the TT career progression of up-and-coming riders. Some do actually burst onto the scene with a podium finish, but most serve an apprenticeship over several years. In addition to the established stars, the early 1950s brought developing TT careers for men like Bill Lomas, Rod Coleman, Ken Kavanagh, Ray Amm, Cecil Sandford, Reg Armstrong, Bob McIntyre, John Surtees and several foreign riders.

THE RACING

Winter machine developments often received early-season try-outs on short circuits, but the real test came in June when ridden over the Mountain Course. AJS had cause for optimism in 1952 when they finished practice for the Junior race with the three fastest times. However, come race day, Geoff Duke (Norton) took an early lead, rode to signals that controlled his pace, broke the Junior race average (but not the lap record), and won by 1½ minutes from team mate Reg Armstrong. AJS had to settle for third place with Kiwi Rod Coleman.

The Senior looked as though it might go the same way, with Duke in the lead on the fifth lap, when clutch trouble forced his retirement. This left Reg Armstrong to catch and then hold off the strong challenge of Les Graham (MV Agusta), to win at a race average speed of 92.97mph – about 1mph slower than the previous year. Ray Amm (Norton) was third and Rod Coleman brought the new Porcupine into fourth. Perhaps it was 'the luck of the Irish', but just as Reg Armstrong crossed the line to win the Senior, his primary chain snapped and he lost all drive.

The Lightweight race turned into the expected fight amongst Moto Guzzi riders and went to veteran Fergus Anderson from Enrico Lorenzetti, at a record race average speed of 83.82mph, with Bruno Ruffo setting the fastest lap at a new record speed of 84.82mph. Perhaps indicative of the passion that Moto Guzzi put into their racing, Fergus received a congratulatory telegram from the president of Moto Guzzi, Giorgio Parodi, worded 'Bravo, Bravissimo. I kiss you'.

The Ultra Lightweight race distance was increased from two to three laps and Cecil Sandford gave MV Agusta their first TT victory at record race and lap speeds, ahead of the Mondials of Carlo Ubbiali and Len Parry.

In winning the Senior Clubmans race on a Triumph twin at over 80mph, Bernard Hargreaves still fell slightly short of the race and lap times set by Geoff Duke back in 1949. The Junior Clubmans did see a new race average speed record for winner Eric Housely (BSA) and a record fastest lap for Bob McIntyre (BSA). It was the fourth consecutive Junior victory for BSA.

A magazine of the day summed up the 1952 TT by saying, 'it was richly rewarding, whether viewed through the eyes of the spectator in search of thrills or those of the technician in search of data'.

1953: A RECORD YEAR

Wherever one looked at the 1953 TT there were record-breaking statistics. Entries for the International races were the highest ever, foreign machines and riders were there in the greatest numbers yet seen and records were broken in most of the racing. It was only in the Clubmans classes where numbers were down.

By March the returning BMW marque had its sole representative, Walter Zeller, spending three weeks on the Island learning the course on an R68 road bike. He was followed by NSU teamsters Bill Lomas and Werner Haas. Norton tried to fit in a quiet visit, but as they brought their experimental 350cc 'kneeler' streamlined model, they became the centre of attention.

There were fifty-one finishers in the 1952 Junior TT – twenty-three rode AJS 7R models like this one, seventeen were on Nortons and eleven on Velocettes.

Every manufacturer seemed to have new developments, most in the pursuit of power, but same aimed at increased reliability and stability. For the latter, there was evidence of steering head angles being steepened slightly to suit telescopic forks, while several were using Earles-type leading link forks, with scope to vary the pivot spindle locations. Suspension travel in general was approaching 4in at the front and slightly less at the rear. In a hint of things to come, NSU and Moto Guzzi had a hint of streamlining around the forks and tank. The scale of manufacturer involvement varied. NSU showed its intent by bringing two lorries, a service van, two cars, twelve factory personnel and ten race machines for its two riders to contest the 125 and 250 races.

Ray Amm pilots the Norton Kneeler during practice for the 1953 TT.

MV Agusta now had a 350cc four to join the 500cc entries of Les Graham and Carlo Bandirola, while in the Ultra Lightweight class there were fifteen entries on a mix of MV works and over-the-counter racers.

Probably the biggest story in 1953 was that Geoff Duke left Norton and signed to ride a Gilera four in the Senior race. Geoff gives the full story in his autobiography *In Pursuit of Perfection*, but the fact that he instantly doubled his earnings had something to do with it. The need to extricate himself from a contract to race cars before he could ride the Gilera meant that he came to the TT with very little practice. Quite happy with the 60bhp on tap, he did not criticize the Gilera's handling at the time, but in later years told that its 'road-holding on the bumpy Mountain circuit was something else entirely'. Also entered in the Senior on Gileras were Reg Armstrong, Dickie Dale and Alberto Milani.

There had been little change to the course, although the adjustment of cambers at Union Mills and Signpost Corner was of benefit to the racers, as was major widening on the inside of Bedstead. This gave a quicker run from Signpost to the Nook, so allowing more seconds to be saved.

The spectators who sat on the banks at Governor's Bridge on race days in 1953 were unlikely to be quite so elegantly attired as those shown on the cover of the race programme.

SPEEDS

The TT Special newspaper had timed riders on the Sulby Straight on the same evening for several years, but that became known to riders, so it changed the evening, saying 'it had become anticipated – and perhaps there has been some foxing!' In the 1953 timing session there was a strong side wind, which was felt to be of benefit to riders. It certainly seemed to assist those riding bikes of more than one cylinder, for fastest was Les Graham (MV Agusta) at 137.43mph, followed by Dickie Dale (Gilera) 135.38mph, Bill Doran (AJS) 135.38mph, Geoff Duke (Gilera) 135.30mph, then Reg Armstrong (Gilera) and Rod Coleman (AJS) before, in seventh place came the fastest single, that of Ken Kavanagh (Norton) at 131.43mph. However, Sulby Straight was not regarded by many as the fastest place on the course and speeds quoted in the 1950s were average ones over a distance of a mile, rather than a flash reading taken at the fastest point. This meant that talk of 140mph maximum speed from the fours was clearly credible, and rumour said the Gilera was capable of nearer 150mph. This was all heady stuff on unstreamlined motorcycles, but while speed alone may have been enough to bring victory on some continental circuits, everyone knew that the Mountain Course required handling and stamina to match.

Jack Brett (Norton) was the fastest Junior at 124.14mph, Bill Lomas (NSU) fastest Lightweight at an incredible 118.45mph, and Cecil Sandford (MV Agusta) fastest Ultra Lightweight at 100.57mph.

With such high speed-trap figures allied to fast practice lap times, it came as little surprise when race average and lap records were broken in the Ultra Lightweight race by winner Les Graham (MV Agusta), in the Lightweight by Fergus Anderson (Moto Guzzi), in the Junior by Ray Amm (Norton) and in both Junior and Senior Clubmans races.

Come the Friday of race week, everyone was ready for a record-breaking battle of the 500s – fours, twins and singles. Geoff Duke (Gilera) obliged by setting a new lap record from a standing start to lead at the end of the first lap, followed by Les Graham (MV Agusta) and Ray Amm (Norton). But Graham crashed early in the second lap, meaning Amm inherited second place and Reg Armstrong (Gilera) moved into third. Those positions were held until early in the fourth lap, when Duke slid off at Quarter Bridge and put himself out of the race. That left Rod Coleman (AJS) and Jack Brett (Norton) to dispute third place, until Brett really got into his stride, taking third on the next lap and overtaking Armstrong to take second place behind winner Amm on the final lap. So, yet again, works Nortons took the first two places in the Senior TT. Not only that, but in the face of strong multi-cylinder opposition, Rhodesian

Reg Armstrong takes Ballaugh Bridge on his 4-cylinder Gilera.

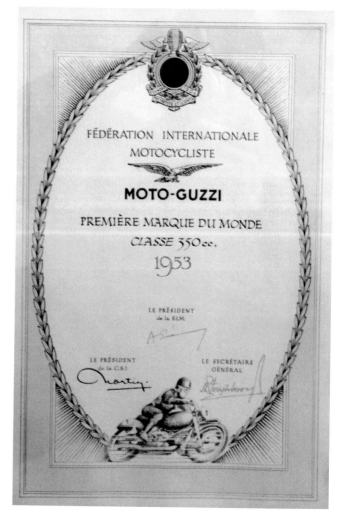

The FIM's confirmation that Moto Guzzi were World Champions in the 350cc class in 1953.

Ray Amm broke the race average and lap record speeds, leaving them at 93.85mph and 97.41mph.

TOO FAST?

Splendid though the racing may have been at the 1953 TT, it saw four fatalities, which included veteran Les Graham, who crashed his 500 MV Agusta near the bottom of Bray Hill. Interviewed in *Motor Cycling* the week before the TT, Graham told how he thought 'present day 500s are both too big and too fast for anybody's good'. Under pressure from Italy, possible power or capacity restrictions were the subject of an agenda item at the FIM Autumn Congress, along with thoughts of Formula racing. The latter would probably fall somewhere between the Clubmans TT and the racing of sports motorcycles, which was popular in Italy.

The proposals to the FIM were aimed directly at improving the safety of riders. In the event, no changes were made, but the issue remained on the agenda.

AMC

Associated Motor Cycles (AMC) owned AJS, Matchless, James and Francis Barnett. In 1953, to quote Mick Woollett, 'they swallowed up Norton Motors Ltd'. Norton director, Gilbert Smith, expressed the hope that things would continue as they were at Norton, on all fronts. And for a short while they did.

1954: SIDECARS RETURN

Early news for 1954 was of the reintroduction of a Sidecar TT race for machines of 500cc. As the available practice time over the Mountain Course was limited, a new course was found for the 'chairs', called the Clypse Circuit. Approximately 11 miles in length, it travelled the reverse direction of the Mountain Course from Cronk ny Mona to Creg ny Baa and then went eastwards over country roads, to return via Onchan to the Grandstand. The Ultra Lightweights also found their race transferred to the Clypse, with both classes due to cover ten laps and 114 miles.

The Clubmans races remained on the Mountain Course, but under the name of Clubmans Trophy and run on the Thursday of practice week. With falling entries, the Clubmans events, deliberately or otherwise, were in the process of being elbowed out of Island racing.

'PLUG CHOP'

For those running British singles, one of the surest ways to check that they were running the correct mixture strength at full throttle was to carry out a 'plug chop'. One of the best places to do this was on the Sulby Straight. At full throttle the rider would pull in the clutch, cut the engine and brake to a standstill at the end of the straight. At appointed times, representatives of sparking plug companies would be waiting there, the plug would be removed and under a knowledgeable gaze the colour would be assessed and pronounced acceptable, or not.

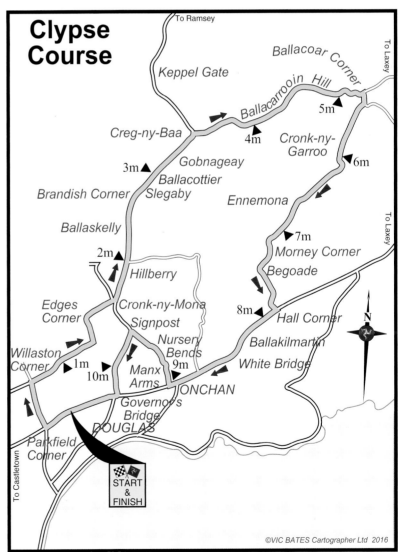

The route of the Clypse Course, introduced in 1954.

KLG used this full-page advertisement to underline their TT successes.

Hans Baltisberger on his 250cc NSU with porpoise-beaked fairing in 1954.

A 100MPH LAP?

Interviewed by Graham Walker back in 1952, Geoff Duke had been asked about the possibility and timescale of someone lapping the Mountain Course at an average of 100mph. Still riding for Norton at the time, he felt that the first 'ton' lap would go to someone on a 4-cylinder bike with good handling that was capable of 150mph. He went on to say that he believed it could happen in 1954, a prophecy he repeated during a public discussion in early 1954. Geoff was mounted on a 4-cylinder Gilera by 1954 and claimed of his machine that 'road-holding (was) much improved by building it lower and narrower, and the weight had been cut considerably by the extensive use of light alloys'. The factory also made improvements to the engine and claimed an output of 64bhp at 10,500rpm.

Gilera were not the only manufacturer seeking to give their riders better bikes, for works Nortons now had over-square engines, an outside flywheel to allow stiffening of the crankshaft and a five-speed gearbox. Unfortunately, the latter proved troublesome and the team reverted to four-speeds for the TT. AJS models were similar to 1953, but came with a lowered steering head and pannier-style petrol tanks to improve aerodynamics, while Moto Guzzi had dohc 350 and 500 engines. The speedy Lightweight NSUs were said to give 16.8bhp in 125cc form with six-speed gearboxes, and a redesigned 250cc engine offered 32.7bhp with a four-speed 'box'.

THE RECORD

Just 37 seconds separated Ray Amm's lap record of 97.41mph from the magic 'ton'. Better machinery would go some way towards reducing that deficit and so would the effect of course improvements. For 1954 there were plenty of those and, in the order a rider would come upon them, they were:

1. Six miles out, at Appledene, a cottage that projected into the road had been demolished, allowing a straightening of the kerb line.
2. Some half a mile before Ballacraine, the substantial change in road level at Ballagarraghan had been reduced, so keeping wheels on the ground for longer.
3. At Handley's Corner the right-hand bank had been cut back to allow the erection of the high wall that exists today.

4. The left-hand bank was cut back at the top of Barregarrow, improving the line and speed.

5. At Ballaugh, the projecting wall at the Raven had been demolished, improving the exit line after jumping the bridge.

6. The two bends at Kerromoar had been widened.

7. Widening at Creg ny Baa to provide those using the new Clypse Circuit with a good line saw the inside of the bend being cut back, to the advantage of those using the Mountain Course.

8. Similar works at Signpost Corner, where the Clypse rejoined the Mountain Course, resulted in considerable widening.

9. The twisty bends from the Nook to Governor's Bridge were eased.

10. The bend leaving Governor's Bridge to join the Glencrutchery Road was widened and was said to give a better exit line.

No one seemed sure of how much time would be saved from all of the above, but it certainly would have been measurable in seconds and heightened expectation that 1954 would be the year of the first 100mph lap.

DISAPPOINTMENT

With big increases in lap speeds in the Junior race of 1954, where Ray Amm (Norton) added 3mph to his own record, and a similar situation in the Lightweight with Werner Haas (NSU) putting almost 6mph on the previous best for a 250, race followers fully expected to see high speeds in the final race of the week, the Senior TT. But it was not to be. Wet and misty weather worsened during the race and brought its curtailment after four laps, with victory going to Ray Amm (Norton) with a fastest lap of 89.82mph. Geoff Duke rode his Gilera into second, feeling that he had suffered unfairly from the timing of the stewards' decision to stop the race.

Over on the Clypse, Rupert Hollaus (NSU) took victory in the Ultra Lightweight race at an average speed of 69.67mph, while Eric Oliver (Norton) led the three-wheelers home at 68.87mph.

While some might have left the 1954 TT feeling disappointed, it certainly was not members of the NSU team, for their performance in winning the Lightweight and Ultra Lightweight was most impressive. Amongst those admiring the 1954 NSUs, and taking many photographs, was Soichiro Honda. The head of the Japanese firm was on a fact-finding mission, with a view to building race machines to contest the World Championships.

1955: BIG-NAME DEPARTURES

Early in 1955, a shock announcement from Norton revealed that they were withdrawing from the World Championships and, in their words, 'reverting to a policy of racing a type of machine which can be sold to private owners'. That meant over-the-counter racers. However, they did intend to send works machines to contest the TT, ridden by two 21-year-old riders, John Surtees and John Hartle, adding that their machines 'would probably incorporate features that would be included in next season's production models'. Norton partly explained their action by decrying the specialist nature of 4-cylinder race machines, the move from road circuits to purpose-built tracks and the use of streamlining.

A week later, AJS and Matchless announced they were to follow the same route as Norton. Their decision marked the end for the factory Porcupine and left the AJS 7R and Matchless G45 being manufactured for sale to the public.

Norton, Matchless and AJS were three marques whose names went back to the early days of the TT and their works entries would be missed in the bigger classes of champi-

Pip Harris (Norton) makes a spirited turn at Willaston on the Clypse Course, pursued by Fritz Hillebrand (BMW). Notice the sidecars mounted on different sides.

onship racing. Amongst the Lightweights, the highly suc-cessful NSU concern also decided to withdraw its 125 and 250cc works bikes, although it did go on to produce the 250cc Sportmax production racer. With an output of 30bhp, it proved a competitive machine.

On more general issues, the fuel to be used at the TT was still 80 octane, there was a straightening of the road at the pits, resurfacing elsewhere and several minor improve-ments. The Clubmans was moved to the Clypse, where all races were reduced to nine laps.

Tyres gave little trouble at the TT, but Dunlop brought a new directional rear, which included knife cuts across the blocks and on the sides to improve grip under wet condi-tions. This was not a special wet weather tyre, for it would also be used in the dry. While hoping to supply plenty of tyres for racing, Dunlop also supported riders by fitting their tyres and by providing tubes, rim tapes, security bolts, balance weights, stout rubber bands, French chalk for handlebar grips, and by checking pressures and tem-peratures before and after a race.

Streamlining was now in common use in continental races, but some riders were concerned about the effect of cross-winds on the Mountain Course. Accordingly, a mix-ture of streamlined and unstreamlined bikes were out dur-ing practice sessions. It was still early days for this form of wind-cheating, but it was said to give a gain equivalent to 4bhp, usually allowed a raising of gearing and reduced fuel consumption, but put more demands upon the brakes.

The first three finishers in the Junior race were on fully faired models – Bill Lomas (Moto Guzzi), Bob McIntyre (Norton) and Cecil Sandford (Moto Guzzi). Lomas lifted the race average speed record by almost 1mph in his non-stop run, but the lap record stayed intact, while second-place McIntyre reported streamline-induced handling dif-ficulties in some of the windy locations. It was a race in which flies gave trouble, as they plastered fairings, screens and goggles, interfering with riders' vision. Thirty years earlier, Graham Walker had given his personal remedy for that problem: 'a sucked glove finger quickly applied [to the goggles] on a fine day will remove squashed flies before they congeal'.

MORE DISAPPOINTMENT

Come Friday's Senior race of 1955, the 100mph lap was again on peoples' minds. Geoff Duke (Gilera) broke the existing lap record from a standing start and thereafter pulled away from his team mate Reg Armstrong, further upping the lap record as he went. Upon completion of his third circuit it was announced that he had achieved the 100mph lap and there was cheering in the crowded Grand-stand. Shortly after, it was announced that he had actu-ally just missed the 100mph lap, recording 99.97mph, less than a second short of the elusive 'ton'. Grandstand crowds booed in disappointment, but Duke rode on unaware and intent only on taking victory. In this he was successful, and after his seven laps he finished 2 minutes ahead of Reg Arm-strong, setting new race average and lap records. Both Gileras had modest handlebar fairings, although it was said that fully faired versions were some 20 seconds a lap faster in calm weather.

With works teams from only Gilera, Moto Guzzi, Norton and Matchless contesting the Senior race it was left to British over-the-counter racers to make up most of the field of seventy-seven starters. Among them were some forty-five Manx Nortons and nineteen Matchless G45s. The latter model had become popular, and one gave Derek Ennett a sixth-place finish. A report of the time told that G45 engines had to show a minimum of 48bhp on the factory test bench before being installed in a new machine.

Geoff Duke rides his Gilera to victory in the 1955 Senior TT, taking the bridge at Union Mills with both wheels off the ground while cranked over.

Some private owners looked after their own race bikes, while others, in search of that elusive edge over the opposition, employed tuners to prepare either just the engine or the whole machine. Both Norton and AMC provided a race service to private riders at the TT, with a garage, mechanics and spares to keep them mobile.

There was to be further disappointment for Geoff Duke late in 1955, when a vengeful FIM banned him from racing for six months for supporting private riders protesting about poor levels of start money at the Dutch TT. Sixteen others, including Reg Armstrong, were also suspended for periods of four to six months. As their suspension periods ran from 1 January 1956, it put some of them out of the TT.

1956: FEWER VISITORS

The 1956 TT saw a fall in visitor numbers, and most commentators felt that this was due to the absence of Geoff Duke. Of course, the remaining riders were capable of putting on excellent racing, but the glamour associated with the top man was missing and people stayed away. It was another lesson for the organizing ACU, who some felt could have done more to support Geoff at FIM level, although they had worries at the time about the attitude of some factions within the FIM towards the TT and its World Championship status.

MORE RIDERS

Despite the decrease in spectator interest, the TT still held its magic attraction for riders, with increased entries in 1956. There had been the usual off-season turnover as riders swapped race teams, and one was John Surtees, who moved to MV Agusta. John was no doubt attracted by the news that the 500-4 was said to be yielding 70bhp at 10,500rpm, giving a top speed of 150mph. In contrast, Moto Guzzi works runner, Bill Lomas, told how their 500cc single-cylinder gave only 45bhp. However, being light, streamlined, of low build and with good handling, the single could still harass the fours, except on pure power circuits. For 1956, the factory dropped its tubular space frame and reverted to using a large-diameter top-tube version.

During practice in 1956, a limited number of riders were timed on Sulby Straight and John Surtees was the fastest 500 at 135.38mph, with Ken Kavanagh's Moto Guzzi coming in at 133.33mph. On that very limited evidence it seemed that Moto Guzzi were still on the pace, but they felt they were beginning to be outrun and were working on both 4- and 8-cylinder racers.

Gilera tried to recruit Bob McIntyre to ride their 500 at the 1956 TT in place of the suspended Geoff Duke, but McIntyre decided to stay with his sponsor, Joe Potts. Nor-

Travelling marshal Colin Broughton takes his radio-equipped Triumph through the approach to Whitegates at the 1956 TT.

ton brought a three-man team of John Hartle, Jack Brett and Alan Trow, but former manager Joe Craig was no longer with them. AMC were represented by Frank Perris, Derek Ennett and Gavin Dunlop.

Helping to look after rider interests out on the course was a team of Triumph-mounted travelling marshals. Their bikes were equipped with experimental radios as an aid to communications, but with technology that still used glass valves and the like, the radios did not take well to the pounding received over the Mountain Course.

MOUNTAIN COURSE

Apart from a little cutting back of the bank at Rhencullen to improve sightlines and easing of the testing right-hander at Ballagarey, the course was relatively unchanged for 1956. The latter bend was situated at the top of the hill after Union Mills. Some called it Glen Vine. Its importance was recognized by John Surtees, who said: 'If you did it all right, and went through absolutely on the limit, not only was it one of the most satisfying things on earth, but you also got a good run at the hill up into Crosby and down past The Highlander.' Surtees was a thinking rider and knew that maximum effort at Ballagarey would pay dividends in terms of increased mph over the reasonably straight and undulating stretch that followed to Greeba Castle. Those not prepared to put in the commitment at Ballagarey would be slower over those following miles. It was a classic TT situation that was repeated at other points on the course.

The Junior and Senior TT were the only International races held over the Mountain Course in 1956 and it was the Moto Guzzi of Ken Kavanagh that hounded John Surtees' MV Agusta throughout the Junior until Surtees ran out of fuel on the Mountain on his last lap. This allowed Kavanagh to win, although no records were broken.

On a bright and dry Senior race day, when gusty winds took the edge off top speeds, John Surtees took his nose-cone faired MV Agusta to his first TT victory, with a fastest lap of 97.79mph. Bill Lomas (Moto Guzzi) held second until the last lap, when he slowed and finished fifth. Second and third finishers were John Hartle and Jack Brett on their Nortons. It was a race in which the first six places were occupied by five different makes: MV Agusta, Norton, Moto Guzzi, BMW and Matchless.

In a strange move, the National-status Clubmans races took place over the Mountain Course, but on the Thursday and Saturday of the week after TT. They yielded a double win for Bernard Codd on BSA Gold Stars, but turned out to be the final fling for the event, which was then dropped. Codd left the fastest lap speeds for the Clubmans at 82.33mph in the Junior and 86.52mph in the Senior.

CLYPSE CIRCUIT
The two Lightweight classes and the Sidecars continued to have their massed-start races over the Clypse, where winning race average speeds had hovered around 70mph since their first running. Sidecars speeds matched those of the 125cc solos and the variation in lap times between the Lightweight and Ultra Lightweights was only about about 2–3mph. MV Agusta won both solo classes on the Clypse in 1956 with their top rider, Carlo Ubbiali. Second and

Bill Webster pushes a 125cc MV Agusta with full streamlining.

third places in the Ultra Lightweight race went to Spanish Montesa two-strokes and they were fitted with six-speed gearboxes.

Streamlining was particularly extensive on factory machines in the Lightweight classes, sometimes extending to enclosing the rear wheel.

Among the Sidecars, BMW were gaining the edge over Nortons and this was reflected in the result of the 1956 race, when Fritz Hillebrand brought his BMW twin home ahead of the Norton singles of Pip Harris and Bill Boddice. British sidecar racers usually had the sidecar on the left, while continentals favoured the right. This sometimes resulted in them taking differing lines through bends on the narrow Clypse circuit. The three-wheelers were also experimenting with streamlining.

1957: FURTHER WITHDRAWAL
Norton, Matchless and AJS ceased to compete at World Championship level with works machinery in 1955, although they did contest a few other events. In November 1956 they announced a further withdrawal, saying that they would 'not enter an official works team in [any of] next season's racing events'. A statement from AMC said that it was due to 'current circumstances', which required 'that all available technical skill and facilities are devoted to to the development of standard products'. It was not good news, for without development their over-the-counter racers would swiftly become obsolete. It also began a period of unofficial works support that left race followers confused, generally muddied the waters and did nothing to enhance AMC's reputation.

By February 1957 it was known that an unofficial Norton team would contest the TT on what, it was said, were to be 1957 Manx models. Riders were John Hartle, Jack Brett and Alan Trow and they were free to use streamlining. Then, come April, race fans were reading of a three-man team who would be using 1956 AJS and Matchless works mounts at the TT.

According to output curves supplied to the press, in standard form the 1957 Manx 500cc 30M gave about 47bhp and the 350cc 40M showed 35bhp, at a little over 7,000rpm. For the standard 7R, output was given as 37.5bhp at 7,500rpm and for the G45 it was 50.5bhp at 7,200. Whether the bhp figures quoted by the manufacturers of racing motorcycles were directly comparable depended on technical aspects like the form of brake used, whether the measurement was taken at the crank or the rear-wheel, plus the less easy to pin down issue of what message they were trying to put across. The figures were best treated as a guide, for just a few months later, Geoff

Duke, when comparing the performance of John Hartle's 500 Norton with that of a 350 works Moto Guzzi, wrote of Hartle's mount giving 54bhp.

It was a time when there were contrasting views within the sport about the merits of streamlining, and the FIM set up a committee to consider its future in both solo and sidecar classes.

GOLDEN JUBILEE

When the organizers sat down to plan the 1957 event, half a century had passed since a band of pioneers gathered on Tynwald Green for the start of the first race for the Tourist Trophy. There was plenty of general publicity on the run-up to the Golden Jubilee event, plus specific news that Gilera had a 50bhp 350-4 to go with its 500 and that Moto Guzzi would trump them all by bringing its V8 to the Island. Italian manufacturers were also busy with new and developing models in the Lightweight classes.

Entry numbers increased and many of the entries were made by dealers. Without their support, supplying machines, paying entry fees and often contributing towards competitors' travel and living expenses, many talented riders would not have been able to contest the TT. Most dealers were in it for the sport, while also hoping for a little increased business.

There were worries that a period of petrol rationing on the run-up to the TT might affect attendances, but the restrictions were lifted just before the event. Good news for the racers was that fuel would be of 100 octane. This was supplied free of charge by firms like Shell and Esso to riders who were contracted to them. Top riders received generous retainers from the petrol and oil companies, with manufacturers, tuners and dealers also contracting themselves to particular suppliers. Such arrangements certainly helped oil the wheels of motorcycle racing, but could sometimes prove restrictive and prevent riders from moving teams.

Perhaps trying to introduce some novelty to proceedings, the organizers considered sending riders off in batches of six, but decided against it. One change they did make was to extend the 1957 Golden Jubilee Senior race to eight laps, making it 302 miles. They also reduced qualifying times for Senior and Junior runners to 32 and 34 minutes. Over on the Clypse Circuit, Lightweight and Sidecar classes reverted to ten laps, giving them each 107½ miles of racing.

VARIATIONS ON A THEME

Streamlining was still a free for all and various forms could be seen. In the bigger classes, MV Agusta used just a nose cone, Gilera initially used a nose cone but moved to a full front-wheel-enclosing 'dustbin', while the V8 Moto Guzzi used a dolphin shape that left the front wheel exposed, although their singles used 'dustbins'. In the Lightweight classes Morinis wore full front and rear enclosure, while others tended to enclose just the front. It was still a time of experimentation with shapes and materials. On the Isle of Man, the Peel Engineering Company was working with fibreglass to produce streamlining for several competitors. It would later manufacture the 'Mountain Mile' dolphin fairing, which became standard wear for British machines.

Geoff Duke with an experimental version of the Peel Mountain Mile fairing.

The 500cc Gilera of Bob McIntyre is wheeled to the pre-race weigh-in by his mechanic.

In another instance of companies showing a different approach to racing, the 350cc 4-cylinder MVs and Gileras were scaled down 500s and thus weighed almost the same as the big bikes – some 320lb (145kg) for the new 350 Gilera. In contrast, the 350 and 500cc single-cylinder Moto Guzzis were scaled-up 250s. Geoff Duke told that after the Moto Guzzi factory had spent a winter 'adding lightness' to its 350, it came to the 1957 TT with a dry weight of 210lb (95kg). He felt that they had gone too far with weight-saving and that it could be too 'gazelle-like' for the Mountain Course. Duke was a non-starter at the 1957 TT, due to a shoulder injury sustained in a spill at Imola. His place was taken by Australian Bob Brown, who joined Bob McIntyre in the Gilera team.

THE MAGIC 'TON' LAP

The high quality of machines and riders entered for the 1957 races made it difficult for armchair pundits to predict the winners. On the Mountain Course, Bob McIntyre's Senior (Gilera) was now giving 70bhp and he set the pace during practice for the Junior and Senior classes, while on the Clypse Circuit, all-Italian Lightweight machinery scrapped for the fastest solo times, piloted by riders of several nationalities. Among the three-wheelers, drivers of BMWs were exerting what was to become a long-term stranglehold on the Sidecar class, where hydraulically assisted brakes were used by several competitors.

Race week turned into an occasion befitting a Golden Jubilee meeting, with new race average and lap record speeds set in every event. As expected, BMWs dominated the Sidecar race with Fritz Hillebrand, Walter Schneider and Florian Camathias taking the top three places, while Tarquinio Provini rode his Mondial to Ultra Lightweight victory from chasing MV Agustas. His team mate Cecil Sandford did the same in the Lightweight after Sammy Miller (Mondial) grabbed the lead on the last lap but fell at Governor's Bridge – the last corner. The meteoric Tarquinio Provini (Mondial) added almost 5mph to the Lightweight lap record, leaving it at 78.00mph.

Victory in the Junior race went to Bob McIntyre (Gilera), who eventually won by a comfortable 3½ minutes, although he had to lift the race average and lap records by almost 3mph to shake off nearest pursuers Ken Kavanagh (Moto Guzzi) and Bob Brown (Gilera).

The last race of the 1957 Golden Jubilee meeting was the Blue Riband Senior TT, which ran under ideal conditions. Challenged in the early stages, McIntyre rode away from the MV Agusta, BMW and Moto Guzzi opposition on his big Gilera, breaking the long-standing 100mph lap barrier four times and leaving it at 101.12mph on his way to the chequered flag and a popular victory. It was a convincing win, for second-place John Surtees (MV Agusta) was some 2 minutes behind, with Bob Brown (Gilera) third and Dickie Dale, on the Guzzi V8, fourth. Overall race time to cover the eight laps was just over 3 hours for the winner and after those 300 racing miles it was reported that the 'tyres of the first three finishers appeared relatively unworn'. They still ran with a slim 3.50in on the rear.

Members of the trade whose components had been involved in setting the 100mph lap indulged in much post-race advertising. For most it was enough just to be associated with the glory, but Ferodo sought to further impress by adding statistics that Bob McIntyre would have applied his brakes seventy-three times per lap and that they would disperse 250,000 ft/lb of energy in slowing for Sulby Bridge.

HALF A CENTURY

During fifty years of TT racing, manufacturers and riders had striven to achieve ever greater speeds. In doing so, they lifted the average race win-

Bob McIntyre fights his 500cc Gilera through the bottom of Bray Hill in 1957.

ning figure of 38.22mph, set by Charlie Collier in 1907 on his fairly primitive Matchless, up to the 98.99mph race average achieved by Bob McIntyre in the Senior TT of 1957 on his state-of-the-art Gilera. That was far more than anyone could have imagined in the early days: in Chapter 1 we saw how, when Frank Philipp set a record lap speed of 50.11mph in the first TT to run over the Mountain Course in 1911, one publication speculated whether 'a 60mph or even a 70mph TT' was possible in the future.

There was less speculation about future speeds in 1957, for the breaking of the 100mph lap barrier left many feeling that a plateau had been reached.

So much had changed during half a century of TT racing, but one constant remained: despite the advances in technology and many course improvements, racing still took a heavy toll upon machinery, thus highlighting weaknesses and fulfilling much of its original purpose.

1958: ITALIANS QUIT

Perhaps the reluctance to speculate about a speedier future after the Golden Jubilee TT was influenced by the shock decision of Italian makes Gilera, Moto Guzzi and Mondial to withdraw from racing at the end of the 1957 season. This was principally on financial grounds, although Gilera's input into racing had slowed, due to the death of Giuseppe Gilera's son from illness. Their twin passions for engineering and racing would be badly missed.

One Italian firm who did not withdraw was MV Agusta. The race activities of the Gallarate concern were a personal hobby of Count Agusta, his principal business being the manufacture of helicopters. The next few years were to provide the Count with an enjoyable and successful hobby, across all solo classes, even though his number one rider, John Surtees, told that he had to pester the Count to maintain development of the big MVs.

BACKGROUND

TT racing in 1958 felt the effect of several changes. First, of course, was the absence of some of the foremost Italian manufacturers, although one 'new' Italian firm to take up the challenge in the Ultra Lightweight class was Ducati, with its little four-stroke engines sporting desmodromic valve gear and putting out 18bhp at 12,500rpm. The class also saw the appearance of the East German MZs, who were said to almost match that output with their pioneering developments in two-stroke technology.

After considering the issue of machine enclosure, the FIM introduced a ruling restricting streamlining to the dolphin type, which left the front wheel exposed. Thus 'dustbins' and rear enclosure were no more. The same body was still talking of dropping the 500cc class, perhaps in 1960, and there continued to be mutterings about the introduction of Formula classes.

Tyre manufacturers were using racing to develop their products, with nylon carcasses replacing rayon and cotton. Nylon was reckoned to be lighter, while still being robust, flexible and offering cooler running. It was a significant change in construction by both the Avon and Dunlop concerns, which would soon spread to roadster tyres and, like other features that first appear in racing, would be adopted by other firms, even those who did not race.

Among some of the top riders who lost their seats after Italian manufacturers dropped out, Geoff Duke was now on a works BMW for the Senior and Dickie Dale was similarly mounted. Duke was also the recipient of a special 350cc engine from Norton at the TT, plus a five-speed gearbox. Others to receive special engines that were claimed to be 'squarer' were Keith Campbell, Alan Holmes and sidecar man 'Pip' Harris, while Bob Brown was given a complete 500cc machine. Meanwhile, Matchless had been developing a 500cc version of the 7R, and a prototype was to be ridden at the 1958 TT by Jack Ahearn. It would be called the G50 and soon go on general sale.

WEIGHT

Hidden among the race regulations was one that had been largely ignored in previous years. It prescribed that riders must weigh a minimum of 9 stone 6 pounds in leathers. The surprise production of a pair of scales in 1958 saw some of the lighter-looking riders asked to step on them. Among those not reaching the appointed weight were Romolo Ferri, Carlo Ubbiali and Luigi Taveri. The last was 21lb (10kg) underweight, while the diminutive Gary Dickinson was even lighter. They were all required to add ballast to their machines to reach the required weight.

SPEEDS

John Surtees and John Hartle were the MV Agusta works riders and they set the pace in practice in 1958, on models now fitted with dolphin fairings. On one chilly early-morning session, as it was struggling to get light, Surtees put in his fastest ever lap, averaging 99.06mph from a standing start. While he was not openly critical of the MVs, he felt that they were still too tall and heavy. But with the 350 revving to 10,800 and the 500 to 10,400, perhaps he was consoled by the power output, which gave him considerable advantage over the British machines in the field of eighty-two, most of them being Nortons.

Timed on Sulby Straight under perfect conditions, John's was the fastest 500 at 139.56mph, with the Norton of Alan

John Surtees and his 4-cylinder MV Agusta at Signpost Corner in 1958. Smoke from the exhausts was customary when the throttle was shut on the MV, John saying that it was related to the substantial amount of oil carried.

With three solo races run and three victories, come Friday's Senior race, MV Agusta were looking to make it a clean sweep. That was the way it worked out, with John Surtees taking victory at a race average speed of 98.63mph and a fastest lap of 100.58mph. Surtees' team mate, John Hartle, was forced to retire, as he had in the Junior, but this time it was due to a major mechanical fire, which saw his Italian mount burn itself out at the side of the road. This left Bob Anderson and Bob Brown to take the other two podium places on their Nortons.

Trow next at 136.40mph, followed by Bob Anderson (Norton) at 133.33mph. It was Geoff Tanner (Norton) who was the fastest 350 at 126.80mph, followed closely by the Nortons of Bob McIntyre and Terry Shepherd.

MV AGUSTA'S YEAR

Race week started with the Junior TT, where John Surtees gave MV Agusta the first of the four wins it would achieve in the solo classes at the 1958 TT. Pursued home by Dave Chadwick and Geoff Tanner on Nortons, Surtees had no need to try for records.

Wednesday saw action on the Clypse, and Tarquinio Provini had to break race average and lap records on his MV Agusta to fight off team mate Carlo Ubbiali, who finished a few seconds behind. Finishing in a highly creditable third place in his first year at the TT was a young Mike Hailwood (NSU). Ultra Lightweight victory went to Carlo Ubbiali (MV Agusta) and he was followed home by the Ducatis of Romolo Ferri and Dave Chadwick.

Sidecars had their own race over the Clypse on the Wednesday and this saw victory go to Walter Schneider (BMW) at record-breaking speeds.

SPEED

The post-war era started with speeds that did not match those of the late 1930s, due to the poor fuel available. Once that returned to pre-war standards, fastest laps in the Senior class soon overtook the best pre-war figure of 91.00mph and aided by faster 4-cylinder Italian machines, fastest lap speed had climbed to 101.12mph.

END OF AN ERA

Riders came from all over the world to contest the TT races, but apart from the successful participation of the Indian marque in the event's early days, the manufacturers represented and winning in 1958 were almost wholly European and had been for decades. This remained the position even after the 'World' Championships were created in 1949, but change was in the air, for the Honda Motor Company of Japan was about to fulfil Soichiro Honda's ambition and challenge for a Tourist Trophy.

CHAPTER FIVE

EAST vs WEST

The creator of Honda Motors, Soichiro Honda, visited the TT in 1954, armed with camera and notebook to gather as much information as possible about the event and the competing machinery. It was the year that NSU dominated the Lightweight and Ultra Lightweight classes at the TT and in the wider world of racing, so when Honda made its first TT entries in 1959, it was probably no coincidence that the bikes from Japan had more than a passing resemblance to the earlier NSU 125cc Rennmax models. However, no one should underestimate the enterprise shown by Honda

Naomi Taniguchi and his 125cc Honda on the Clypse Course in 1959.

almost sixty years ago and no one can be in any doubt today of the impact they have had on the world of racing.

Based at the Nursery Hotel in Onchan, the company had five entries in the 125cc Ultra Lightweight TT in 1959. Four machines were to be ridden by Japanese riders and the fifth by American Bill Hunt. During their stay they had many visits from the curious and also from the more knowledgeable, including several riders. All were keen to get a close-up view of machines that one journalist described as 'neatly made and technically brilliant'.

1959: FORMULA I

Another new arrival on the TT scene in 1959 was Formula I racing. This was for production racing motorcycles of which at least twenty-five must have been sold. Two races, for 350cc and 500cc machines, were run concurrently over three laps on the Saturday evening prior to race week, but with a combined entry of just twenty-nine riders on Norton, Matchless, AJS and BMW, they were thinly spread around the Mountain Course. It was Bob McIntyre (Norton) who took the 500cc win at an impressive race average of 97.77mph, while his close friend, Alastair King (AJS), was first 350 home at 94.66mph. McIntyre's fastest lap on his 'standard production' Manx Norton in that Formula I race was 98.35mph, which compared well with his best-ever Norton lap on his specially prepared Joe Potts race bike of 99.98mph, set in 1958. King was also fast and his pace matched the Junior TT winning speeds of the previous two years, set by Gilera and MV Agusta.

Apart from knowing that works exotica were excluded, few understood the purpose of Formula I and, according to *The Motor Cycle*, the 1959 event 'was not true Formula I racing, for such machines as the Manx Norton and 7R AJS have yet to be entered on the FIM register'. This was despite the fact that the event had been virtually forced upon the TT by the FIM.

DEVELOPMENTS

With patient development, most recently by Doug Hele at Norton and Jack Williams at AMC, the traditional British singles were putting out ever more power. When launched in 1948, the AJS 7R produced 29bhp at 6,800rpm, but in 1959 it gave 40.5bhp at 7,800rpm and was reckoned to be faster than a standard 350 Manx Norton. A desmodromic version of Norton's Manx engine was brought to the Island for evaluation purposes in 1959 and Terry Shepherd used it in practice.

The Lightweight and Ultra Lightweight classes saw technically interesting machines entered by MV Agusta, Ducati, MZ, EMC, Honda and others. A range of singles, twins, four-strokes and two-strokes filled what was a buoyant class. Whether it was due to the talk of dropping the bigger classes from GP racing is unclear, but in contrast to modest development of their fours, MV Agusta put much effort into improving their Lightweights, the 250 coming with a new frame and said to be capable of topping 130mph – almost matching their 350 four.

Streamlining was now widely used in its regulation dolphin form, but despite obvious benefits, it also created problems. Some users met with general engine-cooling difficulties, others found a need to provide ducting to take air to carburettor inlet areas, while those prone to sparking-plug problems fitted air deflectors to help cool them. Each practice session provided examples of 'panic engineering' applied to deal with such issues, for they were mostly ones that had not revealed themselves on short circuits.

Gary Hocking in the middle of the traditional run and bump start used in racing in the 1950s.

PRACTICE

Running to form in the big classes, the MV Agustas of John Surtees and John Hartle were fastest in practice in 1959, but among the Lightweights prospective winners were harder to pick. Riders of MV Agusta, Ducati and MZ machines all vied for the fastest times.

Over the 2-mile run to The Highlander on the Mountain Course, John Hartle clocked the fastest Senior time at an average speed of 131.42mph and John Surtees 128.57mph. Best single was Alan Shepherd on his G50 Matchless at 123.31mph. In later years a speed trap was located near The Highlander that gave 'flash' readings at close to maximum speeds, but in 1959 the average speeds quoted over 2 miles were usually about 10mph down on maximum.

A newcomer enlivening the racing scene before the TT was Gary Hocking, and he showed well on Reg Dearden Nortons during practice. Reg was often the conduit by which Norton released their special engines at TT time, with Tom Arter being used by AMC.

Mike Hailwood had a stable of eight machines in the garage of Geoff Duke's Arragon Hotel at Santon, with veteran tuner Bill Lacey coaxed out of retirement to help tune them.

MV AGUSTA AGAIN

MV faced serious opposition in all four solo International TT classes in 1959 but, as in 1958, they finished the week with four victories, increasing their speeds in all classes. Tarquinio Provini rode the 125 and 250 MVs to new race average winning speeds and also set the fastest 250cc lap. In doing so he became the first to lap the Clypse Circuit at 80mph, while a new lap record for a 125 went to Luigi Taveri (MZ) at 74.99mph.

Everyone was interested in how the new Hondas would perform in the 125 Ultra Lightweight class and they did not disappoint. With four finishers from five starters, they took sixth, seventh, eighth and eleventh positions in a field that had eighteen finishers. They did not have the speed of the winning MV Agustas, but it was a performance that earned them the Manufacturers team prize and their sixth-place finisher, Naomi Taniguchi, rode fast enough to win a Silver Replica.

Races on the Clypse continued to have mass starts, whereas on the Mountain

Course the system was still for interval starting. New for 1959 was the seeding of the top five runners in the Junior and Senior races, based on their previous year's times, followed by balloting them for the first five start numbers. This was a major change for riders and spectators, with obvious benefits for both.

John Surtees won the Junior race, setting a new race record but falling just short of the lap record, while John Hartle came second after inheriting the place from Bob McIntyre (AJS), who had held the MV rider at bay until he retired on lap five. While competitors in that Junior race were troubled by molten tar, the Senior TT had to be postponed from Friday to Saturday due to inclement weather. When Surtees got away from the start of the Senior just after 10.30am, he rocketed into the lead over dry roads, setting a new lap record of 101.18mph from a standing start. Then the heavens opened with heavy rain, hail, mountain mist and strong winds. Those combined to reduce Surtees' lap speed to some 85mph as he fought the elements and coped with areas of both standing and running water, together with the many slides that ensued as he rode to victory. From sixty-six starters, twenty-two sodden heroes finished the race, the winner being in a state of physical exhaustion after averaging 87.94mph over the full 264½ miles and being in the saddle for over three hours.

1960: CHANGE OF COURSE

In 1960 the Lightweight, Ultra Lightweight and Sidecar races were moved from the Clypse back to the Mountain Course. Other changes saw Junior and Senior race distances reduced from seven to six laps, giving each a race distance of 226½ miles, while the Lightweight class covered five laps and 188¾ miles. The Ultra Lightweight and Sidecars ran over three laps and 113¼ miles. All races now used interval starts. There was no Formula I race.

FINE DISPLAY

The TT races attract visitors for many varied reasons, and in 1960 renowned Australian engineer Phil Irving was there to view the technical developments on show. In his words, the TT was responsible for 'assembling, at the same time, the finest and most varied collection of racing machinery it is possible to see anywhere in the world'.

Following Honda's lead, and with huge support from Shell in Japan and Britain, Suzuki came from Japan to contest the Ultra Lightweight race with twin-cylinder Colleda RT60 models. They had basic piston-controlled induction, separate alloy barrels and ran on a petrol mix. With six-speed gearboxes, they were said to be good for 94mph. Arriving well before the start of official practice, the three

John Surtees holds a tight line through Hillberry in the wet Senior TT of 1959.

Suzuki riders put in many learning laps of the course on road bikes.

In the Lightweight class Honda brought new 4-cylinder RC161 models with over-square engines revving to 13,500rpm and giving 36bhp (some say more), while MZ were claiming 42bhp at 11,000rpm from their twins. As usual, this class had a smattering of cut-down singles from Norton, BSA and Velocette.

The Junior class saw entries of enlarged Lightweights from Morini, Bianchi, Ducati and MV Agusta, while Eddie Crooks was out on an experimental 'Lowboy' 350 Norton. Not all the experimental models entered made it to racing or even practice, however.

With the big MV Agustas now generally reliable, it was the overtuned singles that were more likely to fail in the Junior and Senior races. Thus the latter probably welcomed the reduction of race distance to six laps, particularly as those who went for pannier fuel tanks might be able to run a non-stop race, an option not open to the 22mpg MVs without making them unmanageable in the handling department.

Most sidecars were still ridden in sit-up style, but some were positioning fuel tanks in the sidecar and their riders were moving to kneeler mode, something which Eric Oliver had experimented with back in 1953. Their wheels had become smaller and many utilized short leading-link front forks. Dunlop provided a special new rear racing tyre for the 'chairs', but Avons were the preferred wear for solos. There was nothing like the specialization in tyres that there is in today's racing, although Avon were making something of their use of high-hysteresis rubber, said to absorb and then slowly release shocks, rather than bouncing back. They were also claimed to offer better grip in the wet. However, when asked what tyres he was using, Mike Hailwood replied 'round and black ones'.

SPEEDS

While John Surtees claimed that the 500cc MV Agustas were 'topping 150mph in places', figures from the Sulby speed trap – not the fastest spot on the course – showed that speeds in recent years seemed to have peaked there at just under 140mph. Indeed, it was Mike Hailwood (Norton), on the best single-cylinder machinery that money could buy, who equalled the fastest MV speed in 1960, matching John Hartle's figure of 138.46mph. Hailwood's was an exceptional figure, for next best single was Dickie Dale on a Norton at 128.57mph, although previous years had seen other singles over 130mph.

John Surtees' MV was fastest Junior at 125.91mph, with Bob McIntyre (AJS) next at 120mph. In a sign of the times, Tarquinio Provini (Morini) equalled Surtees' Junior speed with the fastest Lightweight at 125.91mph, as did Bob Anderson on his MZ. Moto Kitano was the fastest Honda at 117.68mph, indicating that the Japanese company's 250cc fours were still down on speed.

In the Ultra Lightweight, Carlo Ubbiali hit 109.77mph on his little MV Agusta, followed by team mates Gary Hocking (107.81mph) and Luigi Taveri (105.88mph). Sidecars were not timed at Sulby, but on the 2-mile stretch to The Highlander the fastest average speed was set by Florian Camathias (BMW) at 111.82mph, followed by Fritz Scheidegger (BMW) with 111.14mph and Bill Beevers (BMW) with 105.88mph. Speeds over that stretch would probably be about 10mph down on absolute maximum sidecar speeds.

ROAD SURFACING

Despite the slightly mixed picture on maximum speeds in 1960, practice week showed a general reduction in lap times, indicating an overall increase in lap speeds. Many felt that this was due to the new lengths of smooth tarmac being laid by the Blaw-Knox-type road paving machine now being used on the Island's roads. Not only did this modern

The Ballacraine Hotel provides a backdrop to John Surtees and his MV Agusta during the 1960 Junior TT.

machine provide a smooth running surface, but it also filled depressions, thus eliminating bumps. With race machines hitting maximum revs in all gears, riders were forced to ease the throttle over bumpy sections, to avoid over-revving as the back wheel left the ground. They liked the new smoother surface for allowing them to keep the throttle wide open for longer. They also liked its grip quality in the dry, although some had reservations about the feel in the wet, where they felt it could suddenly 'let go'.

Among stretches to benefit from the new surfacing was Bray Hill, which, now being smoother, allowed John Surtees to take it flat in top on his big MV, even though the extra speed did induce some tail-weaving after the dip at the bottom. The high-speed run from Creg ny Baa to Brandish also benefited from new surfacing, yielding yet a few more mph and the paring of lap times.

MORE RECORDS

In a change to the race programme for 1960, the Lightweight, Ultra Lightweight and Sidecar classes ran on Monday, Junior on Wednesday and Senior in its customary Friday position. No one was surprised when, in winning the Sidecar race, Helmut Fath's fastest BMW lap of 85.79mph raised the lap record by 28.61mph, for the last Sidecar race over the Mountain Course was in 1925. Equally, everyone knew that speeds in the small classes would be faster than their last ride over the 37¾-mile lap, which was 1953 for Ultra Lightweights and 1954 for Lightweights.

In 1960 the Ultra Lightweight 125 win went to Carlo Ubbiali (MV Agusta) with a fastest lap of 86.10mph, up from the 1953 fastest speed of 78.21mph. The Lightweight

A Paddock shot of Naomi Taniguchi and his new 4-cylinder Honda 250cc in 1960.

250 fell to new star Gary Hocking (MV Agusta), with Ubbiali setting the fastest lap of 95.47mph, up from the Werner Haas' 1954 lap speed of 91.22mph. It was Ubbiali's last TT race, for he retired at the end of the season.

There were no fireworks from the Japanese entries. In the Ultra Lightweight race Honda had five finishers occupying solid sixth to tenth places, while Suzuki's best effort came from Toshio Matsumoto in fifteenth. There was another show of reliability from Honda in the Lightweight race with fourth, fifth and sixth places going to their fours. Reliability was a feature sadly lacking with the speedy MZs, which failed to finish.

The surprise in the Junior race was that the win went to John Hartle (MV Agusta) after John Surtees had set a new lap record of 99.20mph, only to strike gear-selection problems and finish second. Bob McIntyre (AJS) took third. Positions of the first two were reversed in the Senior where Surtees took his fourth premier class win, becoming the first man to set a TT race average speed of over 100mph and lifting the lap record to 104.08mph. It was a race in which Derek Minter (Norton) became the first rider of a British single to lap at 100mph, closely followed by Mike Hailwood (Norton), who also lapped at 100mph and took third place.

There can be no doubt that 1960 was an excellent year for those who liked record speeds and interesting machinery to go with their TT racing. Not known at the time was that it was John Surtees' last TT ride. He had started in fourteen Island races and finished them all. Despite setting new race and lap records, many people felt that Surtees rode his big MV Agustas on the Island with something still in hand. He told how 'the most vital ingredient in racing at the TT is rhythm – getting into an established rhythm and sticking to it'. This seven-times World Champion on two wheels left the sport to race on four wheels, where he also became World Champion – the only man ever to do so.

1961: QUALIFYING

There was no shortage of riders who wished to challenge the Mountain Course. For most it would remain an unfulfilled dream, others might enjoy a once-off adventure of a lifetime, while some got so bitten by the TT speed bug that they returned year after year.

Growing lap speeds saw the organizers reduce qualifying times across all classes in 1961. They became:

Sidecar – 38 minutes
Ultra Lightweight –34 minutes
Lightweight – 33 minutes
Junior – 30 minutes
Senior – 29 minutes

The daily grind of practice sessions gave riders and their support crews early mornings, late evenings and general round-the-clock working on maintenance and rebuilds, for riders put in over 70,000 miles in practice at the 1961 TT. Such a mileage produces its share of incidents. When Jack Findlay fell at Cronk ny Mona, evidence of rider and machine's slide up the road was visible for a distance of 134 yards. Both were bent and scraped, but both were made fit to race.

As ever, there were a number of tuners working with British single-cylinder machines, seeking to extract more power and give their clients the vital edge over opponents. Amongst them were Bill Lacey, Steve Lancefield, Francis Beart and Ray Petty. Their work was based on experience and practical testing, which was a painstaking business. All had their secrets and some extended their 'tuning' to the whole machine, utilizing special brake drums, modifying riding positions, having fairings made to their designs and pursuing lightness. Francis Beart's AJS 7R was said to be 25lb (11kg) lighter than standard, which was almost 10 per cent of the weight of the production model.

Standard 1960 Manx Nortons were now delivered with 11:1 compression ratios for 350 and 500cc versions and priced at £497. However, no one was going to win a TT on a production Manx and that is where tuners came into play. Exactly how much it cost to give a machine sufficient extra performance to enable it to challenge for a podium place at the TT was never revealed by those paying the bills.

Many racers could not afford to buy extra performance, but guidance on preparing engines for racing could be found in books like Phil Irving's *Tuning for Speed*.

Fashionable in 1961 were lightweight telescopic steering dampers pioneered by Honda, and the Amal GP2 carburettor was now in use on British singles.

ADVANCE OF THE LIGHTWEIGHTS

In British eyes, the Junior and Senior races were the principal events at every TT meeting, but for many others it was in the Lightweight classes where the real interest lay. That was particularly so in 1961 when the works teams of Honda and Suzuki were joined by a third Japanese manufacturer, Yamaha, who brought 125cc single-cylinder and 250cc twin-cylinder air-cooled two-strokes, together with a team of eight engineers. They were up against entries of European machinery like MV Agusta, Bianchi, Ducati, Moto Guzzi and Aermacchi, although some of those were private entries, and not everyone turned up to race or survived practice. Other marques like EMC and MZ were present, together with a few specials.

There was much variety in the Lightweights in everything from engine configuration of one, two and four cylinders, to frame construction using cradle, spine and lattice forms. All except EMC were air-cooled. MZ were happy with their Ultra Lightweights, which were said to give 25bhp, and in the long Thursday afternoon practice Ernst Degner completed four laps. That was actually one

The Yamaha entries in 1961 had noticeably bulbous fairings.

lap more than the 125s were required to complete in their race. Things were not so good with the Lightweight MZs, and after troublesome sessions trying to get them to carburate properly, the 250s were withdrawn, as they would not run cleanly over the Mountain.

Come the racing, the improved Hondas showed that they had truly made the grade. In only their third year at the TT and in what was described at the time as 'a scintillating demonstration of high-speed reliability', they took the first five places in the Ultra Lightweight race and then did exactly the same in the Lightweight. Winner of both races was Mike Hailwood at record-breaking race average speeds. New lap records were also established in both classes, with Luigi Taveri (Honda) fastest 125 and Bob McIntyre (Honda) setting the TT course alight with an incredible lap of 99.58mph on his 250cc RC162 model. It was a prelude to the company taking further victories in the 1961 GP season to finish as world champions in the 125 and 250cc classes.

Yamaha did well to take sixth place in the Lightweight race with Fumio Ito on the 35bhp RD48 model with its bulbous fairing, but Suzuki were finding the event very demanding, having no 125cc finishers and managing just tenth and twelfth places with their 250s.

A new name to enter the TT record books after winning the Sidecar race was Max Deubel (BMW). He put 2mph on the race average and lap record speeds to win by half a minute from Fritz Scheidegger (BMW).

MV AGUSTA 'PRIVAT'

With their established 'heavyweight' and 'lightweight' team leaders, John Surtees and Carlo Ubbiali, having retired at the end of the 1960 season, MV Agusta entered just Gary Hocking in all four classes at the 1961 TT. For some reason they tried to indicate that these were not works entries, so Gary's bikes came with 'Privat' stickers on the fairings. Few believed the message they were trying to convey. He did not ride the 125 and retired in the 250 race. Hoping for better results with the fours, he led the Junior for three laps, pursued by Mike Hailwood (AJS), but then was forced to slow, allowing Hailwood to lead for most of the next three until, on the last lap, the gudgeon pin failed on Hailwood's AJS just outside Ramsey. By then it was rising star Phil Read (Norton) who was in position to take over the lead and he held it to the chequered flag.

After dominating the TT for so many years, those early races of the 1961 event saw the 'Privat' MV Agustas being embarrassed on a very public stage. It looked as though Hocking was going to redeem the situation in the Senior, for he led until the fifth lap, but was then forced to retire, leaving Mike Hailwood (Norton) to take victory, followed by Bob McIntyre (Norton) and Tom Phillis (Norton). Hailwood's Norton had been bench-tested at 53.5bhp just before the TT, but he had kept Hocking's 70bhp MV Agusta in sight and finished with a race average speed of 100.60mph and a fastest lap of 101.31mph. Fastest lap of the race went to Hocking at 102.62mph. Both Bob McIntyre and Tom Phillis achieved 100mph laps, with the latter's being on the 'Domiracer', an experimental twin-cylinder, pushrod model based on the Norton 'Dominator' roadster.

In becoming the first rider to take three TT wins in a week, Mike Hailwood justifiably earned the unofficial accolade of 'Man of the Meeting' at the 1961 TT. Norton must also have been proud to achieve another double victory in Junior and Senior races.

Post-race congratulations are exchanged between Tom Phillis (left), Mike Hailwood (centre) and Bob McIntyre after the 1961 Senior TT.

1962: WORKS RIDES

Japanese factory representation at the 1962 TT meant there was fierce competition for a coveted and lucrative works ride with Honda and Suzuki, plus the limited seats available with European manufacturers. Yamaha did not contest the event, staying at home to catch their financial breath and to design more competitive machines.

As yet, Japanese riders had not been able to ride at the same winning level as the top racers from European and Commonwealth countries, who, because of their riding skills, were given some of the Honda and Suzuki factory rides. However, there were more potential stars than saddles available, so the next few years would see top riders giving their all to capture a select works contract. Among men who came to the fore in the early 1960s were Jim Redman, Tommy Robb, Hugh Anderson, Mike Duff, Bill Ivy and Ralph Bryans. They joined established stars like Mike Hailwood, Bob McIntyre, Phil Read, Tom Phillis, Ernst Degner and Luigi Taveri, with the diminutive Kunimitsu Takahashi probably the fastest Japanese rider of the time. There were future world champions amongst those names, men who would show their worth across the most demanding tracks in Europe. By their efforts they would prove themselves to be the best – and all would have the Isle of Man on their racing agendas.

Looking back, it is really no surprise that factors like improved road surfaces, advances in tyre and suspension performance, together with hungry riders and factories demanding success from their ever more advanced motorcycles, all combined to bring increased speeds to the TT through the 1960s.

TIDDLERS

After the reintroduction of the Ultra Lightweight class to the Mountain Course in 1960, riders had shown that 125s could cope with its demands and the lap record stood to Luigi Taveri (Honda) at a healthy 88.45mph. For 1962 the organizers included a race for 50cc machines over two laps, a class recently introduced to the World Championships. The 50s would run on the Friday of race-week, just before the Senior TT.

In every TT race of the day, the field was made up of an elite group on works machines, fast runners on dealer-sponsored bikes, good privateers giving their all and a few at the rear of the field who were simply realizing their ambition to ride over the TT course. This brought a wide variation in machine speed and rider performance in the established classes, something that was to be very noticeable in the case of the 50s, where the sophisticated works bikes of Honda, Suzuki and Kreidler, with top speeds of over 90mph, were in the same field as Itoms, ten of which were clocked at less than 60mph on Sulby Straight. The latter were very much private efforts, for the Itom factory showed little interest in the racers derived from their roadsters. Among the 50cc runners was the first woman to contest a solo TT, Itom-mounted Beryl Swain.

Singles, twins, two-strokes, four-strokes and multiple gears were to be features of the 50cc race, with Kreidler having twelve 'cogs' available to their riders to help keep their bikes in a limited powerband of 11,000–12,000rpm. Honda helped boost entry numbers in small-capacity racing by selling their superb 50cc CR110 and 125cc CR93 production race bikes to the public. They were models that went on to dominate race places behind works machinery.

PRE-RACE

More of the new, smoother surfacing was laid from Crosby past The Highlander, and the downhill section after Crosby Hill was straightened. Also, most of the notorious bumps

The winning combination of Honda's 1962 4-cylinder 250cc and Dunlop's new triangular racing tyre.

on that stretch, which previously saw riders airborne, were removed, saving yet more time and also meaning racers arrived at Greeba Castle going measurably faster than before.

Trade support was no longer as fulsome as in earlier years and Shell was the only fuel supplier supporting the TT. Competitors also had to pay for the 7,000 gallons of petrol provided. Tyre suppliers Dunlop and Avon were present, with Dunlop talking of using its latest rubber compounds and introducing a new triangular-section rear tyre, which they called the RMT1. Designed with a radical new profile that offered more tread to the road when a machine was leaned over, the TT meeting would offer the new tyre a demanding test under race conditions.

Girling were present with experimental upside-down, gas-assisted rear suspension units, which were said to improve damping, reduce oil aeration and maintain constant temperature, so giving more consistent performance throughout a long race. They also offered a saving in weight.

A few privately made five-speed gearbox conversions were fitted to British singles, but while Norton and AMC had experimental examples of their own, they did not offer them to customers. It was something riders could have used to advantage over the Mountain Course.

The organizers increased the Lightweight 250 race distance from from five to six laps and shuffled the order of the races.

Gary Hocking was joined by Mike Hailwood in riding 350 and 500cc MV Agustas in 1962, operating under the same 'Privat' label. However, things went wrong for Hocking early in practice, when he tangled with Graham Smith at Ballacrye. Both riders were thrown down the road at high speed and the MV burnt out. Despite the severity of his fall, Hocking was soon out again, swapping 100mph practice laps with Mike Hailwood. The latter was also to ride a Benelli in the Lightweight class and an Ultra Lightweight EMC.

Bob McIntyre and Tom Phillis had entries on 285cc Honda fours in the Junior race and practice times showed they could be a threat to the 350cc MVs. There was even talk of 'Bob Mac' riding one of the 285s in the Senior race. An 8-gallon tank had been made to allow a non-stop race, although McIntyre was known to prefer the idea of a slick pit stop rather than carry that extra weight of fuel.

One man who featured as a fast privateer at the TT for many years was Arthur Wheeler. He favoured Moto Guzzis and had privately entered examples in the 250, 350 and 500cc races.

RACING

The Sidecar race opened the revised race programme, and for the first time in eight years the win did not go to a

BMW. Instead it went to a BSA twin-cylinder kneeler outfit piloted by Chris Vincent, giving a first International TT victory to the BSA concern. More good news for British race fans was that third place went to Colin Seeley on a Matchless G50. Of course, BMWs were there in the mix, Otto Kolle taking second place and Max Deubel raising the lap record to 90.70mph.

Lightweight and Ultra Lightweight races provided another clean sweep of podium places for Honda, with new race and lap records going to Luigi Taveri on his 125, while Bob McIntyre looked like setting new records on his 250. However, after a fast 99.06mph lap, McIntyre retired and left Derek Minter and Jim Redman scrapping at a slightly slower pace, with Minter taking the win. Suzuki scrubbed their 250cc entries as their bikes were too prone to seizure.

Chris Vincent and Eric Bliss hold a tight line at Sign Post Corner as they speed to victory on their BSA outfit in 1962.

Honda had to give best to Suzuki in the new 50cc race, but took second and third places. After the 50cc race, even the doubters had to acknowledge that winner Ernst Degner's lap record of 75mph was swift going on the Mountain Course. Degner had defected from MZ to Suzuki, and the knowledge of two-strokes that he took with him suddenly saw the Japanese company with competitive race machinery and a first TT win. A different link with MZ by Dr Joe Erlich – some say it involved a trade of Norton forks, which were not obtainable behind the Iron Curtain – saw his new two-stroke EMC put up a spirited performance in the Ultra Lightweight race, with Mike Hailwood holding second until forced to retire and Rex Avery coming home sixth.

Junior and Senior victories were shared by MV-mounted Mike Hailwood and Gary Hocking. Hailwood took the Junior with new race average and lap record speeds, lifting the latter to 101.58mph, while Hocking broke John Surtees' records to win the Senior, his fastest lap being 105.75mph.

Race fans expected to witness record speeds and Honda certainly brought new levels of engineering excellence to the TT. However, the Japanese company seemed to feel that power was all, even though TT history told that power without accompanying standards of handling was a dangerous mix on the Mountain Course.

1963: MIXED NEWS

Bad news for race fans came when the manufacture of Norton motorcycles was moved to AMC's Woolwich factory at the end of 1962, accompanied by the announcement that production of Manx Nortons was to cease. Within a couple of months, AJS and Matchless took the same step with the 7R and G50. A few new machines were assembled from spares, but the outdated British singles would now fall further behind the already faster opposition, particularly over the TT Mountain Course, with its miles of high-speed going.

Good news was that Geoff Duke persuaded Gilera to return to racing under the Scuderia Duke banner. Wheeled out from a storeroom at the Arcore factory, where they had lain since 1957, the machines would be raced without mechanical updating. Derek Minter and John Hartle were

John Hartle prepares for a lap of practice on his Gilera in 1963.

signed to ride them and they had some encouraging early-season results, but a pre-TT spill on a Norton put Minter out and Phil Read joined Hartle for Gilera's Island return.

Yamaha were also back with improved 125cc and 250cc models. Still air-cooled, the 125 was a single with disc valve, six speeds and said to give 25bhp. The 250 was a parallel twin, had seven speeds and was said to give over 40bhp at 11,000rpm, albeit with a narrow power band. The company had limited track testing facilities, but felt that it had eliminated some of its earlier problems of plug-oiling, vibration and carburation, as well as lack of power and durability. Riders were to be Fumio Ito, Hiroshi Hasegawa, Yoshikaza Sunako and Tony Godfrey. In contrast to Yamaha, Honda's only Japanese rider was Kunimitsu Takahashi and the company did not enter the 50cc race.

Suzuki concentrated on the 50cc and 125cc classes. In the former they entered an uprated version with nine gears and a top speed of 93mph. There was more change with their air-cooled, twin-cylinder 125 machine, said to give 26bhp and 114mph.

Joining battle with the Japanese two-strokes were six private entries on Greeves 'Silverstone' machines. Designed for, and successful at, short circuits, their entry into the far more demanding Lightweight TT was a worry to factory boss Bert Greeves and he took the unusual step of writing to each rider, asking them to ride 'with skilled judgement and restraint'.

TT prize money had remained unchanged for over thirty years, but in 1963 the ACU finally agreed to pay riders a contribution towards their expenses. However, £10 for 50cc runners, £15 for other solos and £25 for sidecars would not go far towards paying for two weeks of racing.

Marshalling the 37¾-mile Mountain Course had always proved a headache for the organizers and, due to accessibility problems, there were often long delays in getting injured riders to hospital. In a major contribution to rider well-being, a helicopter rescue service was introduced for race days at the 1963 TT.

Dunlop and Avon's development of tyres to provide riders with better road-holding did not pursue the same direction. Of Avon's latest rear tyre it was said it 'looks more like a trials tyre. There are no ribs at all on the sidewalls, the studs extending right across and they look quite knobbly ones too'. By contrast, Dunlop's triangular racing tyres for solos were gaining ribs and zig-zag tread on the sidewalls.

HOT PACE
Still riding 'Privat' machines for MV Agusta, during practice for the 1963 TT, Mike Hailwood gave the returning Gileras a clear idea of the challenge they faced. In Mike's words: 'I deliberately set out to demoralize them by covering every lap of practice at over 100mph'. Come the Senior race and Hailwood continued his hot pace, riding to victory at a new race average speed of 104.64mph and setting a new lap record of 106.41mph. John Hartle and Phil Read were second and third on their Gileras, with Hartle setting a race average of 103.67mph. That was good going for a machine that had received no development since 1957, when Bob McIntyre took one to victory at 98.99mph. While it is always a mistake to make direct year-on-year comparisons of TT races without fully assessing riders, race conditions, machinery and so on, there had to be a reason for an

Mitsuo Itoh rounds Governor's Bridge to take victory on his 50cc Suzuki in 1963 and become the first Japanese rider to win a TT race.

increase of over 5mph in Gilera's winning speeds between 1957 and 1963, particularly as it was achieved with dolphin-type, rather than full streamlining. Was it due to improved road surfaces, better tyres, different rider? Nobody seemed to address the topic at the time, but with no obvious single reason for the 5 per cent increase in race speed, it must have come from a combination of those factors.

Mike Hailwood's MV Agusta faced a stronger challenger in the Junior race from Jim Redman on his Honda. Starting on damp roads, the two battled closely, with Redman later forced to set the fastest lap at 101.30mph as the roads dried, although Hailwood had to retire. This left John Hartle (Gilera) to take second and Frantna Stastny (Jawa) third.

Under better conditions, apart from melting tar in places, Jim Redman rode his Honda to victory in the Lightweight race, with a speedy Fumio Ito (Yamaha) some 30 seconds behind. The early stages had been enlivened by Yamaha's Ito and Tony Godfrey leading Honda men Redman and Taveri. The Yamaha two-strokes were clocked at 141mph past The Highlander but, after a stop for adjustments, Godfrey later fell at Milntown and became the first casualty to be recovered by the new helicopter service. Bill Smith (Honda) was third and Hiroshi Hasegawa brought his Yamaha home in fourth place.

After a delayed start caused by mist on the Mountain, the Ultra Lightweight 125 race turned into a fierce battle between Suzuki team members, with victory and a new lap record going to Hugh Anderson, from Frank Perris and Ernst Degner. It was a victory that Suzuki repeated in the 50cc race, but this time it was Mitsuo Itoh who took the win on his nine-speed 'tiddler' at a new race average speed. It was a first win for a Japanese rider at the TT, in a race that had been increased to three laps and where Ernst Degner set a new lap record of 79.10mph.

Sidecars ran their three-lap race in excellent conditions, with a comfortable win going to Florian Camathias on his BMW-based FCS, followed by Fritz Scheidegger (BMW). Camathias increased the race average speed to 88.38mph but fell just short of the lap record.

1964: THE PACE STEADIES

There was a temporary lull in the upward growth in speeds in some of the classes at the 1964 TT, although there was no shortage of class machinery and riders. Mike Hailwood was on MV Agustas and Jim Redman on Honda's full 350 four. Honda also had a 125 four and a 50cc twin, which was said to rev to 20,000rpm, with some reports saying 22,000rpm. Tarquinio Provini returned on a Benelli 250, Alan Shepherd was on further-developed MZs, Suzuki had unreliable water-cooled 250 fours and EMC came with

redesigned frames and an experimental form of transistorized ignition, when most were still relying on magneto or coil for their sparks. Yamaha sought to build upon the proven speed of their machinery by employing Mike Duff and TT winner Phil Read, who would ride improved 250cc twin-cylinder RD56 models. They also made a late appointment of Tommy Robb to their team. Not unusual for the day was that works riders Duff and Read would both ride a Matchless G50 in the Senior and an AJS 7R in the Junior. Development of the 7R had not ceased, being pushed by enthusiastic entrants like Tom Kirby, who claimed to be getting 45bhp at 8,600rpm from his special short-stroke engine.

Adding interest to the event, British companies Royal Enfield and Cotton fielded entries in the Lightweight race, while Florian Camathias was present with his sidecar hitched to a Gilera 4.

The 1964 Lightweight 250 race promised much, but in words of the time 'turned out to be a wholesale exercise in machine mortality'. An impressive entry of ninety-five was reduced by some failing to appear, others having major problems in practice and a few not qualifying, meaning that sixty-four riders came to the line. A close tussle between Jim Redman (Honda) and Phil Read (Yamaha) ended with Read's retirement on the fifth lap after a spate of plug troubles, leaving Redman to win from Alan Shepherd (MZ) without setting any records. Just nineteen riders finished the race.

An unwell Mike Hailwood was forced to listen to the radio commentary on Wednesday's Junior race from his sickbed. It was one where Jim Redman was in total control, winning by 7 minutes from Phil Read and Mike Duff, both AJS-mounted. All but two of the remaining thirty-eight finishers were on Norton and AJS machines, leaving many

Ellis Boyce takes his Yamaha TD1 around Ramsey Hairpin in 1964.

to wonder about the future of the 350cc class. However, Yamaha had recently started selling their 250cc TD1 production racer in Britain and would later turn their attention to the 350s. Initially in short supply, they were models that would change the face of racing in years to come.

A third win in the week went to Honda in the Ultra Lightweight 125 race. With competition fierce between team mates Jim Redman, Luigi Taveri and Ralph Bryans, speeds were lifted by over 2mph as Taveri took victory by just 3 seconds from Redman and Bryans. There was also a hard-fought battle amongst the 50cc machines, resulting in both race average and lap record speeds being left at over 80mph by Hugh Anderson (Suzuki), as he led home Ralph Bryans (Honda) and Isao Morishita (Suzuki).

On the entry list of ninety riders for the 1964 Senior race, Mike Hailwood's name was the only one to have an asterisk beside it to indicate that he was a previous winner. That was very different from the 1930s, when the same list, with about half the number of entries, would show three or four past winners, all of whom would be contesting the race on similar machinery. While not fully recovered, Hailwood was fit enough to race his 'Privat' MV Agusta in Friday's Senior and, provided he kept going, was assured of victory. That is how it worked out, comfortably, at some 4mph less than record pace.

Living rather on past glories, Norton Motors advertised at TT time, 'Norton have won more admiration and TT races than any other machine'. Derek Minter was the only podium finisher on a Norton, with second place in the Senior.

1965: TWO vs FOUR
By 1965 the TT was well into an era of two-stroke versus four-stroke in the three smaller solo classes, 250, 125

Plugs by the hundred – a scene in the Yamaha camp.

and 50cc, with the products of Honda, Suzuki and Yamaha the main protagonists and quite evenly matched, although the two-strokes did lose out on reliability. Much of that stemmed from 'plug trouble'. So notorious did the two-strokes become for the problem that, even if there was a more serious issue, it was often blamed on the sparking plugs, a reason that no one questioned.

For many years, riders of big four-strokes would carry a couple of spare plugs in a pocket in their leathers and a plug spanner stuck down a riding boot. That era had largely gone, but two-strokes had never rid themselves of temperament towards sparking plugs and their riders usually carried spare ones and a spanner, sometimes in a small pouch fitted inside the streamlining. Tommy Robb joined Yamaha in 1964 and after using all his spare plugs during one early morning practice, he actually resorted to 'borrowing' one from a tractor in a field by the course. It got him back to the start.

Another unpleasant trait of two-strokes was their tendency to seize if carburation was not spot on. Suzuki had redesigned their 250-4 for 1965, but works rider Jack Ahearn nicknamed his bike 'Whispering Death' and riders of two-strokes usually rode with at least one finger of the left hand resting on the clutch lever. This was while trying to watch the road, the rev counter, the temperature gauge and fight its poor handling. Ahearn's Suzuki was timed at 139mph, but a spill in the last practice session put him out of the race. With team mate Hugh Anderson not willing to ride the 250, it was left to Frank Perris to ride the seizure-prone four. Frank described how he rode with four fingers on the clutch lever to enable him to catch piston seizures, but even that was not enough if the disc valve seized, for that would lock the engine solid. Just as they seemed to be making progress, Suzuki pulled the four from competition later in 1965. In the words of Mike Nicks, it was a bike that 'stretched design talents and rider courage to the very limit'.

The top Japanese manufacturers were seeing huge growth in their motorcycle sales as they took over existing markets and established new ones. Racing their products was a valuable means of gaining worldwide publicity and they poured money into it. Phil Read was one to benefit, writing of the time, 'We swept through a show-piece of classic racing competition that was boosted by an open chequebook, the like of which we may never see again'. He also explained why he was racing only Yamahas in 1965: 'aiming to reach the top, what do you need – no matter how good a rider you are, the answer is *speed*'. Read even titled his first autobiography *Prince of Speed*. Bill Ivy joined the Yamaha team and 1965 was his first TT as a works rider.

Joe Dunphy tackles Brandish Corner on his 250 Greeves in the 1964 Lightweight TT.

While Yamaha works machinery was reserved for a select few riders, their TD production racers were by now available to private individuals who wanted to go racing with fast machinery, which came at reasonable cost and was backed by factory resources. The 250 TD1A had various problems, not least of which was an appetite for crankshafts caused, many said, by having the clutch mounted on the end of the crankshaft. It had now reached the c35bhp TD1B stage, after several years' upgrading of cylinders, pistons, heads and exhausts, plus improved suspension, weight-saving and some increase in reliability. Costing £520 in Britain, it was raced worldwide and attracted a host of tuners offering their own improvements to the standard product. This was not just to the engine, but to exhausts, gear ratios, clutch, frame and suspension. Despite shortcomings, the TD1B was a successful production racer. Many over-bored them by a few cc and used them in 350cc races, but a few years later Yamaha marketed the successful 350cc TR2 model, while private owners converted 125cc roadsters into racers. Such popularity meant that the sight, sound and smell of two-strokes was everywhere in racing.

Several British manufacturers attempted to benefit from the burgeoning 250cc race scene, and the products of Greeves, Cotton and Royal Enfield enjoyed success on the short circuits. However, finding TT racing more demanding of speed and reliability, they did not really feature in the results, although Greeves did achieve success at the MGP.

SPEEDS

The TT Special did not time riders at the same place every year. In 1965 it took speeds over the 2-mile stretch to The Highlander, showing Mike Hailwood to be the fastest 500

at an average of 150mph, with the best single being Derek Minter on a Norton at 136.4mph. The MV's average speed was up on previous years, for all the course smoothing with modern tarmac-laying techniques meant that the fours could use maximum power for more of the time. Unfortunately for the singles, this served to take away some of the handling advantage they had previously enjoyed and, allied to their deficiency of 20bhp compared to the fours, it meant ever less of a contest.

In the Junior class MV Agusta had a much harder battle on their hands and brought a new 3-cylinder model in 1965. Phil Read was timed as fastest Junior on an over-bored Yamaha RD56 at an average of 134.35mph, followed by Gustav Havel on a Jawa at 131.42mph. Jim Redman was fastest Lightweight on his Honda, averaging 133.33mph, a speed equalled by Bill Ivy's Yamaha. Ernst Degner's Suzuki was fastest Ultra Lightweight at 122.48mph, clear of his team mate Hugh Anderson at 118.45mph. Both Suzuki riders were on the company's new RT65 water-cooled twins. As riders were only timed over one practice session, there were always frustrating gaps in the published figures; for example, how the new MV three compared to the latest Junior Honda was not revealed, because Hailwood was out on the 500 and Redman on a 250.

As well as *The TT Special* occasionally recording riders' average speed over a 2-mile stretch to The Highlander, another magazine had taken to recording flash readings on the descent to The Highlander, which gave higher figures. One man with top-quality machines in four solo classes in 1965 was Mike Duff. It is interesting to compare his Highlander speeds across the classes: 125cc Yamaha – 125.1mph, 250cc Yamaha – 143.4mph, 350cc AJS 7R – 122.9mph, 500cc Matchless G50 – 137.1mph.

NEWCOMERS

Every TT had its share of newcomers to the Mountain Course and for some years there had been an unofficial pre-practice coach tour of the course for any who wished to avail themselves. In 1965 this was made obligatory for newcomers, since when many experienced riders and travelling marshals have conducted riders on such a lap, often stopping at particularly tricky spots and generally imparting wisdom. One man on the coach in 1965 who was to go on and write his name into TT history was Italian Giacomo Agostini. He was MV Agusta-mounted, as team mate to Mike Hailwood.

STILL FASTER

More records were broken in 1965, with the most closely contested races showing the greatest increases. Victory in the Ultra Lightweight 125cc race went to Phil Read on

Jim Redman sweeps through Brandish Corner on his 250cc Honda.

Mike Hailwood with his battered MV Agusta at the finish of the 1965 Senior TT.

his new water-cooled Yamaha twin by just 6 seconds from Luigi Taveri (Honda). Hugh Anderson (Suzuki) mixed it with them for most of the race, and the pressure saw Read lift the race average speed to 94.28mph, which was appreciably faster than the old lap record of 92.14mph. Anderson set the fastest lap at 96.02mph.

Read took his still air-cooled 250cc Yamaha to the front of the Lightweight race on the first lap, when he became the first man to lap at 100mph on a 250, but he retired and Jim Redman (Honda) then went fractionally quicker, to set the fastest lap of the race at 100.09mph. In deteriorating weather, the race pace slowed and Redman took victory from Mike Duff (Yamaha) and Frank Perris (Suzuki). Read was in the mix again in the Junior race, but it was Mike Hailwood (MV Agusta) who hit the front with a new record lap speed of 102.85mph before retiring, leaving Redman to take victory for the third consecutive year in this class. He lifted the race average speed to a record 100.72mph, with Phil Read in second place on a 254cc Yamaha and Giacomo Agostini (MV Agusta) in third.

After Mitsuo Itoh's new water-cooled, twin-cylinder 50cc Suzuki declined to rev to its narrow 16,500–17,000rpm power band during the race, it was left to Luigi Taveri (Honda) to take the win in wet and windy conditions at slightly slower speeds than in 1964. Meanwhile, Sidecars were advancing their pace around the Mountain Course and Max Deubel (BMW) was the winner in 1965, at new race and lap record speeds – the latter at 91.80mph.

Conditions for Senior race day were mixed, with wet roads in places, particularly under tree-lined sections. MV Agusta were present with Mike Hailwood and Giacomo Agostini and they were expected to be at the front, while the rest of the field raced amongst themselves. People were not too surprised when first-timer Agostini slipped off

at the tricky uphill bend just after Sarah's Cottage, bent the MV and put himself out of the race. However, they were surprised when the experienced Mike Hailwood did exactly the same, at the same spot, a little later in the race. With broken screen, flattened megaphones and an oil leak being just some of the damage to his MV, Mike managed to restart it and get back into the race, to find that he was being caught by several of the fastest British singles. An unscheduled pit stop on the fifth lap meant they got closer, but he held them off to the finish, taking victory from Joe Dunphy (Norton) and Mike Duff (Matchless). Hailwood's race average speed was a lowly 91.69mph, in what turned out to be his last TT race for MV Agusta.

NAMES

Newcomer Giacomo Agostini had a respectable debut year on the Mountain Course and was to go on to star during the next few years. Among others who would make their mark in Island racing during the second half of the 1960s were Bill Ivy, Peter Williams, Ray Pickrell, Alan Barnett, Stuart Graham, Malcolm Uphill and Renzo Pasolini. Some of those would shine in production racing. Already established on short circuits, there was agitation for this racing of sports roadsters to be brought to the TT, where it was felt that it would aid development of Britain's large-capacity road-going models.

LOTTERY

Britain's racing motorcycles certainly needed assistance if they were once again to challenge the best in the world. Springing from a lottery scheme first introduced at the 1965 MGP, an idea was hatched for some of the lottery proceeds to go towards the design of a British world-beating racer. Many were sceptical of the outcome, but invitations went out for the submissions of designs, which were duly received. Sadly, as predicted, nothing really came of the idea.

1966: INCREASED JAPANESE COMPETITION

This was the year when the TT suffered from a nation-wide seamen's strike that looked as though it would prevent competitors and spectators from reaching the Island, so the event was rescheduled to September. It was also the year a Kawasaki made its first appearance on the Island, with a 125cc machine in the hands of the unfortunate Toshio Fujii. In his book *Japanese Riders in the Isle of Man*, Ralph Crellin tells how: 'Experiencing severe gearbox problems early in

Stuart Graham on the Honda 6-cylinder 250 at Quarter Bridge in 1966.

the week, Fujii was unable to continue practice until the final session on Friday evening, where he was required to complete three laps to qualify. On his first lap he crashed heavily at May Hill, Ramsey, and although he did not appear to be seriously hurt, he died later that evening.' Bridgestone was another Japanese manufacturer due to make its debut at the TT, but after poor early-season performances in Europe, they did not appear on the Island.

Benelli were present with veteran Italian star Tarquinio Provini, but he crashed on the approach to Ballaugh in practice and was seriously injured. Initial thoughts were that he was blinded by the low sun, but a respected magazine later related that his bike had been subject to a mechanical 'bodge' that caused the engine to lock. Gilera also made another return with Derek Minter, but he fell at Brandish, suffering an arm injury that prevented him from racing.

Fierce competition in the Lightweight class in the early 1960s had seen Yamaha and Suzuki air-cooled twins become water-cooled fours and Honda upping its four cylinders to six, accompanied by claims of an output of 53bhp. Those who heard the six at close quarters had little reason to doubt the claim, while talk was of Yamaha's water-cooled and eight-speed 250 giving between 50 and 60bhp, depending who you listened to. However, Suzuki still could not get their 250-4 to run reliably and did not bring it to the TT. Handling was not the strongest feature of any of the 'big three' Japanese 250s, but riders were paid to get results, so they rode them to their limits – there was always someone waiting to take over a coveted works seat from any rider who underperformed.

Practice times did not always tell the full story of a rider and machine's performance potential at the TT, but it was as good a pointer to race week as race fans were going to get. Having moved from MV Agusta to Honda for 1966, Mike Hailwood's practice performances showed that he would again be the man that the others would have to beat.

SIDECARS

BMW was the dominant marque in sidecar racing, with the limited production RS54 model the one to have. In very short supply, owners used the 'Renn Sport' as the basis for their development efforts to produce the best three-wheeler and it ruled sidecar racing for many years. There were thirteen BMWs in the list of fifty-seven starters in 1966, but the most popular engine was Triumph, which powered twenty-one outfits. In a closely fought contest over three laps, Fritz Scheidegger took victory from Max Deubel by just 0.8 seconds, with Georg Auerbacher third. All rode 500cc BMWs. Scheidegger took 10 seconds off the previous best race time at an average speed of 90.76mph. Commercial interests then created a row over the make of fuel used by the winner, followed by his disqualification and later reinstatement.

SOLOS

Honda paid Mike Hailwood well to race their motorcycles, but they sought their money's worth in return: he was entered in four of the five solo classes in 1966, even though he was really too big for a 125. The company did not produce racing motorcycles with good handling and in 1966 the worst handler was to be their most powerful machine, the new 500-4, which was said to develop 85bhp at 12,500rpm. Any doubts as to who was to be the main man in the Honda team at the TT – Jim Redman or Mike Hailwood – were resolved when Redman suffered an arm injury that kept him out of the event. Honda brought in Stuart Graham, son of TT legend Les, in his place.

In the first solo race at the 1966 TT, the combination of Hailwood and Honda's 6-cylinder 250 proved unbeatable in the Lightweight class. Hailwood blasted off from the start to set a new lap record of 104.29mph on his first lap. That was more than 4mph faster than the existing record and highlighted the fantastic combination of bike and rider. He eased off after the first lap but still finished several minutes clear of Stuart Graham on a similar six. In fairness to Graham, he was new to the bike and had a lengthy pit stop. Works Yamahas and MZs retired from the race.

The middle of race week was reserved for the Ultra Lightweight 125 and Junior 350cc races. In the 125 race, the exotic 5-cylinder works Honda four-strokes were no match for the speed of the two-stroke Yamahas and Suzukis. Bill Ivy and Phil Read were on their twin-cylinder Yamahas and Ivy rode to victory at a new race average speed of 97.66mph, setting a new lap record of 98.55mph. Both figures were substantially up on the previous record times and the little Yamahas showed reliability that had been missing with the company's 250s. Mike Duff came in fourth to help Yamaha clinch the Manufacturers' Team Prize, an award that makers held in high regard.

Giacomo Agostini was riding the only MV Agusta entry in the Junior race. It was his 63bhp, 3-cylinder model and it was expected that he would battle with Mike Hailwood on his 4-cylinder Honda. However, spectators were disappointed when the latter dropped out on the first lap. Perhaps Agostini was also sorry not to be able to pit his developing TT riding skills against Hailwood, for although relatively unchallenged, he broke both race average and lap records, finishing 10 minutes ahead of second-placed Peter Williams (AJS). Of the seventy-one starters, fifty-eight were still riding British singles from Norton and AJS.

Works Hondas and Suzukis dominated the massed start 50cc race, with victory going to Ralph Bryans (Honda), who, in round figures, lifted the race average speed from 80 to 85mph and set what was to be the fastest ever official lap speed by a 50cc machine of 86.49mph, clocking well over 100mph in the process. As in other classes, the works bikes were far faster than the production race machines. Many of the latter carried the name Honda on the tank and dominated the lower placings, being far too good for Suzuki's production TR50 'tiddler'.

Giacomo Agostini leaps Ballaugh Bridge on his MV Agusta.

Luigi Taveri and his 50cc Honda in Parliament Square, Ramsey.

Minter on Nortons in the early 1960s. Bad news for their owners in 1966 was that the principal spares manufacturer for Manx Norton, AJS 7R and Matchless G50 models – AMC – was in financial difficulty. Spares for the singles were already in short supply and very expensive, with some tuners having items specially made in order to keep their machines running. In a prophetic forecast, the magazine *Motorcycle Sport* wrote of a future where private contractors produced more such spares, finishing with: 'The only major items which cannot be easily, or economically, dreamed up are castings – cylinder heads, camboxes and crankcases are the bugbear. Eventually even these obstacles may be overcome.'

Of the eighty starters who came to the line for Friday's Senior race, forty-one were on Nortons and thirty-one on Matchless, with the balance made up of single entries from other marques, chief of which were the MV Agusta of Giacomo Agostini and the Honda of Mike Hailwood.

MV's relatively new 3-cylinder 350cc had been able to challenge the 350 Honda in world racing and so the Italian company produced enlarged versions to compete in the 500cc class. In 1966 Agostini's '500' was only of 420cc capacity but in the Senior race he harried Mike Hailwood initially, forcing Hailwood to set a new lap record of 107.07mph and, even with rain falling at Ramsey on the last lap, to increase the race average speed to 103.11mph. Hailwood won by nearly 3 minutes, Agostini having slowed towards the end.

British machines finished well behind, with their race speeds being below those set by the likes of Hailwood and

SPEEDS

In 1966 *Motorcycle News* timed riders on the drop from Creg ny Baa to Brandish, a stretch that many felt to be the fastest on the course. The published results showed the fastest riders as follows:

50cc	Ralph Bryans (Honda)	108.4mph
125cc	Bill Ivy (Yamaha)	132.4mph
250cc	Bill Ivy (Yamaha)	150.6mph
350cc	Giacomo Agostini (MV Agusta)	144.6mph
500cc	Giacomo Agostini (MV Agusta)	151.9mph
	Mike Hailwood (Honda)	151.9mph
Sidecar	Max Deubel (BMW)	125.0mph

In the period 1959–1966, covered by this chapter, fastest lap speeds in the Senior category increased from 101.12mph to 107.07mph.

CHAPTER SIX

TROUBLED TIMES

From the earliest days of the Tourist Trophy meetings, manufacturers offered pseudo-racing versions of their products for the road, often giving them designations like 'TT Model' or 'TT Replica'. Among catalogued machines of the 1960s, there were some classed as sports machines, which reflected the continued wish of buyers to project the racer-on-the-road image. They came with items like clip-ons, rear-set footrests, twin carburettors, single seats and so on. Anyone with a standard machine could equip it in similar fashion from the many suppliers of aftermarket extras, many of whom had sprung up to meet the demand for the popular café-racer style machines of the day.

Racing of catalogued production sports machines was a familiar sight on British short circuits in the mid-1960s, and for 1967 the ACU introduced such a Production race to what was the Diamond Jubilee TT meeting. Run on the Saturday before the main race week, it catered for three classes, 250cc, 500cc and 750cc. It had a Le Mans-type start, setting riders off in three capacity waves and was scheduled for three laps. While welcoming its introduction, those who had seen the handling problems created for production sports machines by comparatively smooth-surfaced mainland circuits expressed serious concerns about how they would fare when ridden to their limits over the ordinary public roads of the Mountain Course.

ROADS

The modern equipment used for surfacing the Island's roads had improved them for racing through the 1960s and contributed to faster lap times. However, the TT course was not up to race-track standards and it was subject to the wear and tear of daily traffic outside race periods. This meant that within a year or so of a new smooth surface being laid, it would receive a coat of tar and chippings to prolong its life. Fortunately, the methods used in that treatment had also improved, with chippings being smaller and more evenly spread, so generally avoiding the nasty 'tramline' effects of earlier days. But surface wear was not even and although the tar retained the chippings better than before, in heavily trafficked areas they could be scuffed off, leaving

the tar exposed. On hot days that could melt, creating a serious hazard for racers. Regrettably, there was little the organizers could do about it, given the nature of this public roads course.

Being ordinary roads, the course also incorporated cambers not designed to suit the racing line. It was edged with concrete kerbs, had sundry steel manhole covers embedded in the surface and was regularly dug up to repair burst water mains and the like. All along it were solid roadside banks,

The logo of the Diamond Jubilee TT meeting in 1967.

walls, telegraph poles and other hazards, with unguarded ditches replacing kerbs at the road edge on upland stretches. The TT Mountain Course was not to be compared with Silverstone. For most riders that was the attraction, but for a few it was a cause for complaint and, unfortunately, their voices would become increasingly strident in years to come.

1967: THE MACHINES

Honda dropped their support of the 50 and 125cc racing classes for 1967, but continued to develop their bigger race bikes. The 250-6 came with increased power to try to counter the speed of Yamaha's fours, plus a new frame to improve handling. The 350 was redesigned with six cylinders giving 70bhp and also had a new frame. In typical Honda fashion, the 500 also received more power, when what it really needed was improved handling. The man due to ride all the above, a frustrated Mike Hailwood, commissioned his own frame for the 500, but Honda would not risk 'losing face' by letting him use it. They contented themselves with a little additional strutting of the rear sub-frame.

MV Agusta and Giacomo Agostini continued with development of their 3-cylinder models but early-season events showed that the 350 was now down on speed compared to Honda's new 350-6.

Phil Read and Bill Ivy were Yamaha's works riders, together with newcomer Akiyasu Motohashi. They would use the 4-cylinder 125 in 1967. It was said to give 41bhp at 17,000rpm, had ten gears and could reach 130mph, with the company's 250-4 being some 20mph faster. The development of Yamaha's earliest models into these potent racers had been a step-by-step process through the 1960s for the engineers making up its race department in Japan.

Suzuki were present with 50 and 125cc machines and a new batch of riders, although their new V4 125 was not yet ready to race, while Dave Simmonds rode the nearest thing to a works bike from Kawasaki.

Renzo Pasolini was flying the flag for Benelli on their 350 and 500cc 4-cylinder models, and while his all-action, lean-out riding style endeared him to the crowds, there were questions about Benelli reliability.

Apart from the above and entries from MZ with Heinz Rosner and Derek Woodman, the field in all classes was made up of production race machines – not to be confused with production sports bikes – from the likes of Honda, Yamaha, Suzuki, Bultaco, Aermacchi and, still, a multitude of British singles. If any records were to be broken in the solo classes, however, everyone knew they would come from the works entries.

Motor Cycling's speed trap showed Bill Ivy hitting 153.8mph on his 250 Yamaha, with heavier team mate Phil Read at 148.8mph, while in the 500cc class, Mike Hailwood (Honda) managed 154.5mph, with Giacomo Agostini (MV Agusta) clocked at 152.5mph. The 500s were still running on narrow 3.50 rear tyres and the 80bhp being put through them was beginning to create concern about wear rates over a six-lap race.

DISC BRAKES

A few competitors experimented with disc brakes, but all the top runners still relied on drum brakes. They were usually twin-leading shoe on the front and single rear, having grown in size down the years, to cope with the extra work needed to stop faster race bikes in shorter distances. Some drum brakes almost filled the wheel, and others came with substantial cooling fins and air-scoops, to help shed heat. Ferodo contributed to the growth in stopping power, by developing special racing linings.

Rather like the introduction of streamlining in the 1950s, the fitting of disc brakes did not guarantee instant reward, for it could create problems just as easily as solve them. The potential for extra bulk and their fiercer action increased weight transfer to the front wheel, resulting in heavier loading of forks and tyres that were not designed for them. There could also be a problem with the rear wheel going light under heavy braking, thus upsetting the balance of the bike. Nevertheless, people could see the potential of disc brakes and there was a feeling that their day would come.

BATTLES CONTINUE

The TT was a round of the World Championship and riders came to the Island for the 1967 Diamond Jubilee event having already been in competition with each other on European circuits. After the customary practice sessions, they were ready to renew battle over the unique Mountain Course, where a win still meant so much to riders and manufacturers.

Mike Hailwood had been a major force at the TT almost since his debut in 1958, and 1967 was to be a year in which he dominated the major classes riding Hondas. In the Lightweight race he set new record race average and lap speeds ahead of Phil Read (Yamaha). In the Junior he added 3½mph to his own lap record from a searing standing start and raised the race average speed by a similar amount, leading home Giacomo Agostini (MV Agusta) by 3 minutes.

The Senior race of 1967 has gone down as one of the great ones in TT history, with, in words of the time, 'Agostini on the sleek and manageable MV. Hailwood on the brutish

ABOVE: **Mike Hailwood exits Governor's Bridge on his 6-cylinder Honda at the 1967 TT.**

BELOW: **Giacomo Agostini leaves Parliament Square and heads for the Mountain climb on his 3-cylinder MV Agusta in 1967.**

Production race winners in 1967, John Hartle, Neil Kelly and Bill Smith. It was a time of plain black leathers and no advertising.

and ill-mannered Honda'. Hailwood knew he had a fight on his hands but he was up for it, swapping the lead with 'Ago', as he was increasingly being known, over the opening laps at record-breaking speeds. At his refuelling stop at the end of the third lap, Hailwood lost valuable time hammering a loose twist-grip back in place, then rejoined the fray. With only seconds between them, the outcome was in doubt until nearing the end of the fifth lap, when the Italian's chain snapped at Windy Corner and he was out of the race. Still troubled by his loose twist-grip, Hailwood rode on to win from Peter Williams (Arter Matchless), leaving the race average speed at a new record figure of 105.62mph and also setting a record fastest lap at 108.77mph.

After the race, Mike Hailwood generously expressed the view that Ago might well have won for he also lapped at 108mph, but those who knew the Honda man felt that he would not really have let that happen. A true master of the Mountain Course, he now had twelve TT victories to his name, more than any other rider at that time.

Speeds in the Ultra Lightweight 125 race matched those of the previous year and Phil Read (Yamaha) took victory by a little over 3 seconds from Stuart Graham (Suzuki). In the 50cc race, speeds were slightly down on the previous year, and Suzuki achieved a one-two-three finish with Stuart Graham, Hans-Georg Anscheidt and Tommy Robb.

BMW riders continued to battle for supremacy in the Sidecar class, where Siegfried Schauzu led home Klaus Enders and Colin Seeley, taking 10 seconds off the previous fastest race time.

In the new Production race, the winners were: 750cc Class, John Hartle (Triumph Bonneville) at a race average speed of 97.10mph; 500cc Class, Neil Kelly (Velocette Venom Thruxton), 89.89mph; 250cc Class, Bill Smith

(Bultaco Metralla), 88.63mph. It was considered to be a satisfactory debut for the new class, which set target speeds for future years. As was the norm in Production racing, there was dissent between riders and organizers over compliance with the regulations for the event.

1968: MORE RACES

Short-circuit racing in Britain was suffering from falling attendances but spectator and competitor interest in the TT remained high. Among road-riding motorcyclists there were still kudos to be gained from being able to tell your mates, 'I'm going to the TT'. The Diamond Jubilee of 1967 had seen record entries, boosted by the new Production race. That level was maintained for 1968, where the Sidecar race was split into two classes, run concurrently, for up to 500cc machines and 501–750cc ones. The latter gave an opportunity to use big BSA and Triumph engines, although among the entries of fifty 500s and forty 750s, the 500cc 'Renn Sport' BMWs remained the fastest. It was a year in which riders from over twenty countries came to ride the Mountain Course.

Colin Seeley had purchased the manufacturing rights for Norton, AJS and Matchless race machines and operated a service depot on the Island, providing support for the many riders still using them. As well as uprated engine components and such, he produced the Seeley frame and complete Seeley race machines.

Really bad news was that Honda and Suzuki would not be on the Island, having pulled out of World Championship racing. Yamaha were present with works bikes, but were expected to reduce their commitment to top-level racing after the TT. MV Agusta fielded Giacomo Agostini and, for the first time in eight years, John Hartle.

A rejig of the race programme saw the Sidecars run on Saturday evening, 50cc and Lightweights on Monday, Production and Junior on Wednesday, with Ultra Lightweight and Senior on Friday. Spectators were by now used to hearing full race commentaries from Manx Radio, which helped their understanding of what was going on around the course.

Dunlop had new KR83 tyres available for solos, which, in cross-section, gave a more rounded profile. This allowed a smoother transition between vertical and lean, with the new tyres also being able to handle more power. By the end of the 1968 TT, Dunlop were advertising that the first three finishers in every race used their products.

For those who thought all road surfaces on the TT course were better than they used to be, numerous complaints early in practice about the bumpy nature of the stretch after Ballacraine through Glen Helen showed that improvements were still needed. There were also unkind words uttered about loose chippings at Creg ny Baa, particularly by those riders who were first to come across them. The reality was that course conditions varied from year to year, with maintenance and even reconstruction carried out to cope with ever increasing amounts of traffic.

Practice sessions did not throw up any major surprises, although one early session at sluggish speeds was explained away with the headline, 'Slow Speeds as Riders are Hit by Flies'. In a later session, John Hartle showed he was a worthy team mate to Giacomo Agostini by matching his 104-plus mph laps on the Junior MV. When Hartle last raced a Junior MV at the TT in 1960, he had won the event at a race average speed of 96.70mph with a best lap of about 98mph, so there must have been big changes in the intervening years to put over 6mph on his lap speed. Was it man,

machine or the course? As ever, it was probably a combination. Also impressing with his speed was 1960 Sidecar TT winner Helmut Fath. Indeed, the speed of his home-engineered 4-cylinder URS outfit proved a worry to the top BMW boys.

THE RACING

With the ever-increasing number of races at the TT, this book cannot hope to chronicle all the results, so given that its theme is 'speed', it will concentrate mostly on those that set new records. For the previous few years the Sidecar lap record had hovered around the 91.80mph mark, but in 1968 Klaus Enders (BMW) produced an extra-special lap to lift it to 94.32mph. That pace proved too hot for him to finish the race and Siegfried Schauzu (BMW) took the win at a record race average speed of 91.09mph. Fath (URS)

Bill Ivy and his Yamaha speed towards victory in the 1968 Lightweight TT.

finished fourth, unable to use full power, as the handling of his outfit did not match the demands of the Mountain Course. In the new 750cc class, Terry Vinnicombe (Kirby-BSA) was first at a race average of 85.85mph, from the BSAs of Norman Hanks and Peter Brown, while Chris Vincent, on yet another BSA, set the fastest lap of 89.11mph.

Bill Ivy started the Lightweight 250cc race as he hoped to continue, smashing the lap record from a standing start on his complex RD05A model and leaving it at 105.51mph. His Yamaha team mate Phil Read was intent on matching Ivy's pace and moved into the lead on lap three before being forced out with a puncture. Meanwhile, Ivy had 'a moment', when he caught his foot under the footrest out on the course. Slightly detuned, he slowed the pace but was still fast enough to take victory from Renzo Pasolini (Benelli) and Heinz Rosner (MZ). What may have seemed an easy victory came at a price, for as well as damaging his foot, Bill Ivy finished most TT races with blistered hands, from fighting his machine and the course in his 'never say die' manner.

Ivy and Read were on the true works Yamaha racers, but excluding winner Ivy, five of the first ten finishers were Yamaha-mounted on twin-cylinder production racers. Each of those would have been much enhanced by the entrants with the best tuning aids of the day. The standard Yamaha production racer had now reached the TD1C model and its use of a new five-port cylinder provided more speed and reliability, transforming it into a truly competitive racer.

Come Wednesday and speeds rose slightly in the bigger Production classes, Ray Pickrell bringing a Dunstall Dominator home as first 750. It was one fitted with double-disc front brakes, from Dunstall's catalogue of components for racing. Ray Knight was first 500 home on a Triumph and Trevor Burgess (Ossa) finished as top 250, at a speed slightly slower than in 1967. There were the customary protests after completion of the Production race, including seventeen with regard to the 250 result.

John Hartle put himself out of the afternoon's Junior race on the MV Agusta after crashing his Triumph in the morning's Production race. This left the two Italians Giacomo Agostini (MV Agusta) and Renzo Pasolini (Benelli) to fight things out on their 4-cylinder 350cc four-strokes, with two-stroke-mounted Heinz Rosner (MZ) looking for third place. That was the way it went initially, with their respective straight-line speeds given as 152.5, 152 and 140mph, with Bill Smith on an ageing Honda at 130.4mph. When Rosner dropped out, Smith inherited third place. At the finish Agostini was nearly 3 minutes ahead of Pasolini at a slightly improved race average speed of 104.78mph, but the lap record stayed intact. Smith finished third, a further 10 minutes in arrears. While the race at the front may not have

been particularly close, there were almost ninety other runners and there were many close battles for the lower order places. Some of those took place wheel to wheel out on the track, whilst others were fought against the clock, without the riders seeing each other. That was the nature of TT racing, where everyone had their private race(s), though few had a chance of gaining a win. For the majority the TT was all about the opportunity to ride the Mountain Course at racing speeds, something that they made huge financial and personal sacrifices to achieve.

Yamaha-mounted Read and Ivy were in a race of their own in the Ultra Lightweight, with Read taking victory at a record race average speed of 99.12mph and Ivy setting a new lap record of 100.32mph. It was the first time a 125 had lapped the course at the 'ton' and it was a figure that was to stand for many years. An indication of what Bill Ivy had to do to achieve that lap comes from the words of a spectator who watched his progress down the hill after Barregarrow crossroads:

> Ivy streaked down the hill standing on the footrests, wrestling with the bike in an effort to control a terrifying tank slapper. The front wheel was flopping about all over the place and the bike was doing its best to tie itself into a knot. But Ivy didn't shut down a scrap – he just stood up and fought it with the throttle wide open at 130mph.

That record-breaking 125 TT of 1968 is part of TT history, not least because Bill Ivy actually stopped at Creg ny Baa towards the end of the race, ostensibly to enquire of his race position, although the real reason was to comply with Yamaha team orders that Phil Read should win.

Last race of the week was the Senior TT, and this provided Agostini with his first double win in a week. Run at a slower pace than the Junior, Ago still finished some 9 minutes ahead of second-place Brian Ball (Seeley), who was a mere 0.4 seconds ahead of Brian Randle (Petty-Norton). John Hartle's MV comeback ended when, with gearbox problems, he tried to ride through Cronk ny Mona without changing down, but clipped the kerb and was thrown down the road.

So ended a record-breaking TT meeting, but it was one that missed the presence of works machines from Honda and Suzuki, together with their star riders.

1969: MORE CHANGE

The FIM introduced major changes to racing motorcycles for 1969, designed to curb the runaway technical development of Japanese manufacturers, who had left others floundering in their slipstreams. New regulations restricted 50cc machines to one cylinder, 125 and 250 to two cylinders, and 350 and 500 to four cylinders, with all classes limited to a maximum of six gears. This had a major impact, halting the design of ever more advanced race machines, turning existing works exotica into museum pieces and opening up the field for over-the-counter production racers, particularly in the smaller classes. The TT complied with the new restriction and a look at the numbers entered of the most common makes in the racing classes at the 1969 event showed:

125cc: Bultaco 19, Honda 16
250cc: Yamaha 45, Bultaco 11
350cc: Aermacchi 28, Norton 27, Yamaha 20
500cc: Norton 44, Matchless 25
500cc Sidecar: Triumph 27
750cc Sidecar: Triumph 35

Many other makes were represented, but in lesser numbers.

While part of the thinking behind the imposition of restrictions might have been to reduce costs, the fastest race bikes would still be found in the hands of the manufacturers, sponsors and riders who spent the most on them. Just as with British singles of the 1950s and 1960s, there were tuners who could make a standard product go faster than the next man's. Sometimes this was based upon putting a bike together properly, 'blueprinting' in current jargon, but usually it meant spending much money on special pistons, barrels, exhausts, ignition systems and so on, to gain a race-winning edge over the opposition. The influence of those tuners and suppliers on race results was always apparent, and such was their importance that they began to add their names to the machines they supplied to top riders, often putting it in front of the makers: Kirby-Matchless, Petty-Norton, Padgetts-Yamaha. The FIM's restrictions opened up a new era in which sponsored riders would dominate motorcycle racing.

Jack Findlay rode Francis Beart's special Aermacchi to third place in the 1969 Junior TT.

Looking at some of the makes mentioned above, Aermacchi – an abbreviation of Italian plane makers Aeronautica Macchi – had been around the British racing scene since the early 1960s, initially with a long-stroke, four-speed model, with spine frame supporting a near horizontal, pushrod-operated engine that lacked reliability. A new short-stroke, five-speed unit arrived in 1963 and earned a following in 250 and 350cc forms, the latter being preferred by many to the ageing AJS 7R.

Bultacos were mostly 125s and 250s and did not have the best of reputations in Britain. Noted two-stroke man Brian Wooley described them as 'of variable build quality' with 'a name for fragility'. Initially air-cooled, the later water-cooled TSS versions were better.

Honda 125s were mostly the reliable CR93 four-stroke, twin-cylinder bikes, which met with much success. Yamaha TD1B two-stroke, 250cc twin-cylinder models arrived in Britain in small numbers in the mid-1960s and also achieved success. A few were used at the TT, but most riders felt they were not sufficiently reliable for the event. The TD1C arrived in limited numbers in 1967 and proved a much faster and more reliable racer, with improved handling. Seemingly, Yamaha had at last matched ports, timing and exhausts, all features that could make or break the performance of a two-stroke engine.

In 1969 Yamaha brought out improved production race bikes with the 250cc TD2 and the new 350cc TR2. Still air-cooled, output of the 250 went up from 39bhp to 44bhp at 10,000rpm and a factory quoted maximum speed of 133mph via a five-speed gearbox. Closely resembling the 250, the 350 TR2 gave 54bhp at 9,500rpm and a speed of 139mph. Initially in short supply, those production Yamaha race bikes quickly became the machine of choice for the majority. They were also the ones whose results were most noticeably influenced by who had prepared them and how much had been spent upon them, for out on track substantial differences in performance could be seen from what were nominally the same machines.

Race bikes came with manufacturers' recommendations to replace major components like pistons and crankshafts after a prescribed number of racing miles. That could be an expensive business and not every owner complied. Given the mixed quality of preparation that was carried out with machines in the hands of so many different owners, production race bikes did not have the strongest reputation for reliability over the TT Mountain Course, while those riding super-tuned versions were even less certain of reaching the finish of a 226-mile TT race. Phil Read's machines would have been among the best prepared, but after some mechanical issues during practice one year, he commented

that the 'Mountain Course was designed to produce great bikes as well as great riders'. Yamaha provided an element of semi-works support through its European arm to a select few riders, including TT runner Rod Gould, who also had access to a 125cc twin.

While Yamaha supplied the majority of over-the-counter 250 and 350cc racers, others were available at different times from Suzuki, Kawasaki, Greeves, Cotton and so on. Some, like the Kawasaki 250cc A1-R and 350cc A7-R, were 'proper' racers, while others converted models like the 250cc Suzuki Super 6 roadster into machines for the track.

NAMES

With some top riders no longer paid to race and retiring from the TT scene, the way was open for new names to come to the fore in Island racing. Names like Kel Carruthers, Rod Gould, Dave Simmonds, Paul Smart, Charles Mortimer, John Williams, Charlie Williams, Tony Jefferies, Brian Randle, Mick Grant and Tony Rutter were increasingly seen on the leader board although, as will be seen, not all stuck with the event.

TRADE SUPPORT

Less prominent than in earlier years, when the majority of needs to be met were the fairly standard ones of British singles, major component suppliers were still present to support TT runners. The greater variety of machinery being raced meant a wider range of items had to be carried by those supplying sparking plugs, carburettor spares and so on, while in the world of tyres, Dunlop were increasing their specialization and now developed different tyres to suit different machines. In 1969 they had three types of tyre and five different tread styles for solo and sidecar use. As yet they did not produce special wet-weather versions, but they did introduce 'grip cells', comprising 2,000 small-diameter holes moulded into the tread pattern, which were said to offer benefits in the wet.

THE RACING

The 500 and 750cc Sidecars were given separate races, which tempted some of the BMW runners to fit enlarged barrels to their 500s and tackle the opening 750 race in the hope of earning extra prize money. It was a tactic that proved successful for Siegfried Schauzu, who took his 550cc BMW to victory at record-breaking speeds. With 500cc barrels refitted for the smaller-capacity World Championship event, Schauzu finished second to Klaus Enders, who rode a controlled race to set a new race average speed without breaking his own lap record from 1968. Helmut Fath's

4-cylinder URS was timed at 134.8mph, which was 10mph faster than Ender's winning BMW, but Fath's power/handling balance was still not right for the Mountain Course and he was forced to back it off in places, finishing third.

In the Junior and Senior races, Giacomo Agostini and his so-superior MV Agustas were untouchable. In fairness to Ago, his race-winning average speeds were respectable at 101.81mph and 104.75mph. Those figures were some 4mph slower than the pace he was capable of and yet were still almost 7mph a lap faster than Junior runner-up Brian Steenson (Aermacchi) and second-place man in the Senior, Alan Barnett (Kirby-Metisse). To some extent those results showed the folly of believing that speed is all in motorcycle racing. Whilst Agostini 'cruised' around in smooth, unhurried style, riding well within his own and his machine's limits, Steenson and Barnett were all-action and spectators knew they were using every bit of power and racing right up to their limits. In fact, Steenson looked as though he was likely to go over his in places, while the stylish Barnett showed how a British single could be ridden on the edge for 226 miles. Both were in only their second year at the TT.

The absence of former works machinery in 1969 was felt most in the races for 125 and 250cc machines, although FIM restrictions would not be enforced against the 250s until the following year. MZ and Benelli had a works presence in the Lightweight race, with the Benellis ridden by Kel Carruthers and Phil Read. It was Carruthers who took victory, his Benelli being 6mph faster than Read's, but slightly slower than Derek Woodman's MZ and Rod Gould's Yamaha. His race average speed was 4mph down on the previous year. In the Ultra Lightweight race for 125s, Dave Simmonds rode a water-cooled Kawasaki twin to a first TT victory, although here the average race speed was 8mph down on 1968.

The Production race offered spirited competition across its three classes. Among the 750s it was Triumph Bonnevilles, Norton Commandos and BSA Spitfires that were

Phil Read on the Benelli at Quarter Bridge in 1969.

expected to take the honours, with Rod Gould's Bonneville fastest through the speed trap at 140.1mph. Malcolm Uphill's Bonneville was 6mph slower, but Uphill rode it to victory over Paul Smart (Norton Commando) at a new record race average speed of 99.99mph and a lap record speed of 100.37mph. So pleased were Dunlop with this win that they renamed the road tyres that Uphill used the 'TT100' to celebrate his 100mph lap.

In the 500cc class Graham Penny took victory on a Honda CB450 after being chased by fastest lap setter, Tony Dunnell, on a Kawasaki Mach III. Among the 250s, Alan Rogers brought a Ducati home first, a desmo version of which Chas Mortimer hustled past The Highlander at 110mph to finish third, after being slowed by electrical problems. Frank Whiteway slotted a Suzuki T20 into second. In neither the 500 nor 250cc Production classes were records threatened.

1970: THE PRICE OF SPEED

The main business of the TT revolved around speed. The sights and sounds created by racing motorcycles, the tension and excitement generated – they were all shared by those in attendance and by the worldwide fan base. But there was a price to pay for an event that afforded such stimulation, and in 1970 six riders were killed during practice and racing. This left many questioning whether that was not too

Roadworks at the Verandah show the sort of activity that occurs on the TT course when the racers are not around.

high a cost. There were calls for the course to be made safer, a very difficult task given its nature, but the racers themselves accepted the loss and went on with the racing. More than anyone, they knew the potentially high price to be paid for racing over the Mountain Course.

Former Medical Officer for the races, Dr Pat Cullen, when asked what he thought of riders risking their lives racing, said, 'I don't think they are fools, some are brave, some are lacking in imagination – I think one can say that they do not regard life as something which should be held onto terribly dearly'.

Regrettably, the threat of death was, and still is, inseparable from TT racing. Riders adopted different attitudes to riding the course, with some claiming they did not actually 'race', or that they only rode at 'nine-tenths'. But it was journalist Ted Macauley who encapsulated the attitude of the professional racer of the time, who was there to win, when he described Bill Ivy's riding to set the first 100mph lap by a 125cc machine back in 1968. Writing later, Macauley told how Ivy 'threw himself into heart-stopping moments of defiance of the course's terrible promise to anybody who took liberties with it'.

Major works at the Verandah saw its four bends widened and resurfaced prior to the 1970 TT, resulting in a faster passage for riders and a further saving of time.

PRODUCTION RACING

Having proved themselves in three-lap races since being introduced to the Mountain Course in 1967, the seventy-plus riders in what had become the International Production Race were required to race over five laps and 189 miles in 1970. The 'Proddie' race seemed to have caught the imagination of racegoers, boosting visitor numbers for its Saturday race slot, although some argued that it should be part of the main race week. The Saturday running might well have been one of those commercially based TT decisions, aimed at bringing an influx of visitors for a long weekend by offering them the easy-to-follow massed start Production race.

Initially known for their small-capacity road bikes, Japanese manufacturers had been gradually building larger-capacity ones through the 1960s, and Honda CB750 4-cylinder machines were now entered in the big Production class, alongside Triumph Trident 3-cylinder 750s, twin-cylinder Nortons, Triumphs and BMWs. In a slightly strange scenario, while the BSA Triumph Group was able to provide works machines for American racing, it claimed that differences in specifications between American and European racing meant it could not give works support to events at home. A magazine of the day explained how Triumph entries, and those of Honda, were actually made 'through a (pretty transparent) veil of dealer entries'.

This is what a massed start looked like at a Production TT.

One thing that irked private runners in the Production race was that works-supported entries would come fitted with go-faster components, which, although listed as for sale to the public – to comply with race regulations – would actually be impossible to lay hands on.

Conditions for the Production race were good, and those with electric start jumped into the lead at the Le Mans-type massed getaway. Many machines were now fitted with fairings, yet the 500 and 750cc classes seemed not to match either the straight-line or race speeds of previous years. However, the 750 race did see a titanic struggle between Malcolm Uphill (Triumph) and Peter Williams (Norton), with victory going to Uphill by less than 2 seconds, after Williams' Norton spluttered with fuel starvation over the last couple of miles. Only in the 250cc class were records broken, and they went to winner Chas Mortimer on his Ducati MkIII, who finished 6 seconds ahead of John Williams (Honda CB250).

For 1970 the 750cc Sidecar race ran on Monday and the 500cc race on Wednesday. Klaus Enders set new lap records in both races and took victory in the 500cc event. The 750cc race went to Siegfried Schauzu and new race average speeds were set.

The Lightweight 250cc race also ran on Monday, and here Kel Carruthers (Yamaha) rode to victory over Rod Gould (Yamaha) at a faster race average speed than in 1969.

Both Carruthers and Gould wore jet-style helmets, while the majority still wore pudding-basin style. Within a couple of years almost everyone would be wearing full-face versions.

That 250cc race was hit by tragedy when Santiago Herrero crashed his Ossa at the Thirteenth Milestone and was killed while holding fourth place. The Spanish single-cylinder, disc-valve two-stroke, had been timed at 137mph at The Highlander and Herrero was contesting the lead of the 250cc World Championship at the time. Popular with other riders, his death gave weight to a growing undercurrent of opposition among GP competitors about having to race to win over a course that was so very different and difficult to learn, compared to the average GP circuit. Ironically, the Ultra Lightweight 125cc race was won by another rider appearing at the TT primarily to gain points for his World Championship challenge. This was newcomer Dieter Braun on an ex-works Suzuki, who took an emphatic victory after early leader and fastest lapper, Dave Simmonds (Kawasaki), was forced to retire at the Mountain Box. Unusually, second and third places were also taken by newcomers – Borje Jansson (Maico) and Gunter Bartusch (MZ).

Giacomo Agostini achieved runaway victories in both the Junior and Senior races on his MV Agusta in 1970. In the Junior he took just 3 seconds longer than in 1969, with both his lap and race speeds almost identical to the

Peter Williams (3) with Alan Barnett (5) in pursuit on the Quarter Bridge Road.

greatest experience of fast motor-cycle riding in the world'.

THE COURSE

The 1970 event finished with criticism of the TT course by several voluble riders, who called for '1970 roads on which to race 1970 machines'. They had a point. The roads of the course were described at the time by the magazine *Motorcycle Sport* as 'made up of good-class main roads … yet they are not comparable with good-class main roads on the mainland'. Particularly vocal was Lightweight winner Kel Carruthers, whose race average was 96.13mph. Twenty years earlier, the Lightweight TT was won by Dario Ambrosini (Moto Guzzi) at a race average speed of 78.08mph. Ignoring the faster speeds of the works Yamahas from several years before, that showed a growth of 18mph in twenty years, during which time the roads of the course had been improved. Carruthers clearly thought those improvements had lagged behind machine performance, but the Island aimed for normal highway standards, not race-track ones. There were always going to be cambers that did not suit the racers, street furniture that could be a danger to anyone falling off, little in the way of run-off areas and the prospect of molten tar in

previous year's. In the Senior, where his race average was lower than in the Junior, he took over 4 minutes longer to complete the race than in 1969. There were battles aplenty for podium places in both races, with Alan Barnett (Aermacchi) just failing to set the first 100mph lap by a 350cc single while riding to second place in the Junior. He did top the 100mph lap in the Senior on a Seeley before he dropped it at Doran's, while in close company with Peter Williams (Arter Matchless). The latter, who was one of those who claimed not to 'race' on the Island, also lapped at over 100mph on his ride to second place, saying of the Mountain Course, 'there is no doubt that it provides the

hot weather.

The dissatisfaction being expressed by a few was a prelude to more of those who did not like the TT deciding not to race there; although, at the time, the prospect of losing potential World Championship points was usually sufficient to bring them to the Island. As will be seen, this was an issue that was to be linked to wider financial ones.

Several stretches of the course were resurfaced prior to the 1971 TT. While the work was generally well received, the new smooth surface and the eradication of bumps on the Brandish to Hillberry stretch found riders arriving at and riding Hillberry's right-hand sweep measurably faster than before. Showing that you cannot please everyone, some concerns were expressed about this, but there were no real incidents and things seemed to settle down after a couple of practice sessions. Earlier mention was made of the long approach to Hillberry giving riders time to build up their courage to take it at speed, and Peter Williams summed things up nicely by describing this right-hand sweep as 'a bit of a dare'.

The Cronk y Voddy straight was still a bumpy stretch and very testing for Production bikes at speed. It was a location that revealed to experienced watchers how poor their handling was compared with genuine race bikes.

Molten tar on bends was smothered with cement dust.

1971: A NEW RACE

Not content with Production races for Triumph Tridents, Norton Commandos, Honda CB750s, BMW R75/5s and the like, run to a fairly restrictive specification, some contestants wanted to race more highly tuned and modified versions of those big roadsters. Accordingly, what was called the Formula 750 race was added to the programme in 1971. This allowed for more tuning of both engine and chassis. It was run over three laps with the novelty of a clutch start in pairs at 10-second intervals and attracted thirty-nine entries, which included a degree of works support. It also yielded a splendid race, with the first three riders all averaging over 100mph and winner Tony Jefferies (Triumph) finishing at a race average speed of 102.85mph, while setting the fastest lap at 103.21mph. Second was Ray Pickrell (BSA) and third Peter Williams (Norton). Such a result for British racing machinery, which turned out to be faster than Giacomo Agostini's MV Agusta Senior race-winning speed later in the week, was very well received and caught racegoers' attention. What was seen as an experimental race quickly became a permanent one in the TT programme.

MIXED RESULTS

The 1971 race schedule suffered from mixed weather, with the Junior and Ultra Lightweight races being worst affect-

ed. They were won at relatively low speeds by Tony Jefferies (Yamaha) and Chas Mortimer (Yamaha). In a rare occurrence, Agostini struck problems with the MV in the Junior race and retired on the first lap. The announcement of his retirement brought some unsporting cheers. Another rarity was the sight of Barry Sheene competing in the Ultra Lightweight race. Sheene was riding a speedy ex-works Suzuki but slid off at Quarter Bridge on the second lap and decided that was the end of his TT career.

Speeds crept ahead of the previous fastest in the 500 and 750cc Production races, with wins going to John Williams (Honda CB450) and Tony Jefferies (Triumph Trident), but 250cc winner Bill Smith (Honda CB250) was slightly slower than before.

In what was generally portrayed as a belt-tightening world for former works riders now forced to campaign private production racers, Phil Read treated himself to a Rolls Royce Silver Cloud at the start of the season. It was a move that sent out mixed messages, but Read was still a star rider, having his own bikes prepared by a top tuner, employing good mechanics and continuing to receive trade support. In the Lightweight race he brought 250cc lap times back up over the 100mph mark for the first time since 1968, taking a comfortable win from Barry Randle. Strangely, it was Read's first Lightweight TT victory. Not so strange was that Yamaha filled the first twenty-four places in that

Tony Jefferies rides his Triumph Trident to victory in 1971.

race, for their 250cc TD2 and 350cc TR2 production racers, plus their over-bored versions, were well on the way to taking over the racing world, a process strengthened when Yamaha brought out their uprated versions, the TD2B and the TR2B.

The only other improvement in previous race speeds in 1971 was by Siegfried Schauzu (BMW), who set a new fastest lap in the 750cc Sidecar race of 93.44mph, with the win going to Georg Auerbacher on his BMW. It was Auerbacher's first win after ten years of TT racing.

In a delayed-by-a-day Senior TT, Giacomo Agostini took his customary win in less than perfect conditions at a race average speed of 102.59mph, finishing ahead of Peter Williams (Arter-Matchless) and Frank Perris on a Seeley-framed Suzuki TR500 twin.

1972: NO MORNING PRACTICE

Having been the mainstay of TT practice until the late 1930s, when evening sessions were gradually added, early-morning sessions were abandoned for 1972 and practice compressed into just four evening sessions and a long one on Thursday afternoon. Two of those sessions were curtailed

by mist and the general opinion was that newcomers had not been provided with sufficient time to learn the course. Morning practice was later reinstated.

Phil Read was hugely experienced in Island racing, but even he could have done with more practice time, for as well as his customary 250 Yamaha, he had accepted the invitation of Count Agusta to ride one of his 350s in the Junior race. In addition, he was also due to ride a John Player Norton in the Formula 750 event.

Giacomo Agostini was riding both 350 and 500cc MVs and was joined by a Senior entry for seasoned TT runner Alberto Pagani. Ago lapped in practice at 104-plus mph on his new 350-4 and 106-plus mph on the 500-3, but Read and Pagani lagged behind, while Alex George (Kawasaki) and Jack Findlay, on his semi-factory-supported Suzuki TR500, were principal challengers, although well off the pace of Agostini.

Come the racing in 1972 speeds increased slightly in the three Production classes, but no records were broken in the Sidecar races, where both 500 and 750cc victories went to Siegfried Schauzu (BMW). It was the Formula 750 class that people now looked to for record speeds and Ray

Pickrell (Triumph) provided them in what had been increased to a five-lap race. He lifted the race average speed to 104.23mph and the lap record to 105.68mph. On his TR750 3-cylinder, water-cooled Suzuki, Jack Findlay hit a fastest ever recorded speed at the TT of 158.6mph, at The Highlander.

Wednesday's races were postponed to Thursday and the inclement weather was to remain for the rest of the week. In the Lightweight classes, Phil Read (Yamaha) won the 250 race and, receiving support from Yamaha, Chas Mortimer the 125, while Giacomo Agostini took the Junior win on his regular 350-3, rather than the new four. Yet again, race reports proclaimed 'Agostini's Easy Junior Victory'. It was the same scene in the Senior 500cc race, where he took his

Giacomo Agostini leaps his MV Agusta over the hump in the Quarter Bridge Road that is now known as 'Ago's Leap'.

tenth TT win, although an impressive ride from John Williams (Arter-Matchless) saw him hold Alberto Pagani (MV Agusta) at bay until running out of petrol at the Bungalow on the last lap. This allowed Mick Grant to take third place on his Kawasaki HI-R. This 3-cylinder two-stroke was still air-cooled, with handling that was severely tested by the Mountain Course.

TIPPING POINT

The Tourist Trophy races had been run by the ACU since their inception in 1907. Initially indifferent, the Isle of Man Government gradually began to realize the benefit the races brought to the Manx economy and to publicizing the Island's name. Recognizing that the ACU were losing money on organizing the TT, in 1930 the Manx Government began contributing towards the cost of running the event.

As it gradually increased its financial contribution, the government and its Tourist Board sought a greater say in the running of the TT. However, neither the ACU nor the government picked up on the overall mood towards the high cost of racing in the early 1970s and, more importantly, they appeared not to recognize a growing antagonism towards the TT. Promoters of World Championship rounds were notoriously mean in the amounts they paid out in prize money and, with the sum paid to the winning entrant at the Blue Riband Senior TT still the same £200 as it was in 1930, the TT organizers also excelled in

parsimony. Had prize money increased at a rate to match inflation since 1930, a Senior TT win would have been worth c£2,500 in the early 1970s.

The days when the sport was awash with funding from the major Japanese and European factories had gone, and most riders operated on tight budgets, with the two-strokes of the day requiring considerable expenditure on maintenance. For all the tradition associated with the TT, that itself was not enough in the hard-headed world of racing-to-earn-a-living in the early 1970s, and there was growing opposition to the event. There were multiple reasons for this, but many felt that the payment of realistic prize money would have overcome a lot of them and reduced the level of opposition. Few people went into motorcycle racing with the intention of getting rich, but there were some who did go on to develop that notion, and were particularly voluble at the time.

Entered in the Lightweight 125cc TT in 1972 was popular Italian rider Gilberto Parlotti, who was leading the World Championship at the time on his Morbidelli. Having prepared for his TT debut as thoroughly as possible, he came to the line on the last day of race week under wet and overcast conditions. Challenging the experienced Chas Mortimer for the lead on time, during the second lap Parlotti ran wide at the Verandah, collided with a row of concrete posts and was killed. It was a tragedy for racing to lose such a fine rider, and his death was to have serious repercussions for Island racing.

Influential riders like Agostini, Read and Gould, among others, immediately declared that they would not return to the TT and their actions were supported by a growing number of World Championship contestants who did not wish to be forced into competing there. Taking this a step further, they began a campaign to have the TT stripped of its World Championship status.

Sadly, almost a year later, on the approach to the 1973 TT, the World Championship GP series showed that nowhere was really safe in the world of motorcycle racing. At the historic Monza track, top stars Renzo Pasolini and Jarno Saarinen were killed in the 250 race, in an incident that brought down a host of runners on the high-speed Curva Grande. This famous bend was a right-hander with no run-off area, only an Armco barrier, which threw men and machines back into the tracks of following riders. It was a racing tragedy that is remembered to this day.

The incident at Monza added weight to what had been a growing campaign by riders for safer race circuits. It was something that would be difficult to achieve with the TT Mountain Course.

1973: CHANGE

Belatedly waking up to the threat it faced, the 1973 TT came with the offer of much-enhanced prize money: £1,000 for a Senior win, £600 for a Junior, £750 for Formula 750 and slightly less for Lightweights and Sidecars. In the absence of some 'star' entries, previous podium finishers now looked to move up a step or two and reap the benefit of those increased rewards, which had also been extended to the lesser placemen.

That is how things worked out in the Junior and Lightweight 250 classes in 1973, where last year's second-place men, Tony Rutter and Charlie Williams, took first in the 350 and 250cc races, while veteran Tommy Robb took his first TT victory in the 125 race. Despite all the top places being taken by over-the-counter Yamaha production race bikes, whose year-on-year improvements kept them ahead of the

Fly-spattered Klaus Enders and passenger Ralf Engelhardt round Governor's Bridge on their BMW on the way to victory in the 500cc Sidecar race of 1973.

field, there were some interesting and hard-fought races for the watching crowds, who were there in good numbers. The Production race kicked off the week and riders of 750cc machines were the first to be despatched on their Le Mans-style start, followed 2 minutes later by the 500s and then the 250s. The weather deteriorated during the race, resulting in slowish speeds for class winners Tony Jefferies (Triumph), Bill Smith (Honda) and Charlie Williams (Yamaha).

Record speeds were set in the centre-of-attention, non-Championship Formula 750 race, where Peter Williams and his 75bhp John Player Norton upped the race average speed to 105.47mph and the fastest lap to 107.27mph. It gave Williams his first TT win, from similarly mounted Mick Grant. It was also the second-fastest TT race ever, behind the Hailwood/Agostini battle of 1967.

Peter Williams claimed not to race on the limit over the Mountain course, but his personal account of a lap on his Norton in that Formula 750 race had readers feeling that he could not have ridden much harder. It contained graphic phrases like 'hard against the stop … flat on the tank … the front wheel comes off the ground … ride it through there on the back wheel … ignore the bumps … can usually do flat out … back wheel could suddenly go … the front wheel just touches the road here and there … couldn't believe I could take it flat … just heave on the bars … I sit up here but only because I don't like my head bouncing on the tank at 145mph!'

The Sidecar races continued to attract the top World Championship runners, and race average speeds and lap records climbed by some 2mph in both 500 and 750cc categories, which were won by Klaus Enders (BMW) from Siegfried Schauzu (BMW).

Winner of the Senior race and its accompanying £1,000 was Jack Findlay on his two-stroke, water-cooled Suzuki, which came with an output of 75bhp to make it go and triple disc brakes with which to stop. Closest challengers Mick Grant and Tony Rutter, on over-bored Yamahas, both slipped off in Ramsey without injury. To Grant went the fastest lap at 104.41mph. Second place went to Peter Williams with a race average speed of 100.62mph on his Arter-Matchless, fitted with six-speed gearbox, disc brakes and cast alloy wheels. It was the first time a British single had set a race average speed of 100mph at the TT since the great Mike Hailwood did so back in 1961. Senior winner Jack Findlay had made news earlier in the season by winning a Continental GP on a treadless slick tyre, but such rubber was not yet ready for the demands of the Mountain Course.

So finished a TT where, for the first time in over twenty years, the only MV Agusta taking part was the rescue helicopter. A few people pretended the stars had not been missed, but although the racing was keen, everyone likes to see the best riders in action. Unfortunately, the only interest some of those stars retained in the TT was to snipe at it from the sidelines while casting covetous eyes on what was now one of the richest race meetings in Europe.

MORE TIME SAVED

The roads of the Mountain Course continued to receive improvement. In 1973 resurfacing and bump-easing work was carried out through Laurel Bank to Glen Helen, plus slight beneficial realignment at Sarah's Cottage. The effect of those was to increase speed over the combined bends of that tricky section – for those with sufficient skills. Further lengths of fencing were set back on the Mountain, while, as straight-line speeds continued to increase, riders lived in hope that one day the bumps would be taken out of Sulby Straight.

IMPROVED YAMAHAS

Already dominant in the smaller classes of world racing, Yamaha formally marketed an air-cooled 125cc production race bike in 1973, the TA125, putting out 24bhp. However, what really got the racing world excited was the upgrading of what had become their TD3 and TR3 250 and 350 racers with water-cooling and a little more power to create the TZ generation of racers. The TZ250 was now said to give 48bhp at 10,500rpm and the TZ350 yielded 60bhp at 10,000rpm. New six-speed gearboxes helped them towards maximum speeds of 139 and 149mph. Those machines were to extend Yamaha's already huge influence on racing, with the 350, in only slightly over-bored form, able to challenge for wins in the bigger classes. Each bike came with with an extensive spares kit comprising barrels, pistons, crankshaft and so on, for unlike the old British single-cylinder racers, they could not be run for a season without replacement of major components. Buyers found that performance came at a price and many were augmenting the spares kit with the purchase of further replacement parts well before the season end. In 1974 the TZ750 went on public sale. It was, in effect, a doubled-up 350 and was said to give over 90bhp at 10,000rpm in the state of tune in which it was marketed – which was below its maximum.

1974: SUPERBIKES

Away from racing, in the wider world of motorcycling, growing use was being made of the term 'Superbikes' in regard to products from the likes of Kawasaki, Norton, Triumph, BMW, Ducati, Honda, Moto Guzzi, MV Agusta and Yamaha, for all were producing road-going models to support the growing demand for large-capacity sporting motorcycles. Perhaps to reflect this, the upper limit in the Production race was increased for 1974 from 750 to 1000cc. There was certainly plenty of scope for variety among the 'Proddies', although many preferred the faster, noisier and more race-oriented models previously found in the Formula 750 race, which, perhaps to recognize its less restrictive specification, was now named the Open Formula 750 Classic.

On the organizational front, additional contributions were made towards riders' expenses in 1974, and the ACU became more selective about acceptance of entries. This meant that some who had previously entered just for a fast run around the course had their entries returned.

SPEEDS

There were plenty of speedy laps set during practice for the 1974 TT, with ton-up ones now routinely expected from top runners in the larger classes; well over fifty were recorded in practice week. Speed trap figures from The Highlander gave a wide range of figures across each class, but the fastest were:

Ultra Lightweight 125cc	128mph	Yamaha
Lightweight 250cc	140mph	Yamaha
Junior 350cc	140mph	Yamaha
Senior 500cc	156mph	Suzuki
F750 Classic	156mph	Yamaha
Sidecar 500cc	130mph	Busch Spezial
Sidecar 750cc	136mph	BMW

While top capacity in the Production race was now 1000cc, top speed captured was only 132mph, with 130mph for the best 500cc and 112 for the best 250cc. It would seem that they did not catch the 1,000cc Proddies at their fastest, nor did they time any of the quicker 350 race bikes, who should have been over the 140mph quoted above.

Come the racing and the winner's race average speed in the Production 1000 class was 99.72mph, which was just below the previous best of 100.07mph. The winning machine was 'Slippery Sam', the 750cc Triumph Trident, which in 1974 was ridden by Mick Grant to its fourth TT win and his first. With a wrist in plaster, he finished ahead of the 1000cc BMW twins of Helmut Dahne and Hans-Otto

Mick Grant rides 750cc 'Slippery Sam' to another TT win in the Production 1000cc race of 1974.

Butenuth. Keith Martin (Kawasaki) was first 500cc home, setting a new record race average speed of 93.85mph, and Martyn Sharpe (Yamaha) was the first 250cc, lifting the race average speed for his class to 86.94mph.

Mick Grant later wrote of Slippery Sam: 'I suspect it was also as legal as a bent copper – a real factory special full of bits that appeared in official Triumph parts lists but were unavailable to Joe Public at any price.'

A BMW was to the fore in the Sidecar 750cc race, where Siegfried Schauzu raised the race average speed by over 3mph, leaving it at 96.59mph, after Rolf Steinhausen (Konig) set a new lap record from a standing start of 98.18mph. That was an incredible 5mph faster than before, but Steinhausen's two-stroke did not finish the race. Heinz Luthringshauser also rode BMW to win the Sidecar 500cc race, from rising star George O'Dell on his Konig. It was interesting to see O'Dell's Konig followed by Weslake, Yamaha, BSA and Honda-powered outfits. Seemingly, the 500cc BMW's long-term supremacy was under threat, but it had been a wonderful run.

The Ultra Lightweight and Junior races took place in good conditions and Clive Horton (Yamaha) was first 125 home at 88.44mph. It was this class that still had the biggest gap to close on the existing record race average speed, which stood to Phil Read at 99.12mph. Fastest 350 was Tony Rutter (Yamaha), whose race average speed of 104.44mph was very close to Agostini's record of 104.78mph, and Chas Mortimer's fastest lap of 106.39mph was within sight of Mike Hailwood's record 350cc lap of 107.73mph. Clearly, the new water-cooled Yamahas came with sufficient speed to challenge the records set by former works machines, although there was no opportunity to prove that in the Lightweight 250 race, for wet conditions slowed Charlie Williams' (Yamaha) race average winning speed to just over 90mph. Anyone lucky enough to be racing a true works Yamaha racer, a YZR250 or 350, would have noticeably more power in a bike that was much lighter than a standard production TZ model.

The 1974 Senior TT lost its customary Friday slot in the race programme to the Open Formula 750cc Classic race and was scheduled for Wednesday. However, poor weather saw it moved to Thursday and reduced to five laps, when it was won by Phil Carpenter (Yamaha) at 96.99mph. Suzuki's new 4-cylinder RG500s appeared in the Senior in the hands of Jack Findlay and Paul Smart, but did not last the distance. Conditions were slightly better for Friday's Formula 750 race, where initial rain gave way to drying roads. But the expected big-bike bonanza was spoiled (for some) by over-bored Yamaha TZ350s, which took the first three places in the hands of Chas Mortimer, Char-

lie Williams and Tony Rutter, at an average race speed of 100.52mph. Best four-stroke was the Triumph of Percy Tait in fourth place.

So ended an interesting TT, although one in which the solo classes were dominated by the sight, sound and smell of Yamaha two-strokes. A similar situation prevailed in the wider world of racing and attracted a mixed response, leaving race followers wondering if the company should be seen as saviours of racing, or as wreckers, particularly as they now had new 4-cylinder works YZ500 and TZ750cc machines, which they intended to make available to privateers, a few of the 750s already being in the hands of favoured riders.

MORE THAN POWER

While machines of the early 1970s had been gaining more power, there were other important factors that helped riders reduce the time they took to do a lap of the TT course. Race tyres were under continual development from the principal suppliers, Dunlop and Michelin, with most types now available in differing compounds and tread patterns, with the trend being for them to get 'stickier'. Those supplied for Tourist Trophy races were still expected to last for a full six-lap 226-mile race.

Jack Findlay is quoted on a Michelin website as saying that he used slicks while racing on the Island in 1974. This occurred during practice and was not too well received by the organizers. Initially experimental, more riders tried them in 1975 and in 1976 Chas Mortimer won the Junior race on a Yamaha fitted with a rear slick. Mick Grant was also an early user and later described them as 'probably the biggest single leap in grip in the history of motorcycling'. Initially made just for the rear, the suppliers soon came up with versions for the front.

Like many major advances, there was a price to pay for the increased grip and, as well as the fact that riders had to adjust their style to suit them, the new tyres also made the suspension work harder. Both riders and machines had to adapt to suit the tyres. It was also a period when TT races still ran in the rain, over wet roads. Slicks were not suitable for use in the wet, but there were no such things as full wets at the time and tyres used in wet conditions were of road-treaded type, built with racing compounds and carcases.

The TT organizers were initially against the introduction of slick tyres, mostly on the grounds that they could not determine when they were worn. Steps were taken to have them banned at the TT, but that did not occur. However, the ensuing years were to see increased specialization in the world of tyres, which in the longer run was not all good for TT racing.

Most machines still ran telescopic front forks and twin rear suspension units, with the former becoming larger in fork-stanchion diameter and offering an increasing range of adjustments. Rear units were now available with a range of springs, and could be gas- or oil-filled.

Drum brakes were gradually giving way to discs to help stopping and this brought further changes to fork legs, upon which front-brake calipers were normally mounted.

All these changes interacted with one another and manufacturers tried to develop machines in a balanced manner, although, inevitably, one feature often had more impact than another. With the above improvements combining to create better racing motorcycles, it was no surprise that TT lap times were reducing and thus lap speeds increasing, although perhaps not quite as rapidly as might have been expected.

1975: RACE PROGRAMME

Major changes for 1975 were that the Ultra Lightweight 125cc race was dropped, and the Production race became a ten-lap affair for 1000 and 500cc machines and nine laps for the 250s, with each bike ridden by a team of two riders. The 750cc Sidecar race now became the 1000cc Sidecar race and the Formula 750 race also had its capacity increased and became the Classic 1000cc race, with machines from 300cc eligible to take part. Some know the latter race as the Open Classic.

The above reflected the fact that most manufacturers' flagship roadsters had been growing in capacity and, increasingly, that was where TT race bikes were being derived from – production models.

The TT still counted towards the World Championship in its relevant classes, but rumblings about it losing that status were getting louder and there seemed an inevitability about the outcome.

RECORDS

No records were set in the traditional Senior 500, Junior 350 and Lightweight 250cc race classes in 1975, where wins went to Mick Grant (Kawasaki), Charlie Williams

The colourful green-and-white combination of Mick Grant and his 3-cylinder 500cc Kawasaki in 1975.

(Yamaha) and Chas Mortimer (Yamaha). However, reminiscent of the former days of Norton, Yamaha's current domination was demonstrated by the first thirty-three finishers in the Junior and the first forty-four in the Lightweight all being on the Japanese two-strokes. In the Senior, Mick Grant on his Kawasaki KR 500 triple had the bike seize early on the first lap, but continued at reduced pace. With others falling by the wayside, this was enough to give him the win. The Kawasaki was followed home by a dozen Yamahas, before the trusty Matchless of David Hughes in thirteenth place and similarly mounted Selwyn Griffiths in fifteenth.

Taking Slippery Sam to yet another Production TT victory, the pairing of Dave Croxford and Alex George did grab a new lap record, when George circulated at 102.82mph. Charlie Williams and Eddie Roberts rode a Honda to victory in the 500cc class, while Chas Mortimer and Billy Guthrie (Yamaha) were first riders home on a 250.

Biggest news on the speed front from the 1975 TT was that Mick Grant broke the absolute course record of 108.77mph, set by Mike Hailwood back in 1967. Riding his 3-cylinder, water-cooled Kawasaki two-stroke, Grant completed the second lap of the Classic 1000cc race at 109.82mph to become the fastest man around the Mountain Course. The Kawasaki snapped its chain on the next lap and it was John Williams who took victory on his Yamaha, at a race average speed of 105.33mph, just short of the race record.

Claimed to be giving 110bhp, Grant's KR 750 Kawasaki was reckoned to be prone to chain trouble, caused by the flexing of its engine in its rubber mounts. While he was pleased to have broken Mike Hailwood's absolute lap record, Grant acknowledged that he was on a 750 that was fitted with disc brakes and running on slick tyres and that the breaking of Hailwood's record was long overdue.

Sidecars had changed enormously since the mid-1950s, when BMWs had started to monopolize the winning positions. They were now low, streamlined, kneeler machines, employing various forms of hub-centre style steering, rather than telescopic forks, and with little suspension movement at the rear. They used a variety of power sources, including some adapted from marine engines, which gave over 80bhp in 500cc form, with larger versions offering considerably more. All this was conveyed to the road through wide-section racing tyres on small wheels, usually 7.00 × 13 on the front and 9.00 × 13 on the rear. The fat rear tyres and extra weight of an 'outfit' put additional stresses on transmissions, while the minimal suspension gave a jarring ride that tested overall build quality on the still bumpy Mountain Course.

In 1975, victory in the 500cc Sidecar race went to Rolf Steinhausen on a Busch-Konig at a record race average speed of 95.94mph, with a new record fastest lap going to second-placed Mac Hobson (Yamaha) at 96.71mph. It was a year when there were few BMWs entered in either the 500 or 1000cc Sidecar races, but multi-TT winner Siegfried Schauzu gave the marque what was to be its final TT victory when he won the big class at record-breaking speed. 'Siggy' lifted the race average to 97.55mph and the lap speed to 99.31mph. It was a final flourish from BMW that fell just 10 seconds short of the first 100mph lap by a three-wheeler, but left a target for the ever more powerful machines that were to follow.

1976: MORE RECORDS BROKEN

Between the 1975 and 1976 TT meetings, several speed-restricting curves on the stretch between Braddan Bridge and Union Mills were eased. Known locally as Snugborough, the road-straightening saved riders a few seconds on their lap times.

The Sidecar races again saw advances in speed in 1976, although their absolute lap record remained at just under 100mph, with Mac Hobson (Yamaha) setting a new figure of 99.96mph on his way to winning the 1,000cc race. Siegfried Schauzu lifted the 500cc Sidecar record to 97.50mph after troublesome early laps, although the win went to Rolf Steinhausen (Konig).

In the Production race, postponed from Saturday to Tuesday, BMW got their first solo TT win since 1939, when Helmut Dahne and Hans-Otto Butenuth came home first in the 1000cc class, where a new lap record of 103.13mph was set by Roger Nicholls on a twin-cylinder Ducati. The Production TT was a strange form of handicap race, in which the record books show that the fastest 250 was actually given the overall win, at a race pace 10mph slower than the fastest 1000cc machine and having completed one lap less!

The outright lap record of 108.77mph, set back in 1967, was achieved by Mike Hailwood on a 500cc machine. Mick Grant and his big 750 Kawasaki had gone faster during the 1975 Classic 1000 race, but Hailwood's record still stood for the Senior and had been relatively unthreatened during the early 1970s. In what was a step-change for the Senior TT, John Williams lifted both the absolute and Senior lap record to a heady 112.27mph on his works-supported Suzuki RG500. But what had seemed like a certain victory disappeared after Williams had problems at Governor's Bridge on the last lap. The win went to a grateful Tom Herron on a Yamaha, while Williams pushed in to finish an exhausted seventh.

The 4-cylinder, water-cooled RG500 two-stroke had

John Williams on his record-breaking Texaco Heron Suzuki in the 1976 Senior TT.

been around in works and semi-works form for about three years and was known to Suzuki as the XR14. After deciding to switch emphasis from supporting Grand Prix racing via Suzuki GB at the end of 1975, the parent company recognized that there was a shortage of 500cc race machinery and made Mk1 RG500s available for sale. The price was about £6,000 and they were snapped up by privateers. Coming initially with some 95bhp, the RG500 was much developed in all areas during the next eight years, offering opposition to Yamaha and proving the mainstay of the 500cc class.

Records in the Junior class had also been under threat in recent years, particularly from the top men on TZ350s, and in 1976 Agostini's race record and Hailwood's lap record for the class were both broken, the former falling to race winner Chas Mortimer (Yamaha) at 106.78mph and the

latter being taken by second-place Tony Rutter (Yamaha) at a speed of 108.69mph. World Championship contenders Takazumi Katayama and John Ekerold both tried their hands as TT newcomers in 1976, gaining very satisfactory results of fourth and sixth in the Senior, plus a splendid second place for Katayama in the Lightweight. Also making his TT debut in that Junior race was Joey Dunlop. With a start number of 65, he finished in sixteenth position.

Friday's Lightweight and Classic 1000cc races were postponed until Saturday due to poor weather and, as usual, this meant crowds of disappointed spectators leaving the Island rather than run the risk of not being able to get later boat bookings.

Hailwood's race average record speed of 103.07mph was still waiting to be broken in the Lightweight TT. In what had become an age of screaming two-strokes, the former bark of four-strokes generated fond memories, particularly so in the case of the rasping 250cc Honda-six on which Hailwood had set his figure back in 1967. However, the march of Yamahas through racing was irresistible and Tom Herron grabbed a new race record of 103.55mph to take the Lightweight 250 race. Bill Ivy's lap record of 105.51mph remained intact.

Thoughts that the Classic 1000 race might raise the absolute record were not fulfilled, although John Williams did get a win, this time on his Suzuki TR750-3, lifting both race average and lap record speeds to 108.18 and 110.21mph. Such speed increases brought heavy fuel consumption. It was a time when the TT permitted owners to provide their own quick-action fillers, something Suzuki must have been particularly glad to have available.

The 1976 TT had produced a record-breaking race week across six of the event's nine classes, and there was a feeling that

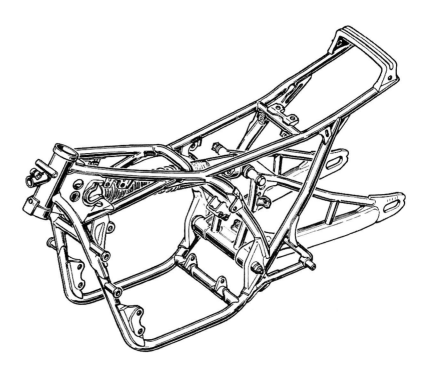

The new frame for the TZ-C series, with monoshock rear suspension.

the quality production race bikes now available would see continued advance in speeds. Yamaha were still developing their smaller racers. Their new TZ250 and 350 C range bikes came with an additional 2–4bhp, monoshock rear suspension and disc brakes all round. Claimed advantages from use of a monoshock were longer travel to absorb bumps and keep the rear wheel on the ground, a wide range of adjustment and an overall improvement in handling. The opportunity was also taken to redesign the TZ frames.

With improved performance in the important fields of power, handling and stopping, plus changes to riding styles, faster laps looked inevitable. But perhaps reflect-ing the relative lack of competition in the Senior class, its fastest laps progressed only slowly through the late 1960s and early 1970s, starting at 107.07mph in 1966 and finishing at 112.27mph in 1976, after a spurt in the last couple of years.

Regrettably, not all was well in the world of TT racing, for it was known that in the months ahead, the FIM were yet again going to review the event's World Championship status. Whatever was decided, what they could not take away was the atmosphere, camaraderie and excitement of the true road racing, which was shared by thousands of TT enthusiasts on their annual visits to the Isle of Man.

CHAPTER SEVEN

A NEW ERA

At the end of 1976 the FIM announced that the Tourist Trophy races would no longer count towards the World Championships. The news came as no surprise, for the influential star riders who wanted to race only on artificial tracks were determined to take the sport away from natural road circuits, both on the Isle of Man and on the Continent. With the decision made, riders could decide which element of the sport they would compete in. Many were happy to do both, but for those of a single mind-set the FIM's decision confirmed the parting of the ways. The gulf between the two could hardly have been made clearer with the news that Britain's round of the World Championships would now be held at the flat, featureless, former airfield of Silverstone. A greater contrast with the TT's Mountain Course could hardly be imagined.

Much was written about the future of the Tourist Trophy races in early 1977, one magazine headline encapsulating the thoughts of many by asking, 'Waterloo or Watershed?' Pessimists forecast that the loss of World Championship status signified the beginning of the end for Island racing, while optimists regarded it as the start of a new era. In support of riders, the race budget was increased to £150,000, with £100,000 going for start and prize money, while to make the event more attractive to visitors, the Island worked hard to create additional attractions at TT time.

1977: RACE PROGRAMME

The 350cc race was dropped for 1977. Previously known as the Junior TT, that title was now given to the three-lap race for 250cc machines, which had been known as the Lightweight TT since 1920. Someone, somewhere, probably knew the reason for the change of name, but race fans saw no logic in the decision. The Production TT was also dropped. A former winner in that event, journalist Ray Knight, felt that it had lost its way, 'due to convoluted rules that permitted manufacturers to build any bike to a specification especially written by themselves for the race'.

Replacing the Proddies came four-lap races for new classes of TT Formula I, TT Formula II and TT Formula III. They catered for road-based sports machines on which fairly extensive alterations could be made to boost performance. Four-strokes were encouraged by giving them a capacity advantage over two-strokes and Formula races went on to develop their own limited World Championship.

Other changes for 1977 saw the 500cc Sidecar race dropped and new two-leg races created for up to 1000cc machines. Each would be of four laps, with an individual winner plus an overall winner based on the best results from the two legs.

A four-lap Jubilee TT race was also in the programme, in recognition of Queen Elizabeth's Silver Jubilee.

YAMAHA

Early in 1977 Yamaha announced it would supply a batch of new race machines to Britain via sporting dealers. There would be forty TZ250s, forty-eight TZ350s and five OW31 TZ750s. It claimed they were being marketed on a subsidized basis with the 250 charged at £2,709, the 350 at £2,884 and the 750 a substantial £6,572. Before production of Norton single-cylinder race bikes stopped in 1962, a rider could buy a new Manx for £572. However, the OW31 was ahead of its rivals in performance, so it was the bike everyone wanted, though few obtained, for only seventy were available to satisfy worldwide demand in 1977.

The names of those who would ride the new Yamahas were publicized and many of them were TT regulars, with most being dealer-supported. The one-year-old models they discarded would be eagerly sought after by those further down the chain, while riders of older machines who could not afford to change bikes would seek more speed by upgrading with later parts, if they fitted.

With the TT races full of Yamahas, the demand for spares was always high and specialist dealers would be on the Island with the full range to keep competitors mobile. The combined distance covered in practice and racing meant that the TT was a high-mileage event for race machinery, and as many major components were good for only a relatively small number of racing miles, it was an expensive business to keep a bike in top order. Despite the expense, the magic of the TT continued to attract riders in large numbers.

Phil Read, on his return to the TT in 1977, speeds through Union Mills on his big Honda.

HONDA

Big news in 1977 was that Honda were returning to the TT with a works machine in the Formula I race and that Phil Read would be returning to ride it. Looking for a profitable TT meeting, Read also put together an RG500 to use, with components gathered from several sources. In the wider world of racing, that model was now on its Mk2 and Mk3 versions and gradually giving more power as Suzuki developed it year on year.

Phil Read's return to the TT was not universally popular. Indeed, it attracted strong anti-Read feelings, with some commentators expressing the opinion that appearance money paid to him could have been better used on others. There were no figures made public, but an ACU spokesman was forced to dampen some of the wilder appearance money claims by announcing that his fee 'was less than half of the £10,000 being spoken of'. By comparison, one of the top sidecar men, George O'Dell, claimed he received £500.

In a move that echoed Ray Knight's earlier comments on problems with Proddie race regulations and one that aroused widespread cries of 'fiddle', Honda arranged for the last-minute homologation of larger carburettors for its Formula I 4-cylinder, four-stroke racer.

THE COURSE

A competitor on a pre-practice reconnaissance lap noted new road surfacing through Union Mills, but said, 'this very smooth half-mile of road only emphasizes how rough the rest of the course is'. The approach to Ramsey had been surface-dressed with tar and chippings some weeks before, but not all had bedded and practice saw competitors returning to the Paddock with broken screens, while others complained of being peppered with chippings when close on the back wheel of another rider.

RACING

The 1977 TT got under way with Junior 250cc and TT Formula I races run in less than ideal conditions and at relatively low speeds. Charlie Williams notched another win in the Junior race dominated by Yamahas, where in the eternal quest for an advantage over similar-powered opposition, several riders were using Seeley, Maxton and Spondon frames to house their Yamaha engines. After making the big decision to return to the TT, Honda were pleased to see Phil Read first home in the shortened TT Formula I race, some 40 seconds ahead of Roger Nicholls (Ducati).

Acting as one of the race scrutineers and thus getting a close-up view of the bikes, Tim Stevens later described the interesting Formula I entry:

Here are riders and motorcycles from all over the world ... with V-twins, parallel twins, and flat twins, with 120-degree threes and 180-degree threes, with in-line fours and a flat four, with shaft drive and chain drive, with telescopic forks and leading links, swinging forks and parallelograms, with pushrods, single and double overhead camshafts driven by chains, bevel gears and belts.

Formula II and Formula III races ran together with less variety of machines entered, and wins went to Alan Jackson (Honda) and John Kidson (Honda), the four-stroke Hondas showing greater reliability than the many two-stroke Yamahas in the race.

It was Phil Read who again showed his class to win Monday's 500cc Senior race at record-breaking speeds on his Suzuki, from Tom Herron and Eddie Roberts. The race was shortened by a lap due to incoming rain and mist, but not before Read had taken advantage of the dry start and raised the lap record to 110.01mph and the race average speed to 106.97mph.

George O'Dell always sought the best race machinery and with it earned a Sidecar TT win and World Championship.

Records were also broken in Sidecar race A. Dick Greasley (Yamaha) set the pace with the first ton-up lap on three wheels, recording 100.59mph, but it was George O'Dell (Yamaha) who then got into his stride, lifting the lap record to 102.80mph and finishing with a record race average speed of 100.03mph. O'Dell was a hard charger on his Yamaha-powered outfit, leaving black lines on the road under both braking and acceleration. The pace was only a little slower a couple of days later in Sidecar race B, where Mac Hobson (Yamaha) won at 99.74mph from Rolf Biland (Yamaha), with first race winner O'Dell charging a bit too hard at the Bungalow and breaking his leg. Two third places for Rolf Steinhausen (Busch Konig) saw him take the overall Sidecar victory. The races were notable for the way in which Yamaha two-stroke engines were becoming the power unit of choice for many of the three-wheeler crews, although they were expensive to run, needing replacement parts at even more frequent intervals than solos. Outfits were also getting longer and lower, with wishbone forms of suspension at front and rear, disc brakes, huge radiators, wide tyres, limited steering lock and several forms of chassis.

Back in 1960 Sidecars had returned to race over the Mountain Course, when winner Helmut Fath's race average speed was 84.10mph on his 500cc BMW. The climb in speed to George O'Dell's 100.03mph average in 1977 came mostly from a lift in capacity to 1000cc and much change in machine design.

Hopes of a hat-trick of solo wins by Phil Read in 1977 were ruined by an open-road crash while testing one of his race bikes. It was an incident that brought him a damaged shoulder and a court appearance. It also meant that he missed the Classic 1000cc race, worth £6,000 to the winner. Happy to take the win was Mick Grant (Kawasaki), at a new record race average speed for the class of 110.76mph and a lap record of 112.77mph. Those speeds would turn out to be the fastest of the week. Grant's big-triple Kawasaki was followed home by the smaller Yamahas of Charlie Williams and Eddie Roberts, after American Pat Hennen (Suzuki) dropped out of second place on the fifth lap.

Come the invitation Jubilee TT race there was a first win for Joey Dunlop on a Yamaha TZ750 hybrid, at a race speed of 108.86mph and fastest lap of 110.93mph, which put him well up with the fastest men around the Mountain Course. Seemingly not rated by the organizers, Dunlop was allocated riding number 30 in the race, so had to cope with plenty of traffic. In addition, concerns about tyre wear late in the race saw him stop in Ramsey to inspect his treaded rear one before racing across the last 14 miles of abrasive

Renold Chain was pleased to announce its TT successes.

mountain roads to the chequered flag. No one knew at the time that Joey Dunlop would go on to win twenty-five more TT races and lift his personal best lap speed from his Jubilee-winning 110.93mph to over 123mph.

1978: EVEN BETTER

Its first year in non-World Grand Prix Championship format had been a good one for the TT, but 1978 was to be even better, for while Phil Read's comeback in 1977 had sparked interest, the news that Mike Hailwood was to return in 1978 really set imaginations alight. The current generation of racegoers would have been aware of Hailwood's long TT history and that he took three record-breaking victories on his last TT appearance in 1967. However, it was only natural that most of them doubted that he could deliver anything like that sort of form eleven years later.

TT fans of an earlier generation could hardly believe they were going to have the chance to see the star of their younger days back in action on the Mountain Course. They

Padgetts provided Mike Hailwood with a Yamaha to film a lap of the Mountain Course during the 1977 MGP – or might it have been reconnaissance for his 1978 TT return?

too would have nursed doubts about how he would perform, for unlike Phil Read, who had been racing at championship level on two-wheels during the whole of his five-year absence from the TT, Mike Hailwood had spent his eleven years away racing cars and picking up a troublesome ankle in the process. In addition, while he was coming back to much the same TT course, the machines he was to ride were very different in terms of power, tyres, suspension, brakes and other parts, all of which now came with a battery of variables in set-up. This was particularly so with the suspension, the potential adjustments of which spanned areas like preload, spring rate, rebound and compression damping. Could he really jump on 1978 machinery, fine-tune it and then challenge current TT stars?

What was in no doubt was that the level of interest generated by Hailwood's return was phenomenal. The press did its bit to fan the flames of that interest and by race week the Island was 'bursting at the seams'.

TRIUMPH AND TRAGEDY

Mike Hailwood's last TT race in 1967 had seen him wearing old-style plain black leathers and boots, with pudding-basin helmet and goggles. Times had changed, and in 1978 his new red and white leathers came splashed with advertising from major names and his trademark white, gold and red helmet colours were applied to a full-face-version. Mike looked the part, but the 38-year-old had to overcome what journalist Ted Macauley described as 'a pack of youngsters on thoroughbred machinery, howling after his reputation'.

Race week opened like a dream for Hailwood's many fans, as he rode an unfancied 864cc Ducati to victory in the TT Formula I race at a record race average speed of 108.51mph and a record fastest lap of 110.62mph. In a quality field, on a bike that was 20bhp down on some of the opposition, Hailwood just rode away from them, catching and passing Phil Read (Honda) who started 50 seconds in front of him, to win by 2 minutes from John Williams (Honda). His last lap was a huge TT spectacle of waving arms and fluttering programmes urging him to the chequered flag. It was an unforgettable occasion, and one that generated a few moist eyes.

Despite what *Motorcycle Sport* described as 'a sparkling cocktail of Yamaha and Martini sponsorship', it was regrettable that a combination of machine failures, running out of petrol and other mishaps prevented any further successes with the Yamahas he rode in other races that week. Even so, the crowds had got what they came for, another TT win by 'Mike the Bike'.

Victory in the Senior race, run on the Monday, went to Tom Herron, who rode his Suzuki RG500 Mk2 at tremendous pace, lifting the race average speed from the previous best of 106.97mph to 111.74mph. Fastest lap went to Pat Hennen at 113.83mph, but in pressing to catch the leader he fell heavily at Bishopscourt, sustaining injuries that ended his racing career.

Pat Hennen's accident brought the all-too-familiar swing of emotions among TT followers, from the high of Hailwood's win to the low of a top runner in hospital fighting for his life. More bad news was to follow, for in Sidecar race A, the popular Mac Hobson crashed his yellow and black Yamaha part-way down Bray Hill on the first lap and was killed, along with his passenger Kenny Birch. Shortly after, in the same race, Ernst Trachsel was killed in another crash at the bottom of the hill. Dick Greasley's win at record speed and Rolf Biland's record lap on his revolutionary Beo Yamaha were received in subdued fashion after such tragedies.

As ever, racing went on, and in mixed weather Sidecar race B was won at slower speeds by Rolf Steinhausen, with newcomer Jock Taylor taking overall victory. In both Sidecar races, winners and fastest lap setters were powered by Yamaha.

While mindful of everything that had gone on earlier in the week, riders and spectators approached Friday's six-lap Classic TT in expectation of a great race. The man who helped fulfil those expectations was Mick Grant, who hurled his big Kawasaki two-stroke around the Mountain Course to achieve victory from John Williams (Suzuki) and

After riding to victory in the 1978 TT Formula I race, Mike Hailwood takes time to sign autographs.

Alex George (Yamaha) at a new absolute record race average speed of 112.41mph and set a new absolute lap record of 114.33mph. Grant was a professional racer who came up via short-circuit, MGP and TT racing, but who also raced GPs with success on Kawasaki 250cc tandem twins. In talking of his preparation for a worldwide season of racing and the arrangements he made for sponsorship, start money and so on, he revealed in his autobiography *Mick Grant – Takin' the Mick* that 'apart from the TT, prize money was almost negligible'.

WORKS SUPPORT

The level of works support received by top riders contesting the TT varied through the 1970s, as it did in the World Championships. Yamaha had years when they were offering support and years when they were busy on development and thus could not give support. Sometimes their support was direct from Japan, sometimes from their European branch in Amsterdam, or from Mitsui in Britain. Usually the support was open and publicized, but at other times it might be 'under the counter'. Suzuki were similar, with Suzuki GB handling the parent company's TT and World Championship machines and riders for several years. Honda had nominally been out of the sport for much of the 1970s, while Kawasaki had limited involvement, mostly with their 3-cylinder production racers. That involvement grew later in the decade with the new FIM F750 Championship and the appearance of their 250 and 350cc tandem twins.

In the late 1970s Yamaha were producing race machines for the 250, 350, 500 and 750cc classes, having dropped the 125 they marketed for a couple of years. By now the 250 and 350 carried the TZF classification and for 1979 the 350 received a substantial upgrade, with redesigned ports, new exhausts and new carburettors with power-jet system operating from 8,000rpm. Said to give another 8bhp, which lifted output to 72bhp at 10,500rpm, when this was allied to considerable weight saving from magnesium cases and aluminium swinging arm, the 350 became noticeably quicker. Far less work went into the TZ250F and its output remained 53bhp at 10,500rpm. Not everyone liked the TZ's handling in standard form, particularly with the extra power, and an ever-growing number of specialist frame makers offered alternatives.

Not a great deal was seen of the YZR500 at the TT, where over-bored 350s tended to challenge for the Senior win, but those lucky enough to get their hands on TZ750s did use them in the Classic race, although to quote Tom Herron: 'Sulby Straight ... now that is something out of this world on a 750 Yam – you have to consciously brace yourself'. Not only did the biggest Yamahas test a rider's bravery and skill, but they were also worryingly hard on tyres over a lengthy TT race, where the latest slick tyres were available to use but where mid-race tyre/wheel changes had yet to be introduced.

Experienced teams and riders would return to the TT each year with some idea of the settings required for carburation, gearing and suspension on the Mountain Course, but much fine-tuning would be carried out during practice to get the right balance. Newcomers often found setting-up to be a daunting task; one whose initial suspension adjustment was out told that, for him, 'Sulby Straight was one big tank-slapper'.

1979: MILLENNIUM

This was not the turn-of-the-century Millennium of 2000 celebrated by the world at large, but the lower key one in 1979 that marked 1,000 years of Tynwald, the Manx Parliament. However, the Manx worked hard to make everything a little special on the Island in Millennium year and the TT was expected to do its bit.

Whatever Mike Hailwood's reasons were for making a comeback at the 1978 TT, it is certain that a profusion of offers of the sort that could not be refused helped make his mind up to return in 1979. The fans were back too, wanting to witness again the seemingly unhurried and almost casual style of the man who, in over twenty years of racing, showed that he could ride anything and usually win. While he would have been guaranteed a good pay day from all of his pre-race contractual arrangements in 1979, there was also the tempting target of a £10,000 first prize for the Schweppes Classic TT and £5,000 for a start-to-finish leader of the Quintin Hazell Senior TT.

Practice week was troubled by poor weather, which made it difficult to tell who was really on form amongst expected front runners like Alex George, Charlie Williams, Helmut Dahne, Tony Rutter, an injured Mick Grant and, of course, Mike Hailwood, who suffered handling problems with his Ducati.

Racing started with the Formula I event on Saturday afternoon and this time Hailwood could not overcome his substantial bhp deficiency compared to the full-blown 1,000cc Honda and Kawasaki fours. The race win went to Alex George (Honda), who raised race average and fastest lap speeds to new records of 110.57 and 112.94mph, leaving Charlie Williams to take second and Mike Hailwood, plagued with problems, to finish fifth. Ironically, in 1979 the Ducati factory had taken a little more interest in his bike than they did in 1978, although not all of it was beneficial.

Suzuki-mounted for the Senior TT, on a bike that had been subject to an extensive weekend engine rebuild, Mike Hailwood simply rode away from the opposition, putting in laps of under 20 minutes and winning by 2 minutes from Tony Rutter (Suzuki), breaking race and lap records along the way with speeds of 111.75mph and 114.02mph. The latter was his fastest-ever TT lap and just 0.31mph off the absolute course record. Second-placed Tony Rutter was a previous TT winner, but he said to Hailwood after the race, 'When you came by I tried to keep up with you, but no way ...' That Senior race was dominated by Suzuki and Yamaha machinery.

The nearest Hailwood came to further glory in 1979 was in the final race of the week, the six-lap Schweppes Classic. In a race-long struggle with Alex George on his big Honda, Hailwood and his 500cc Suzuki got ahead towards the end but lost time going over the Mountain on the last lap. The result was he finished his TT career with second place, losing by just 3.4 seconds to George, who set a new record Classic race average speed of 113.08mph and narrowly missed the lap record.

Mike Hailwood's name had been very much to the fore in 1979, and as an illustration of the reason why it still meant so much at the TT, when Charlie Williams (Yamaha) rode to victory in that year's Junior 250cc race at record speeds, it was Hailwood's long-standing 250cc race record from 1967 of 103.07mph that he broke, along with the lap record of another TT great, Bill Ivy. Williams set impressive new race and lap figures of 105.13mph and 106.83mph on his Maxton-framed bike, during what had been restored to a six-lap race.

SUCCESSORS?

When Mike Hailwood announced after racing had finished in 1979 that his TT career was at an end, people looked around for someone who might emulate his fourteen TT wins. As well as the established riders who shone that year, short-circuit ace Ron Haslam showed in his second year that he was getting to grips with TT racing. Strangely, this may have been aided by a spectacular fall at Ballaugh Bridge, when he admitted he was going for the high-jump record, for it might just have steadied his future pace. Haslam knew that he needed to treat the TT differently from short circuits, telling how Mike Hailwood 'gave me a wonderful riding lesson on the Island … I'd tag on behind him and watch him ride … it was a masterclass'.

Another to excite and grab the imagination of the crowds in 1979 was Kiwi newcomer Graeme Crosby. With his big Kawasaki fitted with high-bars, his wheeling out of slow corners like the Gooseneck brought him to people's notice and he was a definite crowd pleaser. His race performances also revealed his talent, with fourth place in the Formula I race at an average of 107.39mph and a fastest lap of 109mph. They were the fastest laps ever by a newcomer. Among up-and-coming sidecar racers, a young Mick Boddice was another who liked to entertain the crowds at Ballaugh Bridge with height and distance. That was until he began to experience problems with stretched chains, when he decided a more mature approach was required.

PARADING

The TT liked to show off its history and one way was to allow former stars to parade around the course between races. Nowadays that is done in strictly controlled conditions, with the pace set by travelling marshals. At the 1979 TT, the 'parade' was more of a free-for-all.

Fastest in that Millennium Parade was Percy Tait, who lapped in 23 minutes 9 seconds, at an average lap speed of some 97.5mph. Alan Dugdale was second on a Matchless just ahead of Messrs Read and Surtees, whose lap times were 96 and 95mph. Also in the field were past winners like Stanley Woods, Georg Meier, Tommy Wood, Geoff Duke and Bill Lomas. All commented that the course was very much smoother than in their days. Indeed, even the notorious Cronk y Voddy straight had received attention, although it still could not be classed as smooth.

1980: A BUMPY RIDE

There were no complaints from sidecar crews about the

Not a race between John Surtees and Phil Read on MV Agustas, but a parade lap in 1979: here they are entering Parliament Square.

Mick Grant (Honda) and Graeme Crosby (Suzuki) exit Braddan Bridge. They circulated like this for three laps before Grant broke clear to win.

The Cotton/Rotax engine of 1980.

partial smoothing of the Cronk y Voddy straight, for, in frontrunner Trevor Ireson's words, it did away with 'Cronk Y Voddy Cronkiness', which was his name for a type of double-vision that previously afflicted him when he rode it flat out. Come the 1980 TT and the short-travel suspension of sidecar outfits gave their crews serious problems on the bumpy Sulby Straight. Three-time winner Rolf Steinhausen protested, 'I cannot race on such a road', while Nigel Rollason told that if it was not levelled he would not race the TT any more. Seemingly nothing was done, for the following year Jock Taylor talked of having to ease off 'to avoid wrecking the bike'.

In the actual racing in 1980, it was Trevor Ireson who took his third consecutive win in Sidecar race A, with Jock Taylor setting the fastest lap in what were mixed conditions. In the faster B race, an inspired Taylor rode at record speeds that no one could live with to beat Ireson into second place. In doing so he lifted the race average speed to 103.55mph and put over 3mph on the lap record, leaving it at 106.08mph.

It was an unusual year's racing for solos in 1980, because the less than perfect weather for most of the week meant that no records were broken until the last race. However, it was a week with its share of controversy, much of it involving the Honda and Suzuki works teams and their number one riders, Mick Grant and Graeme Crosby. Both teams used their muscle with the organizers to get their way in a manner lesser lights probably would not have managed, with most of the fuss revolving around interpretation of the regulations on issues ranging from fuel-tank sizes to starting order.

Speeds may have been down in some races due to the weather in 1980, but riding skills had to be at their highest to cope with poor road conditions. Mick Grant (Honda) took victory in Formula I, Graeme Crosby (Suzuki) won the Senior in only his second year at the event, Charlie Williams (Yamaha) collected wins in the Junior and Formula II races and Barry Smith (Yamaha) in Formula III. Those FII and FIII races were won on Yamaha's RD350LC and RD250LC machines, which were destined to achieve cult status on road and track.

An interesting machine in the Junior was the third-placed Cotton of Steve Tonkin. It was equipped with a Rotax water-cooled, disc-valve, tandem-twin engine, which was to make its mark at the TT with other makers during the 1980s, so challenging the Yamaha monopoly of the class.

CLASSIC

The closing Classic race of the 1980 TT was open to 1300cc machines, and Mick Grant turned out on a 1060cc Honda, Ron Haslam on a 999cc Honda and Graeme Crosby on a 1084cc Yoshimura Suzuki. Along with Charlie Williams (Yamaha), they were the pre-race favourites (Alex George was absent through injury). Each was backed by what was as close as you could get to works support, with equipment like their quick-fillers saving them up to 40 seconds on each fill against the less well-equipped teams. Understandably, they received the most pre-race attention and the presence of privateer Joey Dunlop on an older TZ750 Yamaha was barely remarked upon.

Canny Dunlop had equipped himself with a huge 8-gallon petrol tank to reduce the number of his refuelling stops, but early in the first lap its retaining straps broke, meaning that for the remainder of the six laps he was forced to hold it on with his knees. Despite this massive handicap he rode

Joey Dunlop – no ordinary road racer.

to a very satisfying victory over Mick Grant and in doing so set a new outright course record, with a lap speed of 115.22mph.

With Dunlop having convincingly beaten the Honda works entries, the only course open to 'Big H' was to sign him up. They did this later in the year and so started a long and unconventional relationship, where the company bent its normally strict rules to accommodate this special road-racing talent.

Joey Dunlop headed an influx of talented Irish riders to the TT in the early 1980s, which included Donny Robinson, Sam McClements, Con Law and Steve Cull. Irish road racing provided its riders with good TT-like training, which yielded a prolific supply of good runners.

SPEEDS

The drop from Creg ny Baa to Brandish was used for the unofficial timing of riders by at least two magazines in 1980, some of them recorded in damp conditions. Fastest speeds achieved were given as follows:

Formula I: Graeme Crosby (Suzuki) – 163mph, Mick Grant (Honda) – 159mph
Classic: Jeff Sayle (Yamaha) – 164mph, George Linder (Yamaha) – 160mph
Senior: Barry Woodland (Suzuki) – 156mph
Sidecar: Nigel Rollason (Barton) – 144mph, Jock Taylor (Yamaha) – 141mph

In total, fourteen riders exceeded 150mph.

A private timing venture at The Highlander in 1973.

SPEED COMPARISON

There had been huge developments in racing motorcycles in the twenty years since the 500cc Manx Norton was at its peak, and in 1980 a good Suzuki RG500 like Barry Woodland's was putting out about 120bhp. That was well over twice the output of a good Manx of the early 1960s. No comparable figures are available to show what speed a Norton reached on the drop from Creg ny Baa to Brandish, but the best-ever published speed of a Norton single from Sulby Straight was Mike Hailwood's 138.46mph in 1960, with several other 500cc singles hitting 130-plus mph there in the same era. Hailwood's 138.46mph at Sulby has to be worth at least 140-plus mph on the drop to Brandish, sub-

ject to gearing, which indicates that big increases in bhp give relatively small increases in mph.

Looking at those situations, which were nearly twenty years apart, if it is assumed that the speed of Hailwood's Senior TT-winning RG500 of 1979 was on a par with Woodland's of 1980, the difference made by the extra top-end speed achieved by Mike's 500cc Suzuki over his 500cc Norton can be illustrated by comparing his fastest lap on a Norton – 101.31mph in 1961 – with his fastest lap on a Suzuki RG500 – 114.02mph in 1979. That gives a gain in lap speed of almost 13mph, which was also a 13 per cent increase. That came after a doubling of bhp available to the rider. However, top speed is not the only factor to consider when comparing the effect of power on lap times, for as well as giving increased maximum, the greater bhp on tap can contribute to a much broader spread of power and improved acceleration. Faster lap times would also have owed something to the improvements made to handling and braking, plus the effect of course improvements.

Back in the 1960s a similar situation had applied to speed/time gains for Mike Hailwood, when he switched from a 500cc Norton to a 500cc MV Agusta. In that move he gained over 20bhp, but even three years later, he had put only 4½mph on his best lap speed. That meant 40 per cent more power gave a 4 per cent gain in lap speed.

Just to throw in another detail – in 1966 Giacomo Agostini (MV Agusta) and Mike Hailwood (Honda) were the two fastest 500s timed on the drop from Creg ny Baa at 151.9mph. Their machines were said to be giving about 80–85bhp.

It is worth mentioning that the only official timing at the TT in those earlier eras was of the time taken by competitors to complete a full lap. The resultant figures were then converted to lap speeds and published by the organizers. All other timing and speeds quoted came from private ventures, whose accuracy was not guaranteed.

1981: EVER FASTER

The 1981 TT was oversubscribed with entries, showing the event maintained its popularity with riders, although some reports said that spectator numbers were down. Those in attendance were witness to dramatic racing, accompanied by manufacturers' protests and the usual examples of good and bad luck. But most of all, they saw ever faster racing and the setting of new speed records over the Mountain Course. Shown below on the left are the race average and fastest lap speeds coming into the 1981 TT and on the right the figures achieved during the 1981 event. It was a special year, for only the rain-hit Senior event failed to improve its figures.

Race	Top speeds pre–1981	Top speeds 1981
TT Formula I	race average 110.57mph fastest lap 112.94mph	111.81mph 113.70mph
Senior TT	race average 111.75mph fastest lap 114.02mph	106.14mph 112.68mph
Sidecar	race average 103.55mph fastest lap 106.08mph	107.02mph 108.12mph
Junior	race average 105.13mph fastest lap 106.83mph	106.21mph 109.22mph
TT Formula II	race average 101.55mph fastest lap 103.40mph	101.91mph 103.51mph
TT Formula III	race average 97.82mph fastest lap 99.37mph	99.66mph 101.31mph
Classic TT	race average 113.08mph fastest lap 115.22mph	113.58mph 115.40mph

Doing the winning in 1981 were Graeme Crosby (Suzuki), who took the Formula I and Classic races, and Mick Grant, who had moved from Honda to Suzuki and won the weather-hit Senior after the first race was stopped and then rerun. Even the rerun was affected by rain showers towards the end, and riding Randy Mamola's Suzuki RG 500 World Championship bike on slick tyres, Grant suffered substantial wheelspin in the wet. Steve Tonkin took the Junior on an Armstrong and so broke Yamaha's long domination of the class, Tony Rutter brought a Ducati home first in the Formula II race, Barry Smith a Yamaha in Formula III and Jock Taylor was dominant in winning both Sidecar races with Yamaha power.

As a sideshow to the racing, Honda and Suzuki renewed their confrontations from 1980, Ron Haslam (Honda) losing the Formula I race after a time penalty that was imposed upon Graeme Crosby (Suzuki) at the start was revoked after protest, so giving him the win. Honda were unhappy with the decision and turned out their three-man team of Joey Dunlop, Ron Haslam and Alex George in all-black livery for the prestigious Classic race as their form of counter-protest. Unfortunately it backfired on them, for Joey Dunlop lost time after running out of petrol near the end of the third lap – an unforgiveable error for a works team – while Crosby and Grant went on to take first and second for Suzuki.

Graeme Crosby was also contesting the World Championships for Suzuki (fifth in the 500cc class in 1981 and second in 1982), but he was a true fan of the TT, saying that what he liked about it was: 'the way the racing is spread out over ten days, the enthusiasm of the fans, dawn practice, hard partying on the days off, the history of the place … it's magic, really, but it's so hard to explain the place to people who've never been there'.

Looking at other features of the 1981 TT, Honda, in what was believed to be a first, carried out a mid-race tyre change for Joey Dunlop in the Formula I race. There was a tightening of regulations for sidecars, aimed at avoiding developments that were making them more like three-wheeled

In Honda's black 'protest' leathers, Joey Dunlop pushes his machine along the Glencrutchery Road to the pits, having run out of petrol. He refuelled but retired later in the race with mechanical problems.

cars; and to improve medical services, a second rescue helicopter was brought into use.

The sum available to pay to riders was increased by 25 per cent in 1981, with a £253,000 fund for prize and appearance payments. It left some claiming that 'the TT was the richest motorcycle event in the world'. Certainly the good money on offer attracted the top road racers and, perhaps indirectly, it thus contributed to faster races.

In the wider world of racing, the FIM announced that 1982 would be the last year of the 350cc class in World Championships and Yamaha's TZ350H of 1981 was their last 350cc racer. It came with a power valve that operated on the exhaust at higher revs and 55bhp was available from an engine that had seen elements of redesign aimed at increasing reliability and component life. There were also minor frame changes and the seat shape had gradually been styled to improve airflow. It was all part of a constant search for more power, increased flexibility and drive, plus improved handling and weight-saving. The aim was to combine all such improvements to help riders reduce lap times.

1982: CONTRARY?

While the FIM had decided to drop the 350cc class, the ACU announced that a race for 350s would return to the TT in 1982 and be run concurrently with 500cc machines in the Senior, even though there was some vagueness about what the 'new' race would be called. It was the only change to the race programme for what was the seventy-fifth anniversary of the first TT meeting. This was recognized by the usual issue of commemorative postage stamps and the minting of 50p pieces bearing an image of Mick Grant. Of rather more importance to competitors was the fact that the weather held good throughout practice and racing.

Missing from the anniversary meeting in 1982 was Graeme Crosby. He had joined a GP team run by Giacomo Agostini, where he found that contesting the TT was not on Ago's agenda.

THE RACING

After 1981's record-breaking spree, it was hardly surprising that some records remained intact in 1982. However, faster

Mick Grant on his 1982 Suzuki XR69 Formula I machine, which he felt was better than the Honda opposition.

Con Law flies high at Ballaugh Bridge on his 250 EMC during his winning ride in 1982.

Jon Ekerold rides the bumpy May Hill, heading out of Ramsey.

speeds were set in several races, including the opening For-mula I event, where Mick Grant, on what he described as his 'trick, super-quick and absolutely loaded with factory bits' Suzuki XR69, tussled with Ron Haslam (Honda) and set a new lap record of 114.93mph before retiring at Ram-sey Hairpin.

The failure of his Suzuki meant that Mick Grant had to sit and watch Ron Haslam race on to his first TT win at a new race record average speed of 113.33mph. Having suffered the disappointment of losing his 'win' in the 1981 race after Suzuki's protest was upheld, Haslam was jubilant, saying 'at last I've done it – I've won a TT! It's something I've always wanted to do – and now I feel great'.

Ron Haslam had served his apprenticeship at the TT before achieving his first win, but after winning the 1981 Senior MGP, Irishman Norman Brown came to the 1982 TT and took first place in the Senior 500cc race. It was a stunning ride at his first attempt, completed at just below record-breaking pace. Mick Grant had been contesting the lead when he tangled with another rider at Doran's Bend and was brought off. Fortunately he did not sustain seri-ous injury at this high-speed point on the course, but ever the outspoken Yorkshireman, he made the organizers well aware of his feelings about 'holiday racers' being allowed out on the same circuit as the stars and creating substantial speed differentials between riders.

Another experienced rider was Charlie Williams. He had several TT wins to his name, but a Senior victory still eluded him. The 1982 Senior 500cc race did not start well for him, as his YZ Yamaha was down on power, so on the second lap he pulled in at the Sulby Glen Hotel to retire. As is the way at such spots, his wheels had hardly stopped turning before a pint of beer was thrust in his hand but, still keyed-up, he prowled round the bike and suddenly spotted a kinked fuel line. Putting his beer aside, the line was straightened to allow a full flow of fuel, Williams put on his helmet and gloves and rejoined the race. Knowing that he had lost too much time to be in with a chance of victory, he was still determined to show what he could do and on his fourth circuit he broke the Senior lap record, lifting it to 115.08mph.

This year the 350s had their own race within the Senior and victory went to Tony Rutter. His race average speed was 108.53mph, which beat Chas Mortimer's record of 106.78mph, set back in 1976 at the last running of a race for 350s. Graeme McGregor set a new lap record of 112.03mph. Race speeds may have changed between 1976 and 1982, but what remained the same was that the old and new figures had all been set on Yamahas, for they were still the dominant race bikes of the day. Change was in the air, however, and despite Yamaha swamping the entry in the Junior 250cc event, it turned into a race of attrition for the marque, with a host of retirements, leaving Con Law to ride his Ehrlich to victory at just below record speed. A tandem twin, the Ehrlich was variously described in the programme and results as a Waddon, a Waddon-Ehrlich and a Rotax-powered Waddon. It was also known as an EMC.

The only record broken in the two Sidecar races was in Race B, where Jock Taylor lifted the fastest lap speed to 108.29mph. Sadly, Taylor was killed later in the summer during the Finnish GP.

Previous year's Formula II winner Tony Rutter was riding a Ducati again and, with an element of works support, lifted race average and lap records by an incredible 6mph. That sort of increase was unknown in TT races in an age when they were being won at over 100mph and it was a performance in which Rutter trounced the opposition, winning by 4 minutes.

No records were set in the Classic race, where Honda brought one of their new V4s for Joey Dunlop to ride only to find during practice that it was not up to the demands of the Mountain Course. Dunlop reverted to his well-tried

In recognition of Con Law's record lap of 110mph on his EMC.

transverse-four, but he was among retirements from the race, as were fancied challengers such as Charlie Williams, Ron Haslam, Mick Grant and Steve Tonkin. Victory went to Dennis Ireland (Suzuki) from Jon Ekerold (Suzuki).

1983: TWO JUNIORS

The Formula III race was dropped for 1983 and the 350cc race machines were now given a race of their own, instead of running with the 500s in the Senior TT, as in 1982. The new race was called the Junior 350cc TT and joined the Junior 250cc TT in the race programme, both running over six laps. The former Blue Riband Senior TT had lost its premier status to the Classic TT in recent years, but for 1983 the two races were combined to give the Senior Classic TT, open to machines up to 1000cc and run on Friday of race week.

The 1983 race programme opened with the customary Formula I race, which went to Joey Dunlop and his new RS850 V4 Honda at record race average and lap speeds, from Mick Grant and Rob McElnea on 997cc works Suzukis. Privateer Trevor Nation (Suzuki) took a fine fifth place on second-hand tyres. Unusually for the TT, the weather was blisteringly hot, taxing the riders even more than usual over their six laps. The Sidecar races were run at a slower pace than in recent years and the A race provided a second win for Dick Greasley on his misfiring Yamaha, while race B gave Mick Boddice his first win after fourteen years of trying. Popular winner of the Junior 350cc race was Phil Mellor, after early leader Jon Ekerold dropped out, while Con Law repeated his previous year's victory in the Junior 250cc race. Law outpaced the rest of the field, setting a new record average race speed of 108.09mph and a record lap speed of 110.03mph on what was now recognized as an EMC, the letters standing for Ehrlich Motor Cycles. Despite Yamaha having increased the power output of their latest TZ250K model, four of the first six finishers in the Junior 250 were Rotax-powered.

Joey Dunlop found time to film a fast lap of the course in 1983. It went on to form the basis of the iconic video **V Four Victory**, which was later watched by many prospective **TT** racers and countless others who could only dream of racing over the **TT Mountain Course.**

Tony Rutter's win in Formula II gave him a hat-trick of wins in the class, in which he raised his own record speeds by a small amount. As in previous years, Graeme McGregor challenged Rutter for the win, but tyre troubles slowed him towards the end of the four-lap race.

The Senior Classic TT lived up to its top billing, with Norman Brown on his RG500 Suzuki setting a new race and absolute course lap record of 116.19mph. However, Brown gambled on getting three laps out of a tank of petrol, but spluttered into retirement at Creg ny Baa towards the end of his third lap. In only his second TT, Rob McElnea (Suzuki) took over the lead and raced to victory from Con Law (Suzuki) and Joey Dunlop (Honda) at a new record race average speed of 114.81mph. Rider speeds were measured at The Highlander by *Motor Cycle Weekly* using a police-type radar gun. The top fastest runners, against a slight headwind in the Senior Classic, were all shown at 155mph.

In a rare TT occurrence, veteran Mick Grant finished the Senior Classic race off the podium, tyre troubles relegating him to fifth place. Suzuki works teamsters Grant and winner McElnea both used the same tyres, but McElnea used a wider rear rim and somehow avoided problems. Unlike days of old, the correct choice of tyres was increasingly important to a rider's chance of race success, but with ever more specialized compounds in use, rates of wear increased and changes of rear tyres at pit stops were now common among the top riders. Principal suppliers of racing tyres at the time were Dunlop and Michelin, with Pirelli also there. Among other members of the trade, Shell Oils proclaimed in post-race advertising that their products were used by most of the winners in 1983.

Riders making names for themselves at the TT in the early 1980s were Barry Woodland, Roger Burnett, Steve Cull, Brian Reid, Geoff Johnson and Gary Padgett.

Showing that the TT races still sorted the men from the boys, the Formula II and Junior 350 TT races were run on the same day, with the several riders who contested both races each putting in ten laps and 378 racing miles.

SPEED

Fastest lap speeds moved from 108.77mph to 116.19mph between 1975 and 1983. While the increases were initially set by 500cc machines, the larger capacities allowed in Formula and Classic TT races saw the bigger-engined bikes setting the fastest laps from the late 1970s.

MANX GRAND PRIX

Running since 1923, the MGP had seen many of its competitors go on to great things at the TT, with Tim Hunt, Harold Daniell, Freddie Frith, Phil Read and Norman Brown among those who went on to become TT winners. While it was not known at the time, those standing on the podium after the Newcomers race at the 1983 MGP were to make a rich contribution to TT racing in the years that followed. They were: first, Robert Dunlop; second, Steve Hislop; and third, Ian Lougher. While it is to be expected that Robert Dunlop's early racing career would be affected by the activities of his elder brother Joey, Steve Hislop tells in his autobiography, *Hizzy*, that it was watching Joey sweep through the Eleventh Milestone at the 1983 TT that inspired him to sort out his life and make a go of his racing.

CHAPTER EIGHT

PRODUCTION MACHINES
TO THE FORE

1984: RACES OLD AND NEW

The 1984 TT programme saw the return of races for Production machines. These offered the chance for manufacturers to show how their roadsters could go over three laps of the Mountain Course, in classes for up to 250, 750 and 1500cc machines. There were other changes, with the Junior 350 TT being dropped after only one year of running. Similarly, although the previous year had seen the combining of the Senior and Classic races into one Senior Classic event, for 1984 they reverted to separate Senior and Premier Classic TT races. Other changes saw the capacity of the Formula I race revert to 750cc, to accord with the FIM's new limit for the class, and among the sidecars, a Formula 2 class was introduced for up to 350cc two-strokes and 600cc four-strokes.

Qualifying times were further reduced to:

Formula I, Junior 250 and Senior 500: 26 minutes
Premier Classic: 25 minutes
Sidecar: 28 minutes

Those times provided an indicator of the spread of machine and rider quality to be found in a TT race, for Joey Dunlop was lapping in just under 20 minutes on a solo and top sidecar man Mick Boddice was getting round in just over 21 minutes with his three-wheeler.

Completely new in 1984 was a Historic TT for 'old' bikes. Rated a hit by most of those who saw the array of Manx Nortons, AJS 7Rs, BSA Gold Stars, Aermacchis and so on, those machines of yesterday were piloted by riders clad mostly in black leather and provided a dose of nostalgia as they trailed Castrol 'R' in their wake. But the three-lap Historic TT was not a particularly quick one and ran for just the one year. It provided a first-ever TT victory for an American rider, the forceful Dave Roper on his G50 Matchless, with Steve Cull taking the 350cc class win on an Aermacchi.

Fierce competition amongst established riders like Rob McElnea, Joey Dunlop, Mick Grant, Charlie Williams, Tony Rutter, Roger Marshall, Graeme McGregor, Phil Mellor and Trevor Nation saw records broken in several classes in 1984. First up was the Formula I race, where Dunlop, on his V4, now reduced from 850cc to 750cc, won by 20 seconds from Honda team mate Roger Marshall, lifting the lap record on his last lap to 115.89mph and hitting 175mph past The Highlander. Come the Senior TT and he raised not only the Senior lap record, but also the absolute record to 118.48mph. Unfortunately, a shortfall of petrol on the last lap saw him hand the win to Rob McElnea. This gave Suzuki their seventh consecutive Senior victory with the RG500. The same 'Rob Mac' restricted Joey Dunlop to second place in the Classic TT, during a fierce battle that included Mick Grant (Suzuki) until he had problems with his clip-ons. McElnea lifted race average and lap record speeds in the process.

Graeme McGregor had a midweek day to remember when he won the Formula II race on a Yamaha from Tony Rutter (Ducati) and the Junior 250cc on an EMC from Charlie Williams (Yamaha). In the latter he also had to fight off the likes of Joey Dunlop (Honda) and Phil Mellor (Yamaha), setting new record race average and lap speeds in both events. It was to be Charlie Williams' last year at the TT, but in third place was Brian Reid (EMC), who would prove to be a worthy successor to him, going on to record five TT wins.

The reintroduced Production races were rated a success, with Geoff Johnson on a Kawasaki GPZ900R taking the 1500cc class, Trevor Nation on a CBX Honda being best 750cc and Phil Mellor on a Yamaha RD250LC topping the smallest class. All were won at higher speeds than at the last running of the event in 1976.

Among the other race machinery, Suzuki were now up to the Mk7 version of the RG500, while Yamaha were marketing the 'L' model of their TZ250. Those bikes were both

Helmut Dahne speeds to second place in the 750cc class of the 1984 Production TT on his Honda VF750.

mainstays of racing and had been developed year on year, incorporating changes to engines, suspension, tyres and so on. With ever-increasing outputs, they were major contributors to faster and faster lap speeds.

Among four-stroke racers there was a trend to fit slipper-clutches, to counter back-wheel chatter and potential over-revving when under fierce braking on the approach to slowish corners.

Sidecars were still setting fast times but without beating Jock Taylor's records. One magazine of the time wrote that 'the development of sidecars has progressed to the point where the motorcycle connection is becoming a little blurred'. But the organizers knew that the three-wheelers were popular with the crowds, so their position at the TT was assured. They were not an easy ride and some experienced short-circuit passengers found the Mountain Course too demanding. It was not unknown for passengers to withdraw their services after a couple of practice sessions.

1985: A SENIOR CHANGE

The organizers had tinkered with the Senior and Classic races during the previous few years, but for 1985 the Classic race was axed and the traditional 500cc Senior TT became the Senior 1000cc race. This was really in recognition of the fact that racing was increasingly based upon production machines, tuned in whichever way the regulations allowed, to compete in separately named races. Not many TT fans knew the intricacies of the rules that saw very similar bikes competing in those slightly different races, but competitors and sponsors welcomed being able to use stock machines that could be upgraded to racers at reasonable cost. It was a trend that was to increase in the years that followed.

Entries were up for the 1985 TT and they were dominated by the Japanese manufacturers Yamaha, Suzuki, Honda and Kawasaki. Proving the Island's lasting popularity with riders, there were nineteen former TT winners among the entry and twenty-nine Manx Grand Prix winners.

This was the year that quick-fillers were finally banned for refuelling, after several years of argument on the issue. Now everyone used the gravity-fillers supplied by the organizers. Being very much slower, they increased the time taken to complete the lap(s) when refuelling took place, thus reducing race speeds.

JOEY'S YEAR

By now known to TT fans simply as 'Joey', William Joseph Dunlop was the undoubted man of the meeting at the 1985 TT, taking three wins. Overcoming the handicap of having been on a fishing boat that sunk coming out of Belfast just thirty-six hours before the start of practice, he was the first to achieve a hat-trick since Mike Hailwood. Both did it on Hondas, all three of Dunlop's having the company's now favoured V-configured engines, including the new Formula I RVF750, which, rather than being a converted production bike, was much nearer a purpose-designed race bike. Happy to ride large or small machines, Dunlop's wins came in the Formula I race where, not pushed, he set a new lap record and won by over 5 minutes; in the Junior 250cc event, where he set new record race average and record lap speeds on what was Honda's return to the class; and in the new 1000cc Senior TT, where he beat team mate Roger Marshall at slightly less than record pace. For that last race of the week, Dunlop chose Honda's RVF 4-cylinder, four-stroke, while Marshall rode their 3-cylinder 500cc two-stroke. The difference in their race times was just 16 seconds. Dunlop loved the RVF750, which was small and fast. It took him to victory in all rounds of the 1985 World Formula I Championship and provided the basis for future TT wins.

Brian Reid (EMC) pushed Dunlop in the Junior 250 race and led by 15 seconds on the last lap, only to run out of fuel at Hillberry. His consolation was to set a new 250 lap record of 112.08mph. He also broke the lap record in the Formula II race on a Yamaha at 110.47mph, but again failed to finish.

No records were broken in the 1500cc class of the Production race, but Mat Oxley (Honda) did raise the race and lap records in the 250cc class. Records were also broken in the 750cc class by victor Mick Grant and by Glen Williams in setting the fastest lap. It was Grant's seventh and last TT victory and was achieved on a new Suzuki GSX-R750, a model that was to go on and carve a name for itself in TT history.

Joey Dunlop at speed over the Mountain.

Ray Knight refuels mid-race in 1986. Journalist Knight 'road tested' the Suzuki for *Motorcycle Sport* **by riding it in the Production, Formula I and Senior TT races.**

THE 'GIXXER'

Ray Knight described the GSX-R750 in its first year as 'an unashamed repli-racer for the road'. It continued a tradition of manufacturers marketing 'TT Replica' models, as they had done since the earliest TT races. Thirty years after its debut, Alan Cathcart reviewed the GSX-R750's impact in *Classic Racer* magazine, by describing it as 'the first Superbike of the modern era'. The term superbike had come into common use in the 1970s and the GSX-R750 gathered together the best big-bike features of the time, plus some of those from Suzuki's successful GP racers, to offer riders what Cathcart called, 'a 750 with the performance of a 1,000, but the handling of a 600 ... a truly revolutionary motorcycle'.

In brief, the engine was a transverse 4-cylinder, 16-valve, dohc and of oil-assisted air-cooled format. That was housed in a GP-derived square-section aluminium chassis, with 'full-floater' monoshock rear suspension and 40mm front forks with anti-dive. It had a short wheelbase, 18in wheels and weighed in some 66lb (30kg) lighter than the opposition such as Honda's 750cc V4 and Yamaha's 20-valve FZ750. Power output was also claimed to be higher than the opposition's, at close to 100bhp, although it was acknowledged that it needed the services of an experienced tuner/blueprinter to get close to that figure from the original model. Other up-to-date features were flat-slide carburettors, large airbox under the fuel tank, hydraulic clutch, six-speed gearbox and cast wheels. With its excellent power-to-weight ratio, the whole package was said to give a top speed of just over 150mph, and Tony Rutter was timed at 155mph on the drop from Creg ny Baa to Brandish.

THE COURSE

There had been no major changes to the Mountain Course for several years, although there were always minor improvements going on. In the winter following the 1985

Virtually every competitor now fitted a steering damper for better control over the bumpy Mountain Course.

TT, work started on stage one of a widening scheme for Quarry Bends. A really narrow and tree-lined section, its several bends ran between closely enclosing banks that limited riders' speeds to around 100mph. Changes from light to shade and retained dampness under the trees were also an inconvenience to riders. It was a spot where they all hoped that they would not come across a slower competitor, for a swift passage through Quarry Bends had a big influence on the speeds achieved on the following Sulby Straight. When the changes were complete, they were reckoned to be worth some 5 seconds a lap.

How much course improvements contributed to faster lap speeds was a long-running topic, and the retired Geoff Duke chipped in with his opinion, comparing his 99.98mph lap in 1955 with Joey Dunlop's 118mph absolute lap record. Duke felt that of the 18mph increase, some 8mph came from course changes, which equated to about 45 per cent. That percentage would have fluctuated down the years. In the earliest days of the TT, when poor course conditions restricted riders from using full power, what small gains in speed were made were probably due to machine and rider. With the rapid spread of tarmacadam surfacing in the early 1920s, there were individual years when the absolute lap record was lifted by 4–5mph. Most of that gain would have come from the course improvements. The rapid gains in lap speeds of the 1960s were probably due to the outstanding works machinery provided to even more outstanding riders like Mike Hailwood. Today most of the speed gain comes from machines and riders, although every so often there is a hike in speed that can be related to a major roadwork.

1986: 'PRODUCTION' INCREASES

Those who liked to spectate at the start and finish area were able to watch from a new Grandstand at the 1986

TT, although it was still mostly open to the elements. Also open to the elements were the many competitors who chose to camp near the Paddock, and early in practice a heavy overnight gale blew down some of their tents. It also blew down the scrutineers' tent and, more importantly to some, the beer tent.

Out on the course, riders returned from early practice sessions with customary complaints of how much bumpier the Mountain Course was than the short circuits on which they were accustomed to racing. Perhaps one of them was Michael McGarrity, who lost control of his Formula I Honda over the notorious bumps of the Sulby Straight and slid down the road for 150 yards. He was lucky to escape with a broken shoulder and abrasions.

Mention was made of the increased use of production-based machines at the 1985 TT and this was an accelerating trend in 1986, both at the TT and in the wider world of racing. High levels of support for the races from Rothmans Honda, Heron Suzuki and Loctite Yamaha teams saw the very best machinery being used over the Mountain Course by top TT riders. The manufacturers also gave support to sporting dealers, for the organizers were keen to have them entering machines in what had become high-profile races.

The three Production classes of 1985 were increased to four for 1986 and named A, B, C and D, with two-strokes and four-strokes having different permitted capacity levels in classes B, C and D. In Class B it was up to 500cc two-strokes racing against up to 750cc four-strokes; in Class C up to 400cc two-strokes against up to 600cc four-strokes; and in Class D up to 250cc two-strokes and up to 400cc four strokes. Class A retained its 1500cc upper limit.

HIGH SPEEDS

At the 1986 TT, where entry numbers were high – some races having 110 riders – and spectator numbers were up, it was the Production classes that delivered quite stunning results. This was particularly so for Suzuki, whose blue-and-white machines took wins in all four classes. Trevor Nation rode his GSX-R1100 to victory in Class A, adding almost 7mph to the race average speed and over 7mph to the lap speed. That was an incredible performance, with Nation becoming the first rider to lap at under 20 minutes on a Proddie machine. He left the race average speed at a record 111.99mph and the lap record at 113.26mph.

Another impressive performance came from Phil Mellor on the latest GSX-R750 with lengthened wheelbase. He added almost 5mph to race and lap speeds in Class B, raising them to 109.23 and 110.69mph, respectively. It was the turn of a Suzuki two-stroke to triumph in Class C. Riding a specially imported 400cc version of the normal 500cc

Trevor Nation advertises Loctite support of his Yamaha efforts.

Gamma, Gary Padgett raced to victory after a wheel-to-wheel battle with Malcolm Wheeler on a Kawasaki GPZ600, which lasted the whole three laps. Padgett's race average speed was 102.98mph and fastest lap 104.43mph. Wheeler was just 1 second behind at the finish. In Class D, Barry Woodland used Suzuki's smaller GSX-R400 four-stroke to take the win at a race average speed of 99.82mph, Mat Oxley (Yamaha) setting the fastest lap at 100.82mph. Both figures were 6–7mph faster than the previous year's 250 times.

With Brian Reid (Yamaha) comfortably breaking race average and lap records in the Formula II event, it really was a momentous year for production-type models, particularly as the majority of the machines entered in the For-mula I and Senior TT races were also production-derived. It was a state of affairs that saw just the Junior 250cc race being contested by some true 'race' bikes, plus a few of the top runners in the Senior, which was won by rising star Roger Burnett on his 3-cylinder, two-stroke Honda. In a rare occurrence, Joey Dunlop slipped off his 250cc Honda at Sulby Bridge in the Junior due to petrol leaking onto his rear tyre. Unhurt, Dunlop remounted, but a damaged exhaust forced him to retire.

The Production races were the undoubted success of the 1986 TT, having received support from manufacturers, dealers, riders and spectators. By doing so, they looked to have re-established the category as an important part of the TT programme, although some had reservations about aspects of the bikes' handling at speed. Strangely, reports of the time failed to mention how the substantial 5–7mph increases in lap speeds were achieved. The winning Suzukis were ridden by good, but arguably not the very best, riders of the day and there had been no major changes to the course. Therefore it would appear to have been down to the machines, with Suzuki putting in much development effort and learning from the worldwide racing successes of the GSX-R750 and its kin.

TYRES

One thing that was changing racing in the mid-1980s and contributing to an increase in lap speeds was the widespread adoption of radial tyres. The old crossply design could no longer cope with the increasing strains imposed by high-powered race bikes, which created a build-up of heat and a falling-off of performance. The new radials were lighter, stronger, cooler running and made the best use of modern materials, utilizing the improved compounds available. Racing would push the development of radial tyres in the ensuing years and riders would benefit from the increase in performance they offered.

1987: FLOURISHING

Ten years after it lost its World Championship status, the TT was more popular than ever with riders who wanted to race on the roads. For 1987 the organizers tried to accommodate as many entries as possible and the upper capacity of the Senior TT was increased to 1300cc. That must have been to accommodate the biggest production-derived machines, for nobody produced out-and-out racers of that capacity. Similarly, although there was little in the way of new 350cc race machinery, the Junior 250 TT was opened up to 350cc machines, becoming just the Junior TT and thus letting in some of the older 350cc Yamahas. Total entries in 1987 were c870, with many riders having multiple entries and riding in as many as six races.

The event as a whole was gaining more publicity from worldwide showing of race highlights on satellite television. On-board cameras were getting smaller, so armchair viewers got an improved and exciting TT experience and almost real-time results were available from information sources like Ceefax – felt to be high-tech in its day.

The rate of machine development by the major manufacturers increased as they strove to take advantage of the growing publicity arising from the racing of production machines, and so improve sales of their roadsters. Their glamorous large-capacity superbikes were now expected to deliver race-track performance on the road, while being equally capable of running down to the shops in traffic and

delivering motorway mile-munching performance when used as sports tourers. They were far more versatile than the production-derived racers and 'TT Replicas' of earlier times and came with ever-increasing use of new technology in all areas, including engine, carburation, suspension, brakes, tyres and electrics.

Competition was particularly keen in the 750cc category, with Kawasaki bringing out its new GPX750 to challenge Suzuki, Honda and Yamaha, while Honda launched its new CBR600, a 'middleweight' tranverse 4-cylinder four-stroke, for which it claimed 'heavyweight' performance. That performance, from a quoted output of 85bhp, would be progressively increased into a far greater figure during its long, and still continuing, production run.

The Mountain Course continued to be the supreme test for any new motorcycle, with one commentator remarking on 'the multitudinous bumps and jumps that are still left on the course in spite of new roadworks every year'. Riders greatly welcomed some smoothing of the worst bumps on Sulby Straight prior to racing in 1987.

WEATHER

Now in its eightieth year of running, the one factor that the TT organizers had never been able to control was the weather, and it affected both practice and racing in 1987. After causing delays and postponements during race week, its worst impact was on the last day's racing, where Production A and C races were cancelled entirely and the Senior was run over a shortened distance of four laps. In conditions that were appalling, Joey Dunlop won at an average speed of 99.85mph, experiencing, in his words, 'more slides than I've had in the rest of my racing life'.

Race week had started well, with Dunlop taking his customary Formula I win on his works Honda at record-breaking race average and lap speeds of 115.03 and 117.55mph. Honda had been good supporters of the TT races, but with a widening area of racing to support and tightening budgets, the late 1980s saw them enter a period where their level of support of the TT varied from year to year. Dunlop was without the ultra-rare RVF for 1987; instead, Mac McDiarmid tells in *Joey Dunlop – His Authorised Biography*, he was provided with 'an American Superbike-spec V-four', still in Rothmans colours.

Records were not threatened in the Sidecar or Junior races, but a first TT win for rising star Steve Hislop (Yamaha) saw him lift the record race average speed in the Formula II race, where Eddie Laycock (Yamaha) set a new lap record of 112.36mph.

In the two Production races that were run – B and D – new records were set by Class B (750cc) winner Geoff

Geoff Johnson rides his Yamaha to victory in 1987 Production Race B.

Johnson and fastest lapper Trevor Nation, while Barry Woodland set new records in Class D (400cc). In a change of manufacturer fortunes, Yamaha took both wins with their FZR750 and FZR400.

Among the rising stars competing in 1987 were Nick Jefferies, Dave Leach, Steve Linsdell, Robert Dunlop, Jamie Whitham and Carl Fogarty, while on three wheels was Dave Molyneux.

1988: CHANGES

The Formula II race was dropped for 1988 although FII runners were accommodated as a separate class within the Junior race. Production Class A and Class B were given individual races and, in a first at the TT, the race for the combined Production Class C and Class D machines was run on the Friday evening of practice week.

The growing profile of the Production races saw the supporting trade offering generous bonuses to winning rid-

ers using their tyres, brake pads, oils and so on. However, in one of those strange twists of racing finance, Honda reduced their level of support to riders, leaving their top man, Joey Dunlop, to put together his own sponsorship deals and fund his racing. Shell Gemini Oils and Michelin were among those to step in with support and he did not let them down, taking the Formula I event on a race-kitted Honda RC30. It was a time when the World Formula I Championship, of which the TT Formula I event was a scoring round and Joey Dunlop a multi-champion, was facing competition from a new World Superbike Championship.

Going on to further reward the faith shown by his many sponsors, Joey Dunlop also rode to record-breaking wins in the Junior and Senior races. In the latter, Steve Cull on his 3-cylinder Honda two-stroke set a new absolute course record of 119.08mph, so bringing the prospect of a 120mph lap firmly into view. Somewhat off that pace were the bikes fielded in the Senior by the returning Norton concern.

Sporting Gemini Oil stickers, Joey Dunlop prepares to depart on yet another lap of the Mountain Course.

Having little connection with the multi-TT-winning maker of the same the name, the Nortons were ridden by Trevor Nation and Simon Buckmaster. With air-cooled, flame-spitting rotary engines, they added interest to the event and both finished the race.

The growing importance of the Production races meant that stakes were higher and that every possible advantage was taken of the rule book in the bid to turn out faster machines. This led to much behind-the-scenes murmuring about eligibility and compliance, but that was the way it had always been in racing, for it was a highly competitive arena. Mick Grant, now in race management, claimed there was a saying in racing: 'you should never fall behind in your cheating, but never get too far ahead'. Not that Grant was advocating cheating, but he firmly believed that the rules were there to be pushed as far as possible. Thus the rule book got ever thicker.

Once again the Production races yielded substantial advances in race average and lap speeds. In the Production A race, Dave Leach upped the race average speed by 2½mph and Geoff Johnson the lap record by 3mph on their Yamaha FZR1100 models, chased home by a batch of Suzuki GSX-R1100s and Kawasaki's new 1000cc ZX-10. In Production B, winner Steve Hislop (Honda) increased the race average speed by 2½mph and Geoff Johnson (Yamaha) the lap record by just over 1mph. A titanic battle in Production C between Steve Hislop and Brian Morrison on their new Honda CBR600s saw Morrison take the win and add almost 6mph to the race average, while Hislop added just over 6mph to the lap record. They were phenomenal increases and only in Production D were things more modest, with winner Barry Woodland on a specially imported Yamaha FZR400R adding 0.43mph to the lap record but leaving his own race average record intact. It was a surprisingly lean year for former Production frontrunners Suzuki, whose best results were fourth in Production A and B. However, they were seriously under-funded at the time, compared to some of the works opposition.

Suzuki did introduce their new GSX-600F roadster in 1988 and, in what was a growing trend to use techno-speak

Barry Woodland rounds Quarter Bridge on his 400cc Yamaha on his way to victory in 1988 Production Race D.

and acronyms, claimed that this bike 'with impeccable racing pedigree' came with 'Twin Swirl Combustion, SACS (Suzuki Advanced Cooling System), Microprocessor Controlled Ignition and Deca Piston Brakes'. All were standard features, available new for £3,199.

SIDECARS

Among the sidecars, top runners like Mick Boddice and Lowry Burton were notching wins and fastest laps of 106–107mph on their Yamaha-powered outfits, but still falling short of Jock Taylor's absolute lap record of 108.29mph, set back in 1982. Roy Hanks was in his twenty-second year of racing sidecars at the TT, but showed that danger was ever-present when he left the road near the Thirty-third Milestone and plunged down the mountainside. The result was broken limbs for him and his passenger-nephew Tom Hanks, but they lived to race again. Their crash brought one of the rescue helicopters to the scene and they became two of the roughly fifteen riders air-lifted to hospital at each TT. Fortunately, many of those require only a check-over. The helicopters are a hugely expensive part of the race organization but are recognized life-savers. Costs increased for 1988 when the Civil Aviation Authority decreed that the single-engined choppers be replaced with twin-engined versions as they needed to fly over built-up areas.

Dave Saville was a regular winner of the Formula 2 Sidecar class, but he lost out to Mick Hamblin in 1988. Average race-winning speeds for the Formula 2 machines were c95mph, with 350cc Yamaha two-stroke engines being the power unit of choice.

1989: MORE CHANGES

New for 1989 were races for Supersport 400 and Supersport 600cc machines, which took the place of the former Production C and D races. Like the Production classes, Supersport machines raced on treaded tyres, but modifications to engines and suspension were allowed. The two remaining races for production bikes were renamed Production 750 and Production 1300. Reintroduced was a race for Lightweight 125s, which last ran on the Mountain Course in 1974. Falling in line with FIM regulations, twin-cylinder four-strokes up to 1,000cc were allowed to enter the Formula I race.

Steve Henshaw and Mark Farmer blast through the bottom of Barregarrow.

All solo and sidecar classes were filled by Yamaha, Honda, Suzuki and an occasional Kawasaki machine. Those looking long and hard at the entry lists might spot a couple of European makers' names, with Steve Hazlett (EMC) best performer with third place in the Junior, but the only others to be seen were a couple of Ducatis in the larger classes. The strong Rotax-powered challenge of a few years before seemed to have faded away.

The top bikes were getting higher specifications and prices, with Honda's RC30 costing £9,500 and Yamaha's OW01 £12,000. The latter was quoted as giving 121bhp, complete with EXUP (exhaust ultimate power valve), aluminium perimeter frame and so on. For those serious about winning, the expense did not stop there, for there were many go-faster modifications that could be applied to a standard machine. Joining the TT party for 1989 was the much cheaper Kawasaki ZXR750, which came in Kawasaki's traditional green.

John Reynolds was a three-times British Superbike champion in the 1990s and 2000s, but only tackled the TT on one occasion – 1989. In his words: 'It pretty well scared me to death'. He told in *Motorcycle Racer* in 2015:

> It was back in 1989; I'd just signed for Kawasaki and they offered me the chance to go out there just to see if I liked it, with no pressure. I was coming up to a place called Barregarrow on a Superbike and Steve Hislop came past me, just as I was shutting off the throttle for the corner. He was still accelerating and changing up a gear as he went into Barregarrow. His bike bottomed out, I saw dust come off the fairing as it ground out on the floor and he disappeared off into the distance towards Kirk Michael. I thought, 'You know what? If that's what you have to do to win a TT, you can keep it – there's no way I'm ever going to do that.'

Joey Dunlop was not fit to ride in 1989, for he was recovering from an early-season injury suffered at Brands Hatch, which would affect his riding of big bikes for some years ahead. There was no shortage of up-and-coming riders eager to take advantage of his absence.

Course conditions from Ginger Hall to Ramsey had always been among the roughest, and in 1989, riders fighting their bikes through the stretch described them as noticeably worse.

RECORD SPEEDS

In a year of eight solo TT races and two sidecar, records were broken in all solo and in one of the sidecar races. It was an outstanding year for speed and American rider Chris Crew wrote of what was required, saying, 'You have to bet your life you know where the next corner is going over the crest of the next hill.' Of those crests, he said, 'you go over wide open in top gear, 155 or 160mph, whatever the bike will pull, with your elbows and toes tucked in, head under the fairing, just watching the white line, trying to see through the bugs'.

Man of the week at the 1989 TT was Steve Hislop. Already a TT winner, 'Hizzy' came with machines from Honda and put his name firmly in the record books with a hat-trick of wins at record speeds, which included the first 120mph lap. Revealing in his autobiography, *Hizzy*, that he was provided with a bike direct from Japan for the Formula I race that, in his words, 'was just so good I couldn't help but go fast on it', he raised race average and lap speeds by 2mph, to leave them at 119.36mph and 121.34mph. Hislop brought the TT into a new 120mph era, which required the rewriting of the lap charts in the Timekeepers' box. With emphatic wins in the new Supersport 600 race and the Senior, he also set new records in those. However, as a reminder that no one is immortal, he had a 140mph fall from his Junior machine at Quarry Bends, from which he was fortunate to escape uninjured.

With three wins to his name in 1989, it was no surprise that everyone wanted to know how Steve Hislop had achieved them. With a response that echoed the comments of many of the great road racers of the past, he advised, 'work at the bends to get the best out of the straights so that you can carry the speed with rhythm and flow, that's the key to TT success'.

Speeds were also increased in the Junior race, won by Johnny Rea, with the fastest lap coming from Eddie Laycock. It was Laycock who took victory in the Supersport 400 race, with Production 1300 going to Dave Leach and Production 750 to Carl Fogarty. Inevitably, records were broken in the returning Lightweight 125 class, where Robert Dunlop lapped at 103.02mph to secure his first TT win.

An indication of what was achieved in this super-speedy year is shown below, with previous records shown on the left and 1989 figures on the right:

Race	Top speeds pre-1989	Top speeds 1989
TT Formula I	race average 117.38mph	119.36mph
	fastest lap 118.54mph	121.34mph
Senior TT	race average 117.38mph	118.23mph
	fastest lap 119.08mph	120.69mph
Sidecar	race average 107.02mph	107.17mph
	fastest lap 108.12mph	108.31mph
Production 1300	race average 114.32mph	115.61mph
	fastest lap 116.55mph	117.27mph
Production 750	race average 112.29mph	114.68mph
	fastest lap 112.98mph	116.91mph
Supersport 600*	race average 108.42mph	112.58mph
	fastest lap 109.83mph	113.60mph
Supersport 400*	race average 102.98mph	105.27mph
	fastest lap 103.79mph	106.90mph
Lightweight 125**	race average 99.12mph	102.56mph
	fastest lap 100.32mph	103.02mph

* Formerly Production Class C and D.
** Previous best figures set by Bill Ivy in 1968.

A study of the results from 1989 showed that several established midfield TT runners, whose best riding days were over, were putting in faster lap times than their previous personal bests. With course improvements limited to the easing of the inside of Brandywell's left-hander, it gave a clear indication that it was faster machines that were responsible for boosting their lap speeds.

A PRICE TO PAY

Everyone — manufacturers, riders, race commentators and spectators — gloried in the high speeds shown at the 1989 TT, but they came at a huge price, for five riders were killed during practice and racing. Passenger Marco Fattorelli lost his life in a practice incident, as did the driver of a separate sidecar outfit, John Mulcahy. At Ballagarey Corner in Friday morning's practice, 23-year-old local man Phil Hogg was killed when he fell from his Yamaha after its engine seized. Come the racing, during Wednesday's Production 1300 race double tragedy struck. Previous TT winner Phil Mellor was killed when he fell at Doran's Bend and, shortly after, Steve Henshaw suffered the same fate after falling at Quarry Bends. Both Mellor and Henshaw were thirty-five and professional motorcycle racers. TT competitors were used to coping with tragedies in their dangerous sport, but this was too much for some, who packed and left the Island in shock before the last of the week's racing.

The 1989 TT closed with doubts being expressed by those close to the racing about just how much faster production bikes could go on standard tyres, brakes and suspension. A less technical view came from some spectators, who claimed they were too quiet and all looked alike.

Riders are dwarfed by the stone wall at the tight 'S' of Handley's Corner.

1990: YET MORE CHANGES

No doubt with the need for safer racing in the forefront of their minds, the organizers dropped the pure Production races A (1300cc) and B (750cc) from the 1990 TT race schedule. This still left the production-derived Supersport 400 and 600 events, where the extra modifications allowed were considered to create machines better suited to racing. A similar situation applied in the Formula I and Senior events, where most of the machines taking part were production-derived, but much modified.

The decision to drop the Production races seemed a drastic one after all the favourable attention given to their racing. Perhaps, though, in their search for publicity and glory, the manufacturers had lost the balance between power and handling, something that has always been essential for machines raced over the TT Mountain Course.

That was not the only change for 1990. Among others were that maximum permitted engine size in the Senior race was reduced to 750cc; competitors were now despatched from the start singly at 10-second intervals rather than in pairs; and in an attempt to improve safety in the pit lane, a 'stop box' was introduced at its entrance, aimed at slowing riders' passage through what could be a congested area.

Sidecars were also subject to a reduction in capacity in 1990, the former limit of 1000cc being dropped, and everyone was required to conform with the Formula 2 engine specifications, races for which had been run in tandem with the Sidecar A and B races since 1984. They permitted two-strokes up to 350cc and four-strokes up to 600cc. Two-strokes had taken all the wins to date and that was repeated in 1990, when Yamaha-powered Dave Saville and his green-and-yellow Sabre-sponsored outfit came home first in both races at record Formula 2 speeds, with a fastest lap of 100.97mph. At this stage the 600cc four-strokes were a little off the pace, but that would change.

Formula I machines were the same as the previous year only faster, with young hot-shots like Carl Fogarty, Steve Hislop, Nick Jefferies, Dave Leach, Trevor Nation, Ian Lougher, Bob Jackson and Phillip McCallen chasing a fat prize purse of £6,000 for a start-to-finish winner. Victory went to Carl Fogarty (Honda) with Steve Hislop (Honda) breaking the absolute lap record in pursuit and leaving it at 122.63mph. Joey Dunlop (Honda) was back in 1990, but not really up to racing a 750 at its maximum. He had to settle for eighth place. With the capacity limit for the Senior TT now reduced to 750cc, riders were using their FI bikes in the Senior, with minor adjustments to suit the rules. However, no real comparison could be made between 1990's 750s and the 1000s of 1989, due to the Senior race being weather-affected. Victory went to Carl Fogarty (Honda), at a relatively lowly race average speed of 110.95mph.

After taking a fine second place in the Formula I race on his works Mitsui Yamaha, Nick Jefferies gave an indica-

Dave Saville and Nick Roche blast off from the start on their Formula 2 outfit in 1990.

Nick Jefferies leans his big Yamaha into Braddan Bridge.

Trevor Nation leads Robert Dunlop through the fast bends of the Thirty-third Milestone on their rotary-engined Nortons.

tion of the commitment required to achieve such a placing by saying, 'The only places it got out of control were those places where you expect to be out of control.' Fast and reliable, Jefferies had been looking for a good finish in the Senior, but it was not to be. In mixed weather conditions, he hit a wet spot climbing Lambfell, lost traction and crashed. He described the aftermath of his 120mph spill with 'Silence! Running feet, shouts, radio messages, the world spinning round.'

The 'new' Norton marque had a good year, with Robert Dunlop taking third spot in the Formula I race and Trevor Nation coming second in the Senior. Spectators loved the distinctive high-revving sound of the rotary Norton, and Dunlop told that with his 9-stone weight, the black-and-gold machine would spin up the rear tyre in all gears, even in the dry.

In good conditions, new race average and lap speeds were set by Dave Leach (Yamaha) in winning the Supersport 400 race and he also set a new lap record in the Supersport 600, where victory went to Brian Reid (Yamaha), at just below record speed. Over half of the sixty entrants in the four-lap Supersport 400 race were mounted on a mixture of Yamaha 400RRSP, Honda VFR400 and Kawasaki ZXR400 machines. None of those were big sellers in the British market, but revving to 14,000–15,000rpm, they were the recognized four-stroke bikes for the race. The two-strokes contesting the class comprised Suzuki RGV250 and Kawasaki KR1250S models, both being closer to race replicas than roadsters.

Steve Hislop (Honda) and Ian Lougher (Yamaha) had a momentous battle in the Junior race, with the lead see-sawing from lap to lap. While Hislop was probably favourite for the win, Lougher held him off by 1.8 seconds to take his first TT victory and at record-breaking speeds. It was a special race and to Lougher went the new race average record of 115.16mph and the new lap record of 117.80mph. Both speeds were 3mph up on the previous best and were to stand for some years. That is perhaps understandable, considering Hislop's words, 'the last lap of that race was without question the hardest I ever had, and ever would ride a motorcycle round the Isle of Man'. Hislop's cause was not helped by a pit stop in which his filler cap was dropped inside the fairing, losing him several fumbling seconds while it was recovered.

Along with Steve Hislop and Ian Lougher, the third member of the talented MGP Newcomers podium of 1983 was Robert Dunlop. In 1990 he took his second TT win, breaking his own records in the Ultra Lightweight 125cc race. Dunlop was Honda RS-mounted, as was every one of the fifty other riders in the race.

Speed was a particularly special commodity to 125s on the Mountain Course and, once gained, they were reluctant to relinquish it, maintaining very high corner speeds and diving over and under bigger race machinery they came across in bends. During a race, slipstreaming other riders was important, as were tricks such as riding in the lee of roadside banks to lessen the effect of the wind. The Ultra Lightweight 125s ran at the same time as the Supersport 400 race and, setting off immediately after the 400s, their top riders were soon mixing it with the bigger bikes. Indeed, they were often held up by them.

The 125s may have been fast for their size, but it was among the big-capacity bikes contesting the Formula I and Senior TTs that ultimate lap records were regularly broken. In the period 1983–90, the outright lap record went from 116.19mph to 122.63mph.

Radio TT broadcast round-the-course commentaries on all races, and in 1990 its commentary box was close to the action at Ballaugh Bridge, where commentator Geoff Cannell would have admired Steve Cull's controlled leap.

CHAPTER NINE

A COSTLY BUSINESS

Racing motorcycles has always been an expensive past-time. Attempts to cut costs by shifting the emphasis to the racing of production-derived machines in the 1980s were partly offset by the never-ending spending on expensive modifications, aimed at gaining an advantage over other competitors. Speed was an extremely costly commodity.

There were a few genuine private runners at each TT, but the majority of riders had their racing sponsored by others. At the top end of the scale this would be full works support with machinery, a riding fee and all expenses paid. In 1991 riders entered by Mitsui Yamaha, JPS Norton Racing, Silkolene Honda Britain and Team Green Kawasaki would have received the highest level of support. Other riders would have their bikes supplied, but have to meet some element of costs. Their bikes would have come from names like Millar Racing, Smith & Aldridge, Shirlaws Motorcycles, Bill Smith Motors and McMenemy Motors Racing. Further down the scale, it was the rider who supplied the bike, with companies or generous friends helping to pay entry and running costs, usually in return for seeing their names on the fairing. Few of those riders had the financial contingency to cope with a major mechanical disaster, which could be quite common over TT fortnight, particularly for those using 'tired' equipment.

In the early 1990s the organizers provided about £250 to each rider to help with costs, plus appearance money to the stars and prize money totalling £129,000. Most of the latter went to the top finishers, and riding the TT still cost a mid-field sponsor or rider thousands of pounds.

While talking of costs, Honda felt the TT was sufficiently important to send two of their RVF750 models for Steve Hislop and Carl Fogarty to use in 1991. Said to deliver 145bhp, the motorcycle press estimated the value of these ultra-special endurance-based models at between £250,000 and £500,000 each. 'Foggy' was riding his in just the Formula I race and Joey Dunlop was to use it in the Senior. Dave Leach was also said to have the use of a full works FVR750 Yamaha – value not quoted.

Yamaha generated much publicity over the fact that 1991 was the thirtieth anniversary of their first participation in the TT. History shows that, along with other Japanese manufacturers, they reshaped the world of motorcycle racing during those thirty years. However, not all of them had totally mastered the demands of the TT – Kawasaki had to withdraw Ian Lougher's entry from the Formula I and Senior races, as they could not get their 750 to handle properly over the Mountain Course.

1991: PRACTICE

It was a time when riders had three early-morning practice sessions, five evening ones and a Thursday afternoon in which to learn their way around 37¾ miles and get up to race speed. It really was not long for newcomers over such a demanding course. Typically, many new riders experienced problems that would see them missing a session, thus reducing the learning time and, as in 1991, the first session was lost to all competitors, due to heavy mist. In one of those vagaries of Manx weather, that mist was between Ballacraine and Kirk Michael and not, as it usually was, over the Mountain. Experienced runners used the practice sessions to reacquaint themselves with the course and learn any changes. They also spent much time fine-tuning their machinery to the particular needs of the Mountain Course so they could ride it to its limits. A rolling-road dynamometer was now available in the Paddock for them to experiment with engine settings, but handling could only be assessed out on the course.

In 1991, riders completed a total of 3,330 laps of practice, with the racing that followed timetabled for Saturday, Monday, Wednesday and Friday.

RACING

A competitive field of past TT winners, plus thrusting young riders with sights set on a first win, like Phillip McCallen, Jim Moodie and Bob Jackson, meant that lap records were unofficially broken in most classes during practice. Steve Hislop and Carl Fogarty held centre stage, alternately lifting each other's speeds from session to session in the premier 750 Formula I and Senior classes. Come the opening Formula I race, the two of them battled wheel

Carl Fogarty (8) and Steve Hislop (11) enter the pits during the 1991 Formula I race to refuel their 750cc Silkolene Honda Britain machines. Hislop was almost 30 seconds ahead of Fogarty at this point in the race.

to wheel in the early laps, before Hislop gradually eased away to win by just over 1 minute, at a record race average speed of 121.00mph and a new lap record of 123.48mph. Joey Dunlop brought his RC30 Honda home in third place. It was a similar situation in the Senior race, where Hislop again used the RVF to win from Joey Dunlop and Phillip McCallen, so making it another Honda-filled podium at record speeds.

Steve Hislop was the man on form at the 1991 TT and secured a third win in the week in the Supersport 600 race at record speeds, riding Honda's updated CBR-F2. As usual, the Junior race was fiercely contested, Robert Dunlop (Honda) taking the win and Phillip McCallen (Honda) the fastest lap, at slightly less than the exceptional record-breaking speeds of 1990.

The Supersport 400 and Ultra Lightweight 125 races were again run together, and while the mixed weather conditions held Dave Leach's winning speed down a little on his 400 Yamaha, Robert Dunlop broke race average and lap records as he took his 125 Honda to a third con-

secutive win. He described riding a 125 over the Mountain Course with the words, 'you just sit there with it buzzing at 13,000rpm and wait for the corners to come'.

Interviewed after a race, many riders will tell of an uneventful ride and no problems, but not everyone rides smoothly to victory. After his Supersport 400 win, Dave Leach told how he thought his race was over when, at the Mountain Box 'I slid on the white line. I was nearly off. The front end just turned under me. My head was down over the front wheel and my helmet hit the mudguard. It was a near miss.' Taking the racing line around the Mountain Course means that riders are frequently crossing the painted road markings while cranked over. Applied in a specially formulated 'non-slip' paint, there are occasional complaints about some lines being slipperier than others.

With two-stroke sidecar specialist Dave Saville unable to compete in 1991 due to injury, Mick Boddice took a double win with his four-stroke Honda, at a little below record speeds. Boddice's win was the start of a takeover of the sidecar class by four-stroke power.

Cranked over and applying power while crossing the white lines.

FASTEST

Clocked by a police radar gun, Steve Hislop's announced speed of 192mph on the Sulby Straight in 1991 had everyone talking – and some doubting. The man himself said 'That's scary, it's frighteningly fast, at the speeds we're doing you just head for the gaps between the green bits.' Hislop and Carl Fogarty pushed each other very hard that year, and both expressed concerns about the speeds being achieved.

THE COURSE

Over the following winter the 2-mile stretch of road from the Twenty-sixth Milestone to the Mountain Box was reconstructed and there were similar works from Windy Corner to the Thirty-third Milestone. At the very least this provided riders with a smoother surface on which to race,

and no doubt a few banks were trimmed back, roadside gutters filled in and cambers adjusted. Competitors would take advantage of every extra inch of extra road offered if it improved the racing line, and those works must have helped reduce lap times.

1992: THE TENSION MOUNTS

Fine performances from solo riders Brian Reid, Phillip McCallen and Joey Dunlop, plus sidecar man Geoff Bell, saw them take wins and break records throughout race week on Yamaha and Honda machinery. In taking the Ultra Lightweight 125cc win from brother Robert, forty-year-old Joey Dunlop equalled Mike Hailwood's total of fourteen TT wins. However, after the stirring 'big-bike' Formula I race that opened the week's racing with a first TT win for

Phillip McCallen (Honda), most spectators spent the intervening days preparing themselves for more battles in the final race of the week, the Senior TT. There was definitely tension in the air in 1992.

A GREAT RACE

Steve Hislop and Carl Fogarty had shown themselves to be the premier racing talents at the previous year's TT. Both were enthusiastic over the event and were proud of the wins they achieved in Island racing early in their careers. But then came a change of attitude as they set their sights on

the wider field of racing and the world stage. Both had left the TT in 1991, indicating that they were moving on. It was a surprise to everyone, not least themselves, to find them back racing at the 1992 event, with Hislop entered on Norton, Honda and Yamaha machinery from several sources and Fogarty on a Loctite Yamaha OW01 for the Formula I and Senior TTs, plus a Supersport machine.

Coming to the TT after just eight troubled laps' practice around Oulton Park on the under-funded rotary Norton, a machine with different characteristics to any other race machinery, Steve Hislop was not optimistic about his

Steve Hislop on his rotary-engined Norton, which became known as the 'White Charger'.

chances, even after respectable showings in practice, on what was a 588cc-rated bike said to deliver 150bhp. However, he was much encouraged by a good second place to Phillip McCallen (Honda) in the week's opening Formula I race, even though it was one in which Carl Fogarty led for the first five laps before retiring with gearbox problems.

The Senior race received a big build-up in 1992, for much was expected of the two young gladiators, Fogarty and Hislop. With Fogarty starting at number 4 and Hislop at number 19, they were 2½ minutes apart on the road, so it was to be a typical against-the-clock race and one in which they did not see each other out on the track. It was also a race in which there were other potential winners, for Phillip McCallen, Joey Dunlop and Nick Jefferies were all riding top machines for Castrol Honda, Robert Dunlop was on another Norton and Trevor Nation on a Ducati 888.

As expected, the 1992 Senior TT turned into a battle royal on track between Steve Hislop and Carl Fogarty. Both knew the Senior TT had recovered much of its prestige, that the manufacturers all valued a win and that, as top TT riders, they had the opportunity to show their worth to the racing world. There was also the small matter of a personal battle to show who was top dog in Island racing. Both gave it their all over 226 racing miles and the lead see-sawed from lap to lap, with pit-stop drama of wheel changes and dropped fuel caps adding to the excitement. On the last lap Hislop held a narrow advantage but Fogarty made a huge effort with the fastest lap of the race and a new absolute course record of 123.61mph. However, it was not enough, for Hislop was only 1 second slower and with the course-side crowds cheering him on, he kept his lead to the flag, to win by just 4.4 seconds. It was no surprise that his winning speed was also a new record average race figure of 121.28mph.

There were scenes of jubilation at this British Norton win, which was backed by Robert Dunlop bringing his Norton into third. The last TT win by a Norton had been Mike Hailwood's in 1961, where his race average speed was 100.60mph and fastest lap 101.30mph.

The 1992 TT was voted a particularly good one and the Senior race was one that would be talked of for years to come. Among riders who caught the eye and looked likely to get a share of the glory in future years were Steve Ward, Robert Holden, Iain Duffus and Mark Farmer.

Trade supporters of the event, like Michelin, were able to advertise that their equipment was used by most of the top solo winners – for example, Supersport 400 and 600 wins achieved on Michelin's standard TX Hi-Sport Radials. Pirelli advertising told that their Kevlar-carcassed MP7 Sports Radial was 'so sticky it can give slicks a run for their

Michelin advertise their TT successes.

money'. Avon's Kevlar belts and computer-designed tread aided their AM22/23 tyres for sports roadsters, while Metzeler claimed to be 'the most successful Production Tyre of the decade'. Tyre manufacturers were in business to increase sales and profits. They knew that racing success contributed to both of those, so they put development effort into producing better tyres. In turn, this allowed riders to go faster, particularly as changing tyres mid-race on the bigger bikes was now becoming more common amongst the top riders, permitting the use of compounds that provided more grip, even if they wore faster.

GETTING TOO FAST?
After the 1992 Senior race, both Steve Hislop and Carl Fogarty called for the introduction of an upper engine capacity limit of 600cc at the TT, for they felt the 750s were getting too fast for the course. Hislop explained: 'it would limit the mind-numbing spots like Sulby Straight and Glen Duff, where the 750s are going so quick on the bumps you can't focus properly'. Not everyone agreed, but Hislop pointed out that there was a huge difference between the

demands imposed while riding a record-breaking 123mph lap and those felt during a good runner's 120mph one. He also knew that bikes would get ever quicker. Easing of the bank at Kate's Cottage, resurfacing the corner at the Creg and slight easing at Signpost Corner after construction of a mini roundabout, meant that the course also continued to get 'quicker'.

1993: JOEY'S RECORD

Messrs Hislop and Fogarty were absent from the 1993 TT, but evergreen Joey Dunlop was there, together with a quality field of potential race winners. Now forty-one years of age, Joey described himself as 'publican and part-time racer' and although he was still not back to his very best form on a 750, he took a convincing win in the Ultra Lightweight 125cc race. What made this result particularly special for Joey was that it gave him his fifteenth win, which was one more than the previous best all-time winner, Mike Hailwood.

The TT organizers worked to give their event more international appeal, and in 1993 riders from eighteen countries were on the Island to do battle with the Mountain Course. It was not a good year for newcomers seeking to learn their way around, for the first practice session was cancelled, several of the following were held in poor conditions and only one lap was possible on what was usually the long Thursday afternoon session. There must surely have been feelings of trepidation amongst those first-timers at the thought of going out and risking their lives in the proper racing that followed.

MIXED RESULTS

Rising star Mark Farmer had to hand back his big Kawasaki during practice, as it did not handle. Fortunate to get a ride on an Oxford Products Ducati, he put it to good use to lead the Formula I race at the end of the first lap, setting what turned out to be the fastest lap of the race, only to retire soon after. Victory eventually went to Nick Jefferies, with

Joey Dunlop (Honda) on the approach to Whitegates, on his way to victory in the 1993 Ultra Lightweight 125cc TT.

This was the power unit of John Britten's unconventional TT race machine.

Phillip McCallen in second. Both were riding for Castrol Honda Britain and after four previous second places at the TT, Jefferies' win gave him the unique record of having won the Manx Grand Prix, the Manx Two-Day Trial and a Tourist Trophy.

New records were set by fractional amounts as Jim Moodie won the Supersport 400 and 600 races, but apart from Joey Dunlop lifting the race average speed in the 125 race to 107.26mph, it was left to double winner of the Sidecar races, Manxman Dave Molyneux (Yamaha), to set the only other new records in 1993, as he lifted the race average and lap speeds of the three-wheelers. The 600cc 4-cylinder, four-stroke engines were beginning to supplant the 350cc two-stroke twins in sidecar racing at the TT, offering a wider power band, increased robustness and improved reliability.

In winning the Junior race for the second year in succession, Brian Reid (Yamaha) set a race average speed of 115.14mph. That compared almost exactly to his winning speed of 115.13mph, set the year before. Victory in the Sen-

ior race went to Phillip McCallen on his RVF Honda. He had been expected to win more, but he was still recovering from pre-TT injuries received at Mallory Park.

DEVELOPMENT

While major manufacturers continued with step-by-step development of their existing race machines, a one-man effort tackled the 1993 TT with a ground-breaking machine designed and built in New Zealand. It was a time when the big firms were actively seeking financial support for their British racing efforts from firms like Castrol and Loctite, so how could an individual afford such a venture, particularly one that radically challenged many conventional aspects of design?

The man sufficiently confident to come from half a world away to race at the TT was John Britten, with fellow Kiwi and first-timer, Shaun Harris, as rider. The new race bike quickly impressed with its speed on the course, while its distinctive sound, looks and colour scheme also caught the attention. Full of Britten's innovative ideas, the chassis was of kevlar and carbon fibre, using the engine as a stressed member. Unconventional suspension and relatively light weight, plus its liquid-cooled, 8-valve, fuel-injected V-twin engine with belt-driven dohc and electronic engine management system, saw its 150bhp deliver plenty of speed for the power-hungry TT course. Come the racing, however, an oil-line failure robbed the Britten of a good finish.

Undeterred, John Britten was back at the 1994 TT with a team of three machines and riders, Nick Jefferies, Mark Farmer and Robert Holden. This time he had an element of sponsorship, going under the banner of 'ICI Autocolour Britten 100'. The huge challenge they faced was brought home to them when Mark Farmer was killed in a practice accident at the Black Dub on one of their machines. It put a damper on their efforts in 1994 and further tragedy struck a few years later, when John Britten died young.

Honda's degree of support to the TT varied year on year. Even when they claimed to be giving full-on works support, riders would complain, saying that they did not have the latest forks or swinging arm. Their RVF750 had done very well in Island racing, but its appearances were sporadic and Honda's top riders would often be on upgraded RC30s. But by 1993 the successful and popular RC30 had lost its edge in the big class, where development was being pushed by superbike racing. Honda's answer was to produce the RC45 and have it homologated for competition at World Superbike level. Borrowing many design aspects from the RVF750, the RC45 was again a V4 four-stroke. Manufacturers were all incorporating the latest technology in their engines and this one had ceramic- and graphite-impregnated cylinder liners, titanium con rods, very short-skirted pistons, fuel-injection and an electronic control unit rely-

The 1994 Honda RC45 in its spectacular Castrol Honda colours. Here, in the Paddock, Steve Hislop's bike receives final preparation before he takes it out for a practice session.

ing on sensors from many different parts of the engine. All that was housed in a substantial twin-spar alloy frame, with single-sided swinging arm, 41mm front forks and multi-pot disc brakes all round.

The RC45 was an example of how technology was moving on, but while some of its new features undoubtedly contributed to faster speeds, they were also intended to aid reliability.

1994: POWER, SPEED, HANDLING

The advent of the RC45 resulted in Honda bringing more powerful machines to the 1994 TT for their team of Joey Dunlop, Phillip McCallen and a returning Steve Hislop. But, as had happened before, the first lap of practice showed that they did not bring the required level of handling to match the increase in performance. As Ray Knight put it in his book *Joey Dunlop – A Tribute*, 'when pitted against

From lapping at 107mph on a TZ350 Yamaha at the 1984 MGP (above), to over 123mph on a Honda RC45 (below), Steve Hislop proved himself to be among the fastest around the Mountain Course.

the Island's undulations, it proved to be something of a wayward beast'. The three Honda works riders expressed themselves far more forcefully on the handling issue but, being paid to race, they spent the practice periods riding ragged-looking laps while gradually improving their times, as they sought to get the elusive balance of stability and high-speed manoeuvrability. Steve Hislop showed his courage and quality by eventually topping the practice leader board at 123.53mph. That was just a fraction under the outright lap record.

Hislop had not wanted to return to the TT, but he was unashamedly using it as a potentially good pay day to help fund his short-circuit superbike racing. This worked out well for him, for he took the RC45 to wins in both the Formula I and Senior races, leading home his Honda team mates in both and lapping at just 1mph below record speed. Saturday's Formula I race suffered from the weather and was stopped after two laps and rerun on the Sunday.

That Sunday race proved a disaster for Robert Dunlop, when the rear wheel of his Medd Racing RC45 collapsed as he was leaving Ballaugh and he sustained serious injury in the resulting crash. Riding in his first TT and also mounted on a Medd Racing RC45 was Michael Rutter. He finished the Formula I race unscathed, but his entry in the Senior was scratched for his back wheel also showed signs of cracking.

While Joey Dunlop was obviously troubled by his brother's accident, he got on with his racing and won the Junior and Ultra Lightweight 125 events. Running with the 125s in 1994 was a new race for machines with four-stroke, single-cylinder engines – the Singles TT. Most of those entered were of about 600cc and featured machines from Yamaha, MZ, Honda, BMW, Kawasaki and others. They were very much roadster-derived engines, although there was a singles class run as a supporting event at World Superbike meetings, which was encouraging development. Lap times of c110mph were forecast and the race was won by Jim Moodie (Yamaha) with a fastest lap of 112.66mph. Moodie also won the Supersport 400 race, while Iain Duffus took the Supersport 600 at a record race average speed of 115.30mph. The latter used the new Yamaha FZR600R, which Yamaha claimed offered 'the ultimate blend of street bike and track cred'. There was certainly an increased blurring of specifications between the two uses.

A new name among the Sidecar class winners in 1994 was Rob Fisher (Yamaha). Winning both legs in just his second time at the TT, he also set a record race average speed of 105.71mph and record lap for Formula 2 sidecars of 106.49mph. As with many of the sidecar riders, Rob brought three complete engines to the event, but returned home with two tired motors and the third a collection of what remained after it 'blew to bits'. The TT is especially tough on the 'chairs', which pull two crew and 16 gallons of fuel around the Mountain Course for three laps and 113 non-stop miles.

The 1994 TT saw its share of high speeds, with some of the fastest laps almost matching record speeds, but it was only in the Sidecar and Ultra Lightweight 125 classes that records were broken. It was remembered as a good year and one that gave double victories to Steve Hislop, Joey Dunlop, Jim Moodie and Rob Fisher, but perhaps it lacked the sparkle of some previous events.

Most spectators show little interest in who takes the Manufacturers Award in a TT race, but the makers do, and Honda were delighted to come away as the major winner in 1994.

1995: CHANGES TO RACE LINE-UP

There had been a change to machine eligibility for the 1994 Senior TT. Previously restricted to machines from 601 to 750cc capacity, it was opened to 201–250 two-stroke twin-cylinder and ACU/FIM Supersport 600cc machines. No one thought that a 250 was going to win a Senior TT, but it did provide the opportunity of an extra race for those riding them.

The race programme was subject to change for 1995, with the title of Junior TT (formerly for 201–350cc two-strokes) now given to a race for 600cc machines to FIM/ ACU Supersport regulations. This resulted in the Supersport 600 race being dropped and the two-strokes displaced from the Junior TT coming back into the programme in a Lightweight race for 201–250cc two-strokes, which was also open to 371–400cc four-stroke, 4-cylinder machines. Inclusion of the latter meant that the Supersport 400 race, which previously catered for them, was also dropped as an individual event, although 'official' results continued to show them under the Supersport title for some years.

Qualifying times were now 22 minutes for the fastest solo classes – Formula I and Senior – and 27 minutes for sidecars. That was a 4-minute reduction from the time allowed ten years before for solos, and 1 minute less for the 'chairs', now operating to the smaller-engined Formula 2 specifications.

DUCATI
Carl Fogarty left the TT for a wider stage and won the World Superbike title for Ducati in 1994. This prompted increased interest in the racing of Ducatis and the 1995 TT saw five entries in the Senior race, to be ridden by the likes of Iain Duffus, Michael Rutter, Trevor Nation and Simon

On his single-cylinder Ducati, Robert Holden tackles the Gooseneck on his way to victory in 1995.

Beck. With quoted capacities of 888cc, 916 and 955cc, these twin-cylinder Italian machines came in various states of tune – and thus performance, depending upon how much had been spent on them. They were twin-cylinder, 4-valve desmos, liquid-cooled and relatively light. At the time they were still considered to be a little fragile for TT course action, but spectators loved the sound of their booming exhausts. With three of them holding second, third and fourth places at the end of the first lap of the 1995 Senior, Ducati hopes were high, but only Duffus was there at the end, albeit in a fine Castrol Honda-splitting second place.

Where Ducati did gain success in 1995 was in the Singles TT. The company built a limited number of costly single-cylinder racers, using much carbon fibre and magnesium for lightness, and Kiwi Robert Holden rode his to a win.

MORE RACING

Among spectators, some wondered what the difference was between machines that contested the opening Formula I

race and the closing Senior race. In short, some could be the same. Both races were open to motorcycles to 'ACU FI Specifications', with the Senior also accepting entries from '201–250 Two Stroke Twin Cylinder and ACU/FIM Supersport 600 machines'.

Once again it was the RC45 Hondas that won the Formula I and Senior races, ridden by Phillip McCallen and Joey Dunlop, with Dunlop also taking the 'new' Lightweight 250 race on a Honda, setting a record race average speed of 115.68mph. He was just a few seconds short of the lap record. Those with long memories could remember when his fellow Irishman, Tom Herron, won the last race to go under the Lightweight 250 name. That was back in 1976, when Herron's race average speed was a record 103.55mph, achieved on the dominant lightweight machine of the time, a Yamaha.

Dunlop rated his 1995 Lightweight win as one of his finest races, telling journalists after the event: 'The bike went 100 per cent, the conditions were 100 per cent – dull and cool – and once I got going I was 100 per cent.' Dunlop readily admitted that if his mood was not right, then he was not always able to give his all. He explained that it was not until he plunged down Bray Hill on the opening lap of a race that he really knew if he was going to be on the pace. Those who knew him well felt that they could tell at the start how he would go. TT commentator of the time, Peter Kneale, was one of those and would tell listeners, 'Joey's got his race face on'.

The only other records to be broken in 1995 were the Ultra Lightweight 125 lap speed, which winner Mark Baldwin (Honda) raised to 109.01mph, and in the Sidecar class, where double winner Rob Fisher (Yamaha) lifted the race average speed to 107.58mph and the lap record to 107.67mph. Coming close to another record, that of the closest finish to a TT race, Mark Baldwin snatched his 125 victory from Mick Lofthouse by just 0.6 seconds, after four

laps and 151 miles of racing. It was doubly disappointing for Lofthouse because he finished before Baldwin and was given to believe that he had won the race.

The 125s were mostly Hondas and competitors were desperate to gain mechanical advantage and speed over each other, so expensive performance-enhancing modifications such as alternative ignition systems, exhausts and so on were incorporated by those who could afford them. In 1995 there was much experimenting with airboxes, which were found to offer a benefit to carburation. But the application of science to the 125s was mixed with 'rule of thumb', and nowhere was this better illustrated than with their water-cooling. With no thermostats, on cool days the use of the correct amount of duct tape on the radiator to control temperature was critical. Joey Dunlop got it wrong that year, had a cold seizure and retired at The Hawthorn, some 6½ miles from the start.

Pictured during his winning ride in the 1995 Formula I TT, Phillip McCallen flies the frightening jump of Ballacrye at over 150mph.

Iain Duffus (Honda) set speeds in winning the 'new' Junior 600cc race that exceeded those of the previous Supersport 600 races. Phillip McCallen (Honda) was an early leader and, while his rather wild-looking, elbows out style always appeared fraught, he usually stayed on. But after passing Duffus on the road, in 'hairy' fashion, he found a false neutral and fell at Waterworks. On his own admission he was 'right up on the banks … sliding it into every corner … real manic short circuit stuff'. Such are the pressures to win, encountered by a professional racer. McCallen was probably the fastest rider at the TT in 1995 and was a man who always gave his riding 100 per cent. He did not believe that you could ride at 'nine-tenths' on the TT course and expect to win. Nor did he favour one part of the course over another, as many riders did. For him it was flat out all the way.

MORE EXPENSE

Not fully supported across all classes by Castrol Honda at the 1995 TT, Joey Dunlop found himself racing a V&M Duckhams Honda in the Junior race. This meant additional expense on a set of new leathers in yellow and blue Duckhams Oils colours, for he could hardly have ridden their machine in the green, red and white of Castrol.

Helping to offset competitors' rising costs — not that Dunlop paid for his own leathers — more money was pumped into the TT the following year, taking the total to over £500,000 for 1996.

1996: PRODDIES RETURN

Knowing that the handling of mid-1990s sports bikes had improved, along with the tyres they used, the organizers felt it was safe to reintroduce the Production race for 1996. Open to machines of 701–1010cc, it was to be run over three laps on Senior race day and was a popular addition to the race programme.

Just like race bikes, production models improved year on year. Back in 1985 the Suzuki GSX-R750 spawned a whole new generation of race replicas for the road and its power output climbed with each batch of modifications. In 1996 a new version was launched that was lighter, had an all new short-stroke engine, twin-spar aluminium frame, ram-air induction, 190 section rear tyre and the by now customary 'computer controlled ignition'. But the Suzuki was only a 750 and at the 1996 TT it faced Honda's uprated Fireblade, which many felt to offer the best overall package of power, handling and stopping. Now of 918cc, with improved aerodynamics and cooling, new frame, modified swing arm, changed damping arrangements front and rear, it incorporated many other minor modifica-

tions and was claimed to deliver 128bhp at 10,500rpm in road trim.

Hondas were the machine of choice for the majority of the Production entry, but 'all-new' Kawasaki ZX-7R and ZX-7RR were also available, along with new Yamaha Thunderace models and a couple of Ducatis of 750 and 916cc. All were claiming outputs of over 125bhp in road trim and as well as the customary range of adjustment for suspension; some offered easy adjustment of steering geometry, ride height and wheelbase.

Production racing was not supposed to be the place where those who spent the most were guaranteed success, but the machines that came to the grid in 1996 were allowed modifications from standard. Most would spend money on things like a new higher-performance rear shock and steering damper, braided hoses, Dynojet kit for the carburettors, a race exhaust to give a few extra bhp and a fibreglass body kit.

For all the claimed advance in technical specifications, what most spectators wanted to know was how much faster would the 1996 Proddies be compared to those of 1989, when the event was last run. The answer was 'not much', for Phillip McCallen's Fireblade win at 117.32mph was less than 2mph faster than Dave Leach's winning race average speed on a 1000cc Yamaha in 1989, and the fastest lap, of 118.33mph in 1996, was only 1mph faster. McCallen did say that he could have gone faster, which probably did not go down too well with Iain Duffus (Honda) who finished just 6 seconds behind him, but it is doubtful if his race figures impressed those who automatically expect ever higher speed at the TT. However, most race fans agreed that 165mph from a Fireblade on Sulby Straight was pretty impressive for a road bike. They also knew that riders faced the old bogey of needing a lot more power and speed to achieve relatively small increases in lap times.

McCALLEN'S YEAR

Taking victory in 1996 in the Formula I race, Junior and Senior races, plus the reintroduced race for Production machines, Phillip McCallen became the first rider to take four TT wins in one week, although it was only in the Junior that he lifted race average and lap speeds to new levels. Nevertheless, it was an impressive performance to leave riders like Nick Jefferies, Joey Dunlop and Iain Duffus in his wake. It might have been five wins in a week if, while running well in the Lightweight 250 race, he had not holed his exhausts on the suspension-bottoming, flat-out bend at the bottom of Barregarrow. This knocked the edge off his bike's performance and Joey Dunlop went on to win. Dunlop also took the Ultra Lightweight 125 race. The only non-Honda solo race win of the week was Jim Moodie's victory in the Singles race on a Yamaha.

'MOLY'

If the solo races of 1996 belonged to Phillip McCallen, then the top performances in the sidecar races justifiably went to Dave Molyneux, who added a substantial 3mph to race average and lap speeds to leave new records of 110.08 and 111.02mph. When the 1000cc Sidecar race was dropped after the 1989 TT, the race record for the Formula 2 machines stood at 99.23mph, but the rapid development of the 600cc four-strokes through the early 1990s had much to do with the increase in F2 speeds, as did 'Moly's' development of his own outfit, known as the DMR (Dave Molyneux Racing). That was the machine on which he did his winning in 1996, with the help of passenger Peter Hill and aided by sponsorship from Team Mannin Collections and others.

There was no recognized large-scale builder of F2 sidecar outfits and most riders used the products of specialist build-ers like Windle, Ireson, Jacobs, Baker and, of course, DMR. With their wind-cheating, streamlined enclosures removed in the Paddock, there was little that remained secret and these makers all borrowed each other's ideas, which helped speed development. The F2 outfits were rather different to GP machines in engine size and chassis construction. They also needed tailoring from their normal short-circuit set-tings to suit the going found over the TT course.

DANGEROUS

There was no hiding from the dangers of the TT Mountain Course and four riders were killed during practice for the 1996 event. But, just as there are some riders who are satis-fied with a five-lap scratch around Brands Hatch, there are others whose ambitions can only be realized by competing in the TT. Two who fulfilled their ambitions in 1996 were John McGuinness and David Jefferies, with the latter tak-ing the award for best Newcomer. No one had any idea at the time of what TT greatness those two would go on to achieve.

Dave Molyneux and Peter Hill on their way to victory in 1996. The many sponsors' names on the bodywork give an indication of the level of support required to go TT racing.

'ROAD RACING CAPITAL OF THE WORLD'

That was the slogan used by the Isle of Man in 1996, accompanied by the claim that: 'Not only is the TT the pinnacle of pure road racing at a world level but it is the lynchpin of a major festival of bikesport and motorcycling.' Spectators of all ages still thronged to see the races, with first-timers and long-term visitors sitting on the roadside banks or at course-side pubs, swapping their TT stories.

Among the subsidiary events in 1996 was a parade of Moto Guzzi machinery to celebrate the seventy-fifth anniversary of their first appearance at the TT. It was headed by an original version of their exotic 1950s V8, ridden by original rider Bill Lomas, and a replica V8 ridden by its builder, Giuseppe Todero. Veteran Lomas rode the full lap, but young Todero threw his £500,000 machine down the road at Braddan Bridge, less than 2 miles from the start. Fortunately the only damage was to the bike's fairing and the rider's pride.

1997: NINETIETH ANNIVERSARY

By 1997 the TT had been running for ninety years and much had changed in that time. The early pioneers who gathered at St John's in 1907 had no conception of the journey that real road-racing would take after they had chugged around in that first race, with most setting lap speeds of under 40mph. Come the early 1990s, the top men were circulating the Mountain Course at over 120mph. In 1997 the race average and lap record speeds of the big Formula I and Senior races were still stuck at those set by Steve Hislop and Carl Fogarty during their epic battle in the 1992 Senior TT. There was a similar situation in the Lightweight 250 class, where Ian Lougher's lap record, set in battle with that man Hislop again, had remained intact since 1990. There had been plenty of growth in speeds in other solo classes and in the sidecar classes, but speeds in those three solo ones remained about 1mph short of the records. It was a position that did not change in 1997.

Mounted on a special, ultra-expensive Honda Britain RC45, Phillip McCallen won both the Formula I and Senior races with best laps approaching, but not quite reaching, the 123mph mark – Fogarty's absolute lap record stood at 123.61mph. In the latter race, second place was taken by Jim Moodie on a Padgetts Honda NSR500 two-stroke, said to cost £90,000 and to put out 135bhp. With a win in the

Phillip McCallen was sponsored by Motorcycle City when he rode to second place in the 1997 Junior TT. He is seen here at the slowest point on the course, Governor's Bridge.

Production race giving him a hat-trick, McCallen finished the meeting on eleven TT wins and a second place in the Junior race, plus a high-speed spill at Quarry Bends while going well on his 250.

Victory in the Lightweight 250 race went to Joey Dunlop on his Honda Britain RS250R from Ian Lougher (Honda). The man who achieved the fastest lap and made his first podium appearance was Aprilia-mounted John McGuinness in third place. Ian Lougher took his 125cc Honda to victory in the Ultra Lightweight race, setting a new race average speed record of 107.89mph and a new lap record of 109.25mph, while Ian Simpson took another Honda to victory in the Junior at record speeds, with his fastest lap at 119.86mph – so close to 120mph on a 600 and a reflection of the development put into those models. The only non-Honda winner of a solo class was Dave Morris on a BMW in the Singles race, where he set a new lap record of 112.07mph.

While Dave Morris was a new name among TT winners, he had been close to victory in the Singles class for a couple of years. Other up-and-comers going well in 1997 were Derek Young, Adrian Archibald, Simon Beck, Adrian McFarland and Mark Flynn.

1998: THE 120MPH CLUB

It was Steve Hislop who set the first 120mph lap back in 1989. Since then, a fairly select group had joined him in the '120mph Club'. Totalling about twenty, some ten of them were present at the 1998 TT, where spectators were still waiting for Steve's absolute race average record speed of 121.28mph and Carl Fogarty's absolute lap record of 123.61mph to be broken. Quite why those records set in 1992 remained intact in the face of manufacturers' claims of ever-increasing outputs from their machines and tyre makers' talk of increased performance from their rubber, was a bit of a mystery. Six years is a long time for a record to stand in TT racing.

Unusually, only one race record was broken in 1998 and that was in the Production TT. Jim Moodie was already a member of the 120mph Club, but in bringing his Honda Fireblade home in first place at record-breaking pace he lifted the Production lap record to 120.70mph, thus bringing Production machines into the Club. Of course, his 4-cylinder Fireblade was of greater capacity than the 4-cylinder 750s of the Formula I class, but it was quite a performance for a sports roadster. Moodie was delighted with the Fireblade, finding the standard set-up 'brilliant' and leading home Nigel Davies on a Kawasaki ZX-9RR, followed by Michael Rutter on another Honda. In fourth place came a rapidly improving David Jefferies on Yamaha's new YZF-R1 – an encouraging display by both bike and rider, reinforced by R1s also taking fifth and sixth places.

Phillip McCallen did not ride the TT in 1998 due to injuries received at Thruxton, and Joey Dunlop was not fully fit. In addition, Iain Duffus suffered a freak accident stepping out of his motorhome in the TT

Robert Dunlop was master of the Ultra Lightweight TT for 125cc machines, winning it on five occasions.

Paddock and broke his leg. Both the Formula I and Senior races went to Ian Simpson (Honda), although some felt that Bob Jackson might have snatched a rare TT victory for Kawasaki had his filler cap not been dropped during his single refuelling stop. The winning/losing margin was just 3.7 seconds. In a Honda CBR600-dominated Junior race, Michael Rutter took one to his first TT victory, while in the weather-hit Lightweight race, Joey Dunlop used all his skills to splash home to a courageous first place, while Robert Dunlop ended his post-accident lean years with a win in the Ultra Lightweight 125 race. Both Dunlops rode Hondas, as did all the other winners, except for Dave Morris taking the Singles race again on a BMW.

Joey Dunlop entering Quarter Bridge on his Honda at the 1999 TT. It was a year in which he rode at number 12, instead of his customary 3.

1999: CAPACITY CHANGES

The TT races have always been shaped to accommodate the popular engine capacities of the time. In the early days they were for 350 and 500cc, with 250cc machines joining in 1920. That was the situation for almost thirty years, until a race for 125cc machines was introduced. There was a brief period in the 1960s when 50cc bikes were catered for, but they were dropped and the next major change was the acceptance of 750cc machines. Thereafter the upper limit gradually increased, touching 1500cc for a while – not that there were any race machines of that capacity. Engine sizes were then reduced to 750cc fours, with up to 1010cc twins allowed into the Senior race.

With manufacturers wanting to showcase their flagship sportsters, which were now tending towards 1000cc, the TT accommodated them by opening up the Formula I race to four-strokes of any engine configuration from 700 to 1010cc. They also accepted 500cc GP machines manufactured after 1994.

The Lightweight 250 TT for two-stroke twins had accommodated the 351–400cc four-strokes, but for 1999 the latter got a separate race – the Lightweight 400 TT. This meant the TT now had ten races, with entries slightly up on the previous year.

A CHANGE AT THE TOP

Honda had dominated the big classes at the TT in recent years with their expensive works RC45s, but in 1999 Yamaha recovered much of their winning ways with a relatively new machine and rider. The machine was their YZF-R1, a 1000cc transverse 4-cylinder four-stroke, said to deliver 140bhp in road trim. More like a 600 in size, it came with a new design feature of a 'stacked' gearbox, which allowed for a reduction in wheelbase. The R1 was very well received by press and buyers as a road bike, with Yamaha advertising proclaiming that it had all the best attributes to attract the sporting rider, saying that it was 'the shortest, lightest and most powerful in its class'. Their advertising extended to the glossy TT programme, where a double-page spread mentioned that 'the R1 delivers levels of performance that were quite simply inconceivable before its launch'. They were bold claims being made to a knowledgeable audience, with the TT Mountain Course waiting to put them to the test against the likes of Hondas, Kawasakis, Suzukis and Ducatis.

However good Yamaha's R1 was claimed to be, it needed a top runner to ride it and a top team to prepare it. No one doubted the talents of the latter in the shape of the experienced V&M Racing, but their chosen rider, David Jefferies, was only rated at number 15 in the organizer's seedings, although he had ridden to fourth place on an R1 in the previous year's Production TT.

It turned out to be a timely choice of rider, whose father and uncle were both TT winners, and whose riding was improving from meeting to meeting in a mixed schedule of short-circuit and road racing. The young David Jefferies had starred at the 1999 North West 200 a couple of weeks before and his performance during TT practice had everyone talking. What is more, he carried his practice performances over into the racing and in so doing helped make it an exceptional year, where speed records were broken by riders in seven of the eight solo races.

One surprise entry was Phillip McCallen, who had missed 1998 due to worries on the injury front. He was back to ride in four races and, in another surprise, he was riding Yamahas. Honda Britain (also calling themselves Honda UK) had their usual strong line-up of Joey Dunlop, Ian Simpson, Jim Moodie and Michael Rutter. In the Formula I and Senior TTs they were all mounted on RC45s, while John McGuinness and Ian Lougher were also Honda-mounted, using NSR500 GP-style V-twins.

THE RACING

Racing got under way with the Formula I event and, as many expected, David Jefferies took his first TT win, circulating at record speed and finishing 15.8 seconds ahead of Joey Dunlop. The race was shortened to four laps, and Jefferies opted not to take a new rear tyre at his single pit stop. To make Yamaha's day, Iain Duffus brought the other V&M R1 into third place. The motorcycle press had a field day at Honda's expense and *Motorcycle News* headlined 'A £20,000 Proddie Bike Shouldn't Humble £500,000 Honda RC45s. Someone Forgot to Tell David Jefferies'. *In later years Classic Racer* described the winning machine as 'a modified street bike which, eight weeks before its first race, was wearing a licence plate and was taxed for the street'. The R1's victory brought to an end Honda's seventeen-year run of success in the Formula I race.

Honda recovered some face during race week with Jim Moodie winning the Junior race, although Yamaha's other threat, their 600cc R6, took second and third places with Jefferies and Duffus. More Honda wins went to Ian Lougher in the Ultra Lightweight 125, Paul Williams in the Lightweight 400 and John McGuinness in the Lightweight 250, with the last two breaking records in their races. For good measure, Honda also took both sidecar races with Dave Molyneux and Rob Fisher, with Moly lifting the three-wheeler's lap record to a heady 112.76mph.

Come the last day's racing and it was very much Honda versus Yamaha again. The three-lap Production race opened proceedings and David Jefferies took his second TT win on an R1 at record-breaking pace, while leading home Jason Griffiths and Phillip McCallen on their R1s.

Honda knew they were up against it in the Senior, so hatched a plan to send Jim Moodie off at a pace that they hoped would lead young Jefferies astray. Moodie certainly set a fast pace, for he broke the absolute lap record from a standing start, leaving it at 124.45mph. But Honda's plan failed when Moodie was forced to retire on the second lap, 8 miles out at Ballig Bridge, with a shredded rear tyre. This

left David Jefferies to complete a hat-trick of wins at a new race average record speed for the Senior, with Iain Duffus second, Ian Lougher third on the first Honda, a NSR500V, Nigel Davies on his Yamaha R1 in fourth and Joey Dunlop an unaccustomed fifth on his RC45.

ROADSTER TO RACER

David Jefferies' TT-winning Yamaha R1 race bike may have been a roadster some eight weeks before, but it underwent much change to make it a winner over the TT course, as did most production-based bikes of the time. V&M racing comprised Jack Valentine and Steve Mellor, who both were vastly experienced in the preparation of competition machinery. Their R1s, for they also built the one ridden by Iain Duffus, received a complete engine strip-down, followed by a rebuild that included things like a lightened, rebalanced and polished crankshaft with new oval section and chrome-moly steel con rods. The cylinder head was ported, flowed and polished, compression ratio raised and special valve springs fitted. They fitted their own camshafts and adopted ram-air induction, special airbox and a radiator twice the size of the original.

Having seen 132bhp from a stock R1, V&M were pleased with the 174bhp available after they had worked their magic, which also included remapping the ignition for the higher revs now available and a special exhaust. The frame remained virtually standard, although a Penske rear shock was fitted, while front forks were re-valved and dropped 10mm in new adjustable yokes. Among other changes it was fitted with new cast iron discs and six-pot calipers, while the petrol tank was enlarged to allow completion of two laps on a tankful. So, no longer your standard R1, but a TT-winning motorcycle that V&M were prepared to replicate for customers on payment of £26,000.

SPEEDS

Everyone had their own view as to Yamaha's resurgence in the big bike classes, with some crediting it to the machine and others to the men riding them. Most debate on the machines centred on whether the 1,000cc Yamaha R1 was faster and better handling than the 750cc Honda RC45s, for without naming the opposition, Yamaha advertising had built up an aura of superiority in those areas.

Information on speeds achieved was hard to come by. Some of the teams now had set-ups from which they could gather data, but it was not the sort of information they made public. Aware of the fascination with speed, the organizers installed an electronic speed check opposite the Grandstand on the Glencrutchery Road, with a digital display of the speed achieved by everyone who passed. The fastest runners in 1999 were Jim Moodie (Honda RC45) at 164.9mph, Iain Duffus (Yamaha R1) 163.8mph, Joey Dunlop (Honda RC45) 163.8mph, David Jefferies (Yamaha R1) 163.5mph and Ian Lougher (Honda NSR500) 163.5mph. It showed that speeds were quite close among the top runners. It was not a point where they hit maximum speed and most were still accelerating as they passed the timing point. On the fastest parts of the circuit, the best riders would reach 180–185mph.

In the Production race, David Jefferies and Iain Duffus on their Yamaha R1s were joint fastest at 153.2mph, followed by three more R1s, while in the Junior race Phillip McCallen (Yamaha R6) and Joey Dunlop (Honda CBR600) were joint fastest at 149.9mph.

As manufacturers produced machines with more speed, riders had to adapt to cope with it. Braking points changed, corner entry now required a rider to tip the machine in earlier, and some sweeping bends that had previously been flat out now required riders to drop a gear. More speed meant more of a challenge. Seemingly, riders could not get enough and previous calls for reductions in machine capacities were no longer heard. However, for all the growth in machine performance, it was becoming increasingly difficult to turn that gain in power, handling and braking into faster laps. Getting past 122mph lap speeds proved particularly difficult and took several years, but in the period 1990–99, the outright lap record did go up from 122.63mph to 124.45mph.

David Jefferies sweeps through Ginger Hall on his winning V&M Yamaha.

CHAPTER TEN

FASTER AND FASTER

The Tourist Trophy race meeting was proud of its long history stretching back to 1907, no more so than at the start of the new millennium in 2000, when people were looking both backwards and forwards, making comparisons with the past and anticipating the future. The event's prospects looked bright, with race enthusiasts anticipating ever-growing speeds around the Mountain Course, where the absolute lap record now stood at 124.45mph.

The term 'TT' became embedded into the world of motorcycling during the twentieth century and with the ever-increasing spread of communications, those same initials were becoming familiar to many in the wider world. It was claimed that 500 million people would watch televised transmissions of the races in 2000 and developing technologies were expected to allow ever more people to tune in and share the excitement of real road racing. Such growth in numbers brought an increase in associated advertising and, in current jargon, the TT would be turned into a 'brand' to be marketed worldwide. But while a few sought to profit from the commercial side of the event, true supporters got their reward from the annual dose of high-speed excitement generated by the top road racers of the day.

Those racers would continue to compete for a Tourist Trophy over the enduring Mountain Course, where, apart from customary resurfacing and maintenance, the only real improvement was to the last of the Quarry Bends. There

Joey Dunlop at Quarter Bridge on his winning 250 Honda in 2000.

the camber had been adjusted in riders' favour, giving an improved exit onto the Sulby Straight and, perhaps, an extra few mph on their speeds.

2000: THE WEATHER

In 2000, practice started on Saturday evening rather than the customary Monday morning and such early-morning sessions were now down to two. However, weather conditions turned poor in the middle of practice week, leaving Newcomers struggling to put in enough laps to qualify and experienced riders still trying to achieve the right set-up for their race machines.

Among those troubled with set-up problems was Joey Dunlop. Armed with a choice of a Honda VTR1000SP-W from World Superbike and a Fireblade for the big races, he found that the former, usually called the SP1, had a stuttering power delivery and that it did not handle. Much of practice was spent doing single laps then coming in to tweak the suspension, before going out again to see if there was any improvement. In the end, reverting to the previous year's type of tyre helped solve the handling difficulties. Other Honda Britain men on Fireblades were Iain Duffus, Jim Moodie and Adrian Archibald. Riding for Yamaha UK on V&M R1s, David Jefferies and Michael Rutter had a good practice. Jefferies' bike was also referred to as an R71, for V&M claimed to have squeezed his R1 motor into a modified 750cc R7 frame.

Joey Dunlop's problems were made all the harder by the fact that he had six machines to get race ready. Seemingly, past settings did no more than provide a baseline when riders returned to the TT, either with a new machine or one that had been subject to a season's racing since it last ran on the Mountain Course. It was an intensely busy time. Grabbing his 250 for an early morning lap, Dunlop found that it had not been fuelled and spluttered to a halt at The Bungalow. Needing to get back to the start to take out another bike, he found a paper cup and borrowed some petrol from a travelling marshal's machine. As his Honda ran on 'petroil', he also needed to find some oil to add to the petrol. With the assistance of a willing spectator and his bike, he removed the drain plug from one of its fork-legs, mixed some of the drained-off oil with the petrol in his tank and was away to complete his lap. Always known as a canny rider, Dunlop had twenty-five years of Isle of Man racing knowledge to call upon to get over his problems. Such hard-earned experience was something that previous TT great Mick Grant described as 'priceless'.

THE RACING

Joey Dunlop showed his enduring class by winning the opening Formula I race at the 2000 TT. Then, in an almost unbelievable display, he went on to take the next two solo races, the Lightweight 250 and the Ultra Lightweight 125. Both of those wins came against stiff opposition. Just halfway through the meeting, Dunlop already had a hat-trick of wins, bringing his total up to twenty-six. The next best was Mike Hailwood on fourteen.

Wednesday afternoon's Junior race at last gave Yamaha a chance to shine, for it was David Jefferies who took over the winning ways. He also went on to win the Production and Senior races, which meant that for the first time at a TT, two riders achieved hat-tricks of wins in the same year. En route to his victories, 'DJ', as he was known to most, raised the race average speed in the Junior to 119.13mph and in the Senior to 121.95mph, topping it all with a new absolute lap record in the Senior race of 125.69mph. He was the first rider to lap at 125mph – yet another TT speed barrier smashed.

Honda's share of the record-breaking came in the Junior, where Adrian Archibald lapped at 121.15mph to become the first rider to break 120mph on a 600.

Now in his fifth year at the TT, John McGuinness was slowly building his tally of wins, taking victory in the Singles race, while Rob Fisher was victorious in both sidecar races, so making it his third double.

In a difficult-to-believe scenario, the declared winner of the Lightweight 400 TT was disqualified when his engine was measured and found to be 600cc. The win was justly given to Brett Richmond.

JOEY – THE ENIGMA

Forty-eight-year-old Joey Dunlop finished 2000 TT week with third place in the Senior race. In doing so he recorded his fastest ever TT lap at 123.87mph, setting it on the very last lap of the race. Some three weeks after receiving worldwide acclaim for his successes at the renowned International TT meeting, Dunlop loaded his 125 Honda into his van, collected long-time supporter John Harris and his CBR600 racer, and set off for Estonia to take part in some local races. That was his style – he did what he fancied. But there, on a rain-soaked surface, he left the road on his 125, collided with trackside trees and was killed.

After twenty-five years' racing over the dangerously narrow roads of his native Ireland and on the high-speed TT course, as well as on short circuits worldwide that earned him several World Formula I championships, the seemingly immortal Joey was dead. Mourned by the world of motorcycling and beyond, his funeral in Ballymoney brought the town to a standstill. Reports talk of 50,000 mourners.

Previously known as the Twenty-sixth Milestone, this spot on the Mountain climb was renamed Joey's in recognition of his twenty-six TT victories.

2002: RACING GOES ON

Heartless as it may sound, like all of the many deaths that occur in the dangerous sport of motorcycle racing, followers quickly accepted that they represented the past. While Joey Dunlop would never be forgotten, race fans now had to look to the future. However, what was scheduled to be the next TT, in 2001, did not happen, for an outbreak of foot and mouth disease in Britain had the Island fearful for its farming activity, so the TT was cancelled.

On the wider stage there was concern that despite the production-based formula of World Superbike racing, costs were spiralling out of control, so manufacturers were looking for ways to reduce them. There was also recognition that many people were now choosing to buy 1000cc road bikes rather than the 750cc ones raced in the World Superbike series.

Two years after its last running, the TT returned in 2002. The Isle of Man welcomed it back, claiming it had 'pulled out all the stops this year to provide great racing and a huge variety of entertainment'. There were changes to the race programme. The Lightweight 400 TT and the Ultra Lightweight 125 TT now ran together, while retaining their separate race identities. A similar situation was created for the Lightweight 250 TT, which was scheduled to run with the Junior 600 TT. The Production TT became two races, on different days. First was the Production 1000 event for four-stroke machines of 701–1010cc to ACU Production Regulations, run on the Monday. The other was the Production 600 TT for four-stroke machines up to 600cc to ACU Production Regulations, run on Friday. The Singles TT was dropped from the race programme.

Among other changes were the introduction of random breathalyzer tests for competitors and trials of bike-fitted transponders to aid lap timing. The organizers also upped the prize money, with a 'bonus' of £5,000 being paid to each race winner.

Crowds returned in 2002, for the TT was an essential part of many peoples' lives. Some were satisfied with the annual two-week 'high' they received from attendance at race time, but for many it was a year-round focus of interest. Much was expected by the speed-seeking element in 2002, for while the TT was a unique event, it was also part of the wider motorcycling racing scene, where development was driven by World Superbike and GP racing. Two years' progress in those fields should have filtered down through the competition departments of firms like Honda, Yamaha, Suzuki, Kawasaki and Ducati, to the benefit of TT machinery.

THE RACING

The man expected to do much of the winning was David Jefferies. However, having switched from Yamaha to Suzuki shortly before the event, there was a question mark over how he would go on a new bike. Along with Ian Lougher, DJ now rode under the TAS (Temple Auto Salvage)/Suzuki banner. Top Honda runners were John McGuinness and Adrian Archibald, while Jim Moodie and Iain Duffus rode Yamahas for V&M Racing.

David Jefferies was by now the crowd favourite and he did not disappoint his many fans, taking record-breaking wins in the Formula I, Production 1000 and Senior TTs of 2002. Not only did that give him his third consecutive hat-trick of wins, but in the Senior he lifted his own absolute course record to 127.29mph. It was a stunning performance, marred only by his smaller Suzuki breaking a valve in the Junior race; a challenging John McGuinness also blew his Honda engine in that race, resulting in Jim Moodie happily taking the Junior win on his Yamaha.

ABOVE: **David Jefferies powers out of the Gooseneck on his TAS Suzuki.**

Rob Fisher and Rick Long at the Bungalow during one of their winning rides in 2002.

The 4-cylinder 600cc motors used in the Junior TT had been subject to much development by manufacturers in their efforts to offer 'fastest in class' to potential buyers of their road machines. Preparation for racing raised engines to an even higher state of tune, and John McGuinness' Honda was redlined at 15,500rpm, a figure that he would seek to reach as often as possible over the four-lap and 151-mile race distance.

Ian Lougher gave solid support to his Suzuki team mate David Jefferies, including winning the Production 600 race. Switching to a Honda, he then came home first in the Ultra Lightweight 125 event, setting new race average and lap records, leaving the latter at 110.21mph. That was some going for a single-cylinder 125cc machine putting out approximately 46bhp.

Among first time winners in 2002 were Bruce Anstey (Yamaha) in the Lightweight 250 and Richard 'Milky' Quayle (Honda) in the Lightweight 400, while Rob Fisher (LMS) achieved another double on three wheels.

If those watching the racing were not convinced from the multitude of new records that bikes were getting faster, the digital speed recorder opposite the Grandstand showed spectators that the highest speed of 165mph recorded in 1999 increased to 170mph in 2002, at a point where the bikes were still accelerating.

The Joey Dunlop Trophy was introduced for 2002 and awarded to the best aggregate performance across the Formula I and Senior TT races. As winner of both, David Jefferies collected the trophy and the accompanying cheque for £10,000.

2003: MINOR CHANGES

Taking its usual late May and early June spot in the racing calendar, the 2003 TT arrived with an entry of 319 individuals, 150 of them being from the seventy-five sidecar crews.

It was to be the last year of early-morning practice, a ritual that had started with the first event in 1907. Many riders complained about early-morning practice down the years, as did some marshals and officials, for they had to be in position well before the racers arrived.

The few Lightweight 250s again ran with the Junior 600s, but without a recognized race of their own, and the Junior race was described as being 'for Machines to TT Supersport 600 Regulations'. The term Supersport was one that would be heard more of in the future. Out on the course the series of bends at the Thirty-second Milestone were renamed Duke's, in honour of star of the 1950s and ambassador for the TT races, Geoff Duke.

Transponders were now mandatory and used to determine race results. Timing strips triggered by the trans-

ponders were located at Glen Helen, Ballaugh, Ramsey, The Bungalow, Cronk ny Mona and the Grandstand. Those timing points generated additional information for race commentators – now sitting in front of computer screens – who were able to quote sector speeds, plus the increasing/decreasing gaps between riders and other information they thought might be helpful to spectators and support teams. The latter included those located in the pits and, for signalling purposes, those out around the course.

HONDA DOWN, SUZUKI UP

Honda had been long-time supporters of the TT, but in 2003 they gave restricted input to the event, limiting their publicized involvement to Ian Lougher and Dave Molyneux. Lougher had Colin Edwards' 2002 World Superbike SP2 and Moly had help with engines. The SP2 was much upgraded in fuelling, frame and engine compared to the earlier SP1 and was said to give 180bhp. Not that Lougher was able to use all of that in the early stages of practice, for the bike had stability problems at high speed. They were eventually ironed out and a good race set-up obtained.

Soichiro Honda, founder of the company bearing his name, knew that success in racing sold road bikes, but something Honda no longer seemed to be the bike of choice for riders to compete on at the TT. Five years earlier, at the 1998 event, there were thirty Hondas in the Formula I race out of seventy entries and seventy-two Hondas in the Junior race out of ninety-one entries. In 2003 there were just seven in the Formula I race and fourteen in the Junior. It was a change that would not have escaped the notice of the motorcycle-buying public.

Honda had done their best to keep their name in the forefront of racing by winning the World Superbike Championship with Colin Edwards in 2000 and 2002, although Ducati probably made a greater impact with their several wins earned by Carl Fogarty and Troy Bayliss. Indeed, their racing successes are said to have transformed the Italian company. But even Ducati's multi-wins did not encourage racers to buy, for there were only seven of them in the 2003 Formula I TT. Yamaha had been successful at the TT of late and there were some twelve R1s entered, but it was Suzuki who dominated the Formula I entries in 2003, filling thirty-nine of the eighty places. Just two years earlier they had replaced their GSX-R1100 with the GSX-R1000, fitted with an enlarged and uprated 750cc engine. The 2003 version was claimed to weigh less, had more power and handled better. There was talk of 180bhp at the crankshaft and 143bhp at the rear wheel for this 180mph motorcycle.

David Jefferies and Adrian Archibald were to ride TAS Suzukis, John McGuinness was on a Ducati 998, which he

Over a wet road and with the sun in his eyes, John McGuinness takes one of the patriotically painted ValMoto Triumphs through Ballacraine.

described as better than his previous year's Fireblade but which needed a roller-starter after pit stops, and Jason Griffiths received Yamaha's support on an R1. Those top men would be looking over their shoulders at established riders like Iain Duffus, Bruce Anstey, Jim Moodie, Sean Harris and Ian Lougher, while also being aware of promising ones like Ryan Farquhar, Richard Britton and Martin Finnegan. Spectators were particularly interested in seeing how a Val-Moto team of Triumphs went, on their first appearance in the Junior race.

A SAD DAY
David Jefferies had been slightly slower than team mate Adrian Archibald in the early stages of practice in 2003, but during the long Thursday afternoon session he was up to

speed and in Archibald's slipstream as they powered downhill into Glen Vine and the sweeping left-hander by the Vicarage, which they prepared to take with barely an easing of throttles. Then it went wrong for Jefferies as the Suzuki slid from under him and both crashed into a roadside wall. In an instant, the brightest TT star of his generation was killed and a family steeped in TT racing was thrown into mourning, along with every race follower. After three consecutive hat-tricks of TT victories, the young superstar was gone. Everyone knew that racing could be a cruel business and the TT more so, for it allowed little room for either rider or mechanical error. A tragedy like DJ's made many think about stepping back from motorcycle racing, but it was an addictive pastime, whatever role a person took – rider, spectator, sponsor, organizer – and most soon returned.

FAST RACING

After the previous year's record-breaking spree, speeds were just slightly down in some classes in 2003. Adrian Archibald rode his Suzuki to victory in Formula I and Senior TTs, but 1mph down on 2002 figures. John McGuinness led both of those races on his Ducati before dropping back slightly and Ian Lougher finished both on the podium, with Jason Griffiths taking two fourth places. In the Formula I race, only the latter three, out of the first thirty-three finishers, rode anything other than Suzuki.

Shaun Harris ensured that Suzuki continued their winning ways by taking both Production 1000 and 600cc races, while fellow-Kiwi Bruce Anstey brought his Triumph home first in the Junior at a record-breaking race average speed of 120.36mph. It was a race in which relative new boy Ryan Farquhar impressed by raising the lap record to 122.30mph. Another lap record went to winner of the Ultra Lightweight 125 race, Chris Palmer (Honda), and he also took the barely recognized 250 win within the Junior 600 race. In a world where the major manufacturers were no longer making 'proper' race bikes for the Lightweight classes, 125 and 250cc riders faced an uncertain future as machines aged and entry numbers fell.

Ian Bell (Yamaha) and Dave Molyneux (Honda) took a win each in the Sidecar races, while runner-up in both was local man Nick Crowe (Ireson).

For several years, entries for the Senior TT had been by invitation, based upon the fastest riders in practice. Allocated number 1 in 2003, Adrian Archibald felt that was not right, as David Jefferies had set a fractionally faster time. Accordingly, he obtained the organizer's permission to contest the Senior under number 0. It was part of Archibald's tribute to a great rider and team mate.

Further tragedy struck away from the TT later in 2003, when eleven-times winner Steve Hislop was killed in a helicopter crash shortly after winning the British Superbike Championship.

2004: NEW ORGANIZERS

The ACU had run the TT races since 1907, with what, at times, had seemed to be the reluctant involvement of the Manx government. But times had changed. The financial value of the races to the Island was recognized and from 2004 the government took a twenty-year licence to run the entire event. It appointed the Manx Motor Cycle Club Ltd to organize the racing on its behalf. Having run the Manx Grand Prix since its inception as the Amateur races in 1923, the club was in a good position to do so. The government also injected some extra effort to attract quality riders, for the TT was in need of a boost.

Like any new broom, the MMCC made its presence felt with changes. Its first action was to do away with early-morning practice, the loss of track time being partially compensated for by the introduction of practice laps after each day's racing. No one gave a definitive reason for the change. It was known that many riders disliked early practice, that marshals were harder to get and, although unspoken, that the growing specialization of race tyres meant they were becoming unsuitable for the mixed damp/dry conditions most likely to be met at six o'clock in the morning.

A surprise move was the reduction of the race distance for the Formula I and Senior races from six laps to four. The reason given here was that statistics showed more accidents occurred late in the race. The majority opposed the change.

The entry system for the Senior TT, whereby the fastest riders in practice received an invitation to take part, was shown to have caused a reduction in the number who turned up to ride. For 2004, entries were invited in advance, as for the other races.

ENTRIES

Overall numbers of race entries were good for 2004 at 731, but, as in previous years, the level of support from manufacturers varied. Honda had no named presence although they may have given Ian Lougher support in the Formula I and Senior races on a CBR-RR through Mark Johns Motors. Ian had other Honda-mounted rides from private entrants in the Junior, Production 1000 and 600, and Ultra Lightweight 125 classes. Official support from Yamaha Motor (UK) Ltd was given to John McGuinness and Jason Griffiths, while Adrian Archibald and Bruce Anstey were with TAS Suzuki. Potential front runners on Kawasakis were Ryan Farquhar and Shaun Harris, while a Newcomer destined to catch the eye was Guy Martin.

RECORDS GALORE

John McGuinness showed his true class as a TT rider in 2004, taking his first hat-trick of wins. He was victorious in the opening Formula I race on a Yamaha, where he became the first to achieve a race average speed of 125mph (125.38mph) and where he lifted the lap record to 127.68mph. He went on to break records in the Lightweight 400 race on a Honda, before reverting to a Yamaha for record-breaking wins in the Junior. Despite his undoubted talent, McGuinness admitted to being 'a bit laid back' in his approach to racing, but in 2004 he had Jim Moodie in his support team and credited him with keeping him focused.

Elsewhere, Bruce Anstey (Suzuki) lifted Production 1000cc records to a new race average speed of 123.72mph and a new lap record of 125.10mph; Ryan Farquhar (Kawasaki) took his first TT win in the Production 600; Chris Palmer (Honda) raised race average and lap records in the Ultra Lightweight 125 race; and Dave Molyneux (DMR Honda) did the same in the Sidecar races. To Adrian Archibald (Suzuki) went the Senior TT win, after initial leaders John McGuinness and Ian Lougher both retired. It was a very good year for those who liked their racing to be faster and faster.

The scale of high-speed activity generated by the TT can be seen from figures showing that riders completed 3,065 laps in practice and 1,780 in the races. Total distance covered was nearly 183,000 miles.

ABOVE: **Dave Molyneux and Dan Sayle (DMR) take a tight line through the sweeping bends at the Eleventh Milestone.**

BELOW: **Newcomers experiencing their first lap over closed roads behind a travelling marshal.**

2005: NAME CHANGES

The organizing MMCC made slight changes to the regulations for bikes contesting the TT in 2005, aimed at bringing them in line with those raced on British short circuits. It also renamed the race classes to reflect what was happening elsewhere. The Formula I race now became the TT Superbike race, Production races were replaced by TT Superstock and the Junior became the Supersport Junior TT. The above were now only open to four-strokes; there was no place in the new race programme for 125 and 250cc two-stroke machines, nor for 400cc four-strokes. It was said that the changes reflected the views of riders and manufacturers, but there was no mention of those held by spectators. Manufacturers Honda, Yamaha, Suzuki and Kawasaki were present to support a seven-race programme, comprising two Sidecar races (A and B), two Supersport Junior (A and B), an opening TT Superbike and closing Senior TT that were, in effect, duplicate races, and one TT Superstock race.

The changes brought no visual differences to the machines raced in 2004 and the harmonization of regulations saw no attributable enhancement of performance. Superbike and Senior TTs reverted to six laps, but the number of individual competitors dropped to 244, with the organizers claiming that they were now concentrating on quality rather than quantity. Many found it regrettable that there were only four non-Japanese machines in the entire solo and sidecar entry – one MV Agusta, one Aprilia and two Triumphs.

In a bid to help Newcomers, they were given their own introductory lap at the outset of practice. Going out in a group, they were shown the way by travelling marshals riding at the head, middle and rear, at controlled speeds. In later years, these orange-jacketed first-timers would be broken into smaller groups and led by former racers.

TYRES

With tyre manufacturers chasing the publicity to be gained from success in racing, their development efforts resulted

Tyre marks on the road show the effect of full throttle being applied on the exit of the last of the Quarry Bends, to gain maximum momentum for the Sulby Straight that follows.

Sweeping through light and shade at Union Mills.

in tyres that now laid continuous black stripes around the entire 37¾ miles of the Mountain Course. There certainly was no secret as to where the racing line was, for it was there on the road surface for all to see, both on the corners and the straights. However, it did reveal differences of opinion as to what exactly was the right line, being up to 2m wide on some corners.

Increased tyre performance came from greater specialization in design and construction. With the Island known for its variable weather conditions, the TT really needed tyres that could cope with roads that were wet and dry during a race, but that flexibility was not a feature of current tyre development. There were tyres for wet roads and tyres for dry ones, but the in-between going often found at the TT presented problems, because 'wets' would soon deteriorate over drying roads and 'slicks' were unsafe in the wet. Such problems were compounded for both solos and sidecars by the ever-increasing power outputs of modern race machines.

The situation was brought into focus during practice for the 2005 TT, when time was lost due to wet conditions.

Clerk of the Course, Neil Hanson, laid down a marker for the future when he stated that he would no longer start a TT race in wet conditions. That decision was taken in the interests of safety, but it was one that would impact upon future events. Indeed, it affected the opening Superbike race in 2005 and saw it postponed until Sunday.

RACING

Whilst Superbike, Superstock and Supersport races introduced new titles to the 2005 TT, it was still reasonable to compare their results and speeds with previous Formula I, Production and Junior races. A fast pace was set throughout the seven-race programme, with records broken in four of them. Bruce Anstey (Suzuki) lifted the TT Superstock (formerly Production 1000) average race speed to 124.44mph and TAS Suzuki team mate Adrian Archibald set a new lap record of 126.64mph. In TT Supersport A (formerly Junior TT), Ian Lougher (Honda) increased the average race speed to 120.93mph, while in the Senior TT, winner John McGuinness (Yamaha) set off with the aim of establishing a lead from the outset and raised the lap record to 127.33mph on his opening lap. McGuinness also won the opening TT Superbike race (formerly Formula I), at just under record speed.

On three wheels, a charging Dave Molyneux lifted average speeds by an impressive 3½mph, leaving the race average figure at 114.90mph and the lap record at 116.04mph. Moly set his new records in Sidecar race B, having struck trouble in race A, which saw a first win for Nick Crowe.

TOO HOT
The TT Supersport races attracted the highest number of entries in 2005 and 2006. The 4-cylinder 600cc machines used in them were subject to development effort by the manufacturers and by race tuners, but, as always, there was a price to pay for speed and in 2005 it showed itself in the form of reduced reliability. There were seventy finishers in race A from eighty-one starters, but only fifty-eight in race B from seventy-five starters. Significantly, amongst those failing to complete the second race were the factory-

supported Hondas and Suzukis, plus the Yamaha of John McGuinness.

While a private runner might have to effect an engine rebuild at the TT in the back of a van, 600cc works engines needed full workshop attention. Notwithstanding the excellent service facilities available from the expensive mobile workshops run by many teams at the TT, they could not undertake the between-races sort of rebuilds required by machines that had been overstressed by the demands of the Mountain Course. The solution chosen by the manufacturers, and accepted by the organizers, was to reduce the TT Supersport to one race for 2006, giving a six-race programme.

2006: LESS RACING
The slimmed-down programme of six races did not go down well with all TT fans, for many remembered when there were ten, and even if some of them were combined to give races within races, they did offer variety in sights and sounds. For others, six races were enough, because a large number of them were present to enjoy the TT scene as a whole, with its varied entertainments and general motorcycling theme. To them, the races were just a part of that scene.

On the organizing side, efforts were being made to attract more quality riders to the event, although the overall number of entries accepted was reduced to give slightly smaller grids. For 2006, there were just 226 individual competitors across solos and sidecar events, with revised timetabling bringing some changes to their race days. They did at least now enjoy free entries, but a new introduction was a 'TT licence', designed to ensure that competitors had recent and relevant racing experience.

The big four Japanese manufacturers were again supporting the TT in 2006, along with major private entrants and sponsors. For Honda it was HM Plant, Suzuki used Temple Auto Salvage (TAS), Yamaha were represented by AIM Racing, and Kawasaki appeared in the colours of McAdoo Racing. As had been the way for some years, the manufactur-

John McGuinness keeps his many sponsors happy by displaying their logos.

ers' efforts were made through such private teams. Quite what their level of support to those teams amounted to was a closely kept secret.

Along with improving the quality of competitors it invited to race, plus better promotion and marketing, the TT was now portraying itself to a growing audience in an increasingly professional manner. In the modern world such factors registered and were important, resulting in grow-ing interest from riders, sponsors, press and TV.

THE COURSE

The Mountain Course still had more than its share of bumps, jumps, off-camber corners, changes in surfacing and other factors that affected han-dling. Part of a rider's TT education was learning how to deal with them. The worst bumps could sometimes be avoided by taking a non-standard line, while jumps needed the correct technique. Newcomer Ian Mackman had not mastered that technique and told of his experience:

> Ballacrye is a 140mph jump following a sixth-gear left-hander. You come around the corner, get the bike upright as quickly as possible and crack the throttle open. I didn't quite get the bike upright and it landed with the wheels out of line. I think the spectators could hear me screaming before the wheels even hit the deck. The bike landed and the rear wheel threw itself from full lock one way to full lock the other repeatedly, eventually straightening itself 200 yards up the road. A big moment.

Road conditions changed from year to year, meaning that the learning process was never complete.

Even 125cc machines 'jump' at Ballacrye, as Nigel Beattie shows at the 2003 TT.

There had been few major changes to the course in recent years, but 2006 saw reconstruction of Windy Corner. An open, windswept bend at a height of 1,220ft (372m), it had seen its share of racing incidents. From the 1930s to the 1950s it was a second-gear corner taken at 55–60mph. Today it is a fourth-gear job, with riders taking advantage of its wide, positively cambered, right-handed sweep to get the fastest run on towards the Thirty-third Milestone. The 2006 improvements were thought to save riders 4 seconds a lap and, apart from the cat's eyes on the inside of the bend having to be lowered after John McGuinness complained that he was catching his knee-sliders on them, the work was rated a major improvement.

The upgrading of Windy Corner was carried out principally on road safety grounds. Other measures introduced for the benefit of the Manx motoring public included a programme of applying 'Shell-grip' at busy junctions and on some bends. A blend of epoxy resin and bitumen with calcined bauxite chippings, it gave enhanced grip, but there was little comment as to whether it offered benefit to the racers.

Practice week normally experienced mixed weather, but in 2006 it was almost completely dry. This enabled the rubber laid on the track to remain and riders felt that this contributed to grip.

RACING

Morecambe's John McGuinness was now recognized as the top TT rider of the era, although he had plenty of challengers for that position. McGuinness was riding works Hondas under the HM Plant banner in 2006 and got off to a flying start with victory on a Fireblade in the opening TT Superbike race, setting a new lap record in the process. With record-breaking wins in the Supersport and Senior TTs, he also raised the absolute lap record to 129.45mph in the Senior and led something of a resurrection for Honda at the TT, where Nick Crowe also used their new 600 engines to achieve a Sidecar double at record-breaking speeds. Having unofficially broken the Sidecar lap record during practice, Dave Molyneux was travelling at 145mph when he managed to flip his outfit onto its back at Rhencullen in a later session and put himself out of the racing.

Only in TT Superstock did Honda miss out in 2006. There victory went to Bruce Anstey (Suzuki) at just below record pace, with Ian Hutchinson (Kawasaki) second and Jason Griffiths (Yamaha) third. The latter was 'Mr Consistent' at the TT, for while never a winner, he achieved multiple podium finishes. In only his second year at the event, Cameron Donald showed that he was a man to watch, with second place in the Senior race, and future star, Manxman

Conor Cummins, made a steady debut, as did William Dunlop.

SPEEDS ON BRAY HILL

This fearsome drop has fascinated spectators and frightened riders down the years, with many and varied claims as to speeds achieved. At the first running of the TT over the Mountain Course in 1911, a local newspaper forecast, perhaps optimistically, that riders would take it at up to 70mph. By the mid-1930s they were timed at 95mph; after some smoothing, Omobono Tenni took it at a highly courageous 120mph in 1948; while in the early 1950s, Manxman Jackie Wood was the fastest at 127mph.

One thing that race followers always wanted to know was were riders flat out coming down Bray? For their part, riders indicated that they were and speeds quoted were usually close to the maximum speed of the day, although, in reality, only the fastest riders kept the throttle wire really stretched to the limit. Lesser riders would usually permit themselves a little slack – and who can blame them?

As machine speeds increased, the pace down Bray Hill also got quicker. By 1967 Mike Hailwood was talking of 'doing about 145mph … and everything bottoms in the dip'. In the 1980s, top riders reckoned they could use full throttle on the popular Suzuki RG500s of the day, which would have been about 155mph.

In the early 1990s Steve Hislop took an RVF Honda and the rotary-engined Norton through the bottom flat in top gear, which he thought equated to 167–170mph, while fastest lapper in the early 2000s, David Jefferies, felt that his Yamaha had too much power, and 'I rolled it back'. However, after moving to a Suzuki he told, 'I managed to do Bray Hill absolutely flat in the Senior race … doing at least 175mph, possibly 180'.

In 2006, John McGuinness explained, 'I normally click the big one into top gear as I crest the brow of Bray Hill … it's about 180mph down there', with Guy Martin confirming 'it must be knocking on 180mph'.

A big enough challenge on a solo, Bray Hill must seem much narrower with a sidecar. In the late 1970s top man Jock Taylor told how he used to be flat out, but how the development of bumps in the road meant he backed off to 120mph. Moving on some forty years, it is perhaps no surprise that many-times winner and current star, Dave Molyneux, holds his self-designed DMR outfit flat out, extracting every bit of power to hit 150mph.

TT CENTENARY 1907–2007

In 2007 the Isle of Man was awash with justifiable celebration, as the TT reached the centenary of its first running over the St John's Course in 1907. It really was a fantastic achievement, for having suffered countless problems down the years, it had overcome them all and reached 2007 in a position of strength, with everyone expecting fast and exciting racing. To that end, as John McGuinness had set a new absolute lap record in 2006 of 129.45mph, people looked to him to make a centenary statement by breaking the 130mph barrier in 2007.

By complete coincidence, the Highway Authority did its bit to speed riders' passage with considerable widening works at Brandish Corner. This previously tightish left-hander, with roadside banks and railings, was thus made much faster. Early in practice, John McGuinness voiced the opinion that the alterations at Brandish had turned a '50mph corner into a 150mph one'. He was probably being a bit conservative in putting the former speed as low as 50mph, but the message was clear – it was now considerably faster. Estimating that it would 'reduce average lap times by three seconds', he added that because it was so smooth and open it would be top gear on a 600, but that he would 'knock it back one and roll it on the big one'.

There was nothing new about course improvements contributing to the reduction in lap times. It had been happening for 100 years and, while it was not possible to make an accurate assessment of the time saved, it certainly amounted to many minutes.

Whatever was going to happen on the race front in 2007, the supporting industry ensured that there was plenty of TT centenary memorabilia available to fans: books were published, commemorative stamps issued, special coins minted, compilation DVDs of former races offered and there were photo exhibitions looking back over the past 100 years, plus a re-enactment of the first TT over the St John's Course.

QUALITY RIDERS

An active rider recruitment campaign meant that the TT was into a period where each year saw new entries from established short-circuit racers who fancied the challenge and potentially good payout TT racing offered them. For 2007, former British Supersport champion and regular British Superbike competitor, Steve Plater, tried his hand on R1 and R6 Yamahas supplied by AIM Racing, while Keith Amor and Gary Johnson were other first-timers. Also, although this was a return from years at British Superbike racing rather than an Island debut, past regular competitor and TT winner Michael Rutter, still only thirty-three, made an Island comeback on Kawasaki ZX-10R and ZX-6R bikes from MSS Discovery Kawasaki.

GROWING SPEEDS

The influx of such quality riders served as a spur to established TT stars and was just another factor that helped contribute to the year-on-year growth in speeds, as everyone upped their game. Its effect would not be measurable but it joined other influences like increased pressure from high-level sponsors, greater coverage and the subsequent gaining of publicity from TV and online activities and, of course, the associated growth in financial rewards available to top riders. All served to heighten expectations and performances.

At the same time, a never-ending stream of machine improvements played a major part in increasing speeds. As it had been for a century, this was a step-by-step process, with the effect of each individual improvement being difficult to quantify. John McGuinness arrived for the 2007 event with his big Honda having a 'new spec' engine with improved engine management electronics, plus new fork yokes. He was confident they contributed to a better bike, but no one could predict or measure what effect that would have on race speeds. As far as straight-line speeds went, McGuinness reckoned his Honda was giving him 195mph on Sulby Straight. It was such Sulby moments that caused him to say, 'when you are on the bike, wide open and flat out, it's the best feeling in the world'. Lesser mortals can only imagine, with envy, the heightening of all senses that must occur in such a situation.

RECORDS ALL THE WAY

The result of 100 years of motorcycle development was showcased at the 2007 TT. Contesting the event had helped manufacturers enhance design and performance across all aspects of the racing motorcycle, with those getting it right returning home in triumph, while for those who got things wrong it was a case of going back to the drawing board.

The pace was hot in practice, and further proof that design and performance were still advancing came when, in the ensuing Centenary race week, records were broken in all classes. However, although nobody disputed that tyres were a factor contributing to advances in performance, their unsuitability for use in mixed road conditions and a claim of poor visibility caused the postponement of Saturday's opening races until Sunday.

With track conditions still not perfect, John McGuinness (Honda) opened his 2007 TT with a win in the postponed Superbike race, leading home Guy Martin (Honda) and breaking both race average speed and lap records for the class, at 125.55mph and 128.27mph. Next day, 'King of the Superstocks', Bruce Anstey (Suzuki), took his third consecutive win in the class in perfect conditions. Again

History is made as the scoreboard opposite the Grandstand records the first 130mph lap.

200bhp available from his Honda, he opened with a standing-start lap speed of 129.98mph, smashed the 130mph barrier on his second lap at 130.35mph and raced on to victory at a new Senior race average record speed of 127.25mph. McGuinness won by 32 seconds from Guy Martin, who was followed by Ian Hutchinson and Ian Lougher. The first four all rode Honda Fireblades.

John McGuinness joined a select band of record-breakers and the 130mph title was truly his, for he was the only one in the race to reach the figure. It was an achievement that set the seal on a memorable and record-breaking Centenary TT.

SPEEDS

Shown below is the progression in speeds since the Mountain Course was brought into use in 1911.

First lap achieved at	Rider	Year
50mph	Frank Philipp	1911
60mph	Jimmy Simpson	1924
70mph	Jimmy Simpson	1926
80mph	Jimmy Simpson	1931
90mph	Freddie Frith	1937
100mph	Bob McIntyre	1957
110mph	John Williams	1976
120mph	Steve Hislop	1989
130mph	John McGuinness	2007

During the period covered by this chapter, 1999–2007, fastest lap speeds increased from 124.45mph to 130.35mph. That was impressive.

records were broken, with Anstey actually getting around faster than the Superbike speeds, his race average being 125.87mph and fastest lap 128.40mph. It was a tremendous performance by the Kiwi on what was said to be a stock bike fitted with a forks kit and aftermarket rear shock but, strangely, Anstey could not get his big Suzuki to handle in the Superbike and Senior races. A welcome sight and sound in the Superstock event was Martin Finnegan bringing a factory-supported MV Agusta into fourth place.

A less than fully fit Ian Hutchinson (Honda) rode to his first TT victory in the Supersport race, setting a new race average record speed of 123.22mph, with John McGuinness (Honda) just 2.84 seconds behind and Guy Martin (Honda) being the first to break the 125mph barrier on a 600. Martin took third place and left the new lap record at 125.16mph. The sidecar races saw two wins for Dave Molyneux using Honda power, although he was just short of his own race average record, but Nick Crowe used his Honda power to break the outright lap record for the three-wheelers, leaving it at a heady 116.67mph. Unfortunately, such treatment also saw Crowe break his Honda engine, so he did not finish the race.

Come the last race of the week, the Senior TT, and the target of a 130mph lap was there for the taking by the top riders. The man who rose to the occasion and put his name into the record books was John McGuinness. With some

ONWARDS AND UPWARDS

2008: ORGANIZATIONAL CHANGES

Every TT brings changes, and the 2008 event had its share. Some affect the average spectator in a way that he or she can see and feel, but many leave them untouched. Coming in the latter category was the news for 2008 that after four years in the hands of the Manx Motor Cycle Club, organization of the races was to revert back to the ACU under the auspices of ACU (Events) Ltd. Of more direct effect on fans seeking to watch from their favourite spots around the Mountain Course, was the introduction of a wide range of restrictions on where they could stand. This came about after a safety review, following an accident towards the end of the 2007 Senior race when a rider and two spectators were killed, and two marshals severely injured. The accident occurred

Spectators get an ultra-close view of high-speed racing at the end of the Cronk y Voddy Straight.

Old hands: top sidecar man Dave Molyneux (right) shares a joke with top solo rider John McGuinness.

at Joey's – the Twenty-sixth Milestone. Despite the imposition of those restrictions, there still remain many places where spectators can stand close the racing and so experience the high-speed thrills of TT-watching.

On the racing front, the second Supersport race returned to the programme for 2008, and the 125 and 250cc TT races were also reinstated. Rather diluting the news of the two-strokes' return was the fact that they would run over the 4¼-mile Billown Circuit in the south of the Island rather than over the Mountain Course. They would be part of Billown's customary Steam Packet Race meeting, run on the Saturday after the Senior TT.

THE YOUNG GUNS
A promotional theme at the 2008 TT went under the heading of 'Young Guns' and featured some of the star young riders contesting the event. The basis of the promotion was that their growing talents showed that the future of the TT was in good hands. Those included were Conor Cummins, William Dunlop, Martin Finnegan, James Hillier, Ian Hutchinson, Gary Johnson, Olie Linsdell and Guy Martin. Of course, 'Hutchie' had already won a TT and Guy Martin had come close to doing so.

Joining his brother William, a young Michael Dunlop rode his first TT in 2008. They were the sons of the late Robert Dunlop, himself a five-times TT winner.

All of the above would have been on high-class machines, but everyone's aim was to achieve a works ride. It was an age where most factories entrusted the preparation and management of their bikes to private entrants like TAS and HM Plant.

Honda had given much support to the TT down the years, but its level had fluctuated in recent times. This was probably caused more by budgetary constraints than a reduction in enthusiasm. In 2008 there were no official Honda works entries at the TT. It meant that John McGuinness was mounted on Padgett-supplied Hondas, which, he was assured, incorporated the best Honda Racing bits. Honda's decision not to support the 2008 TT meant that both Ian Hutchinson and Ian Lougher had to find alternative machinery. Hutchie joined Steve Plater at AIM Racing, where they would race Yamahas. Plater was back at the TT for a second year, having set the fastest-ever Newcomer's lap of 125.61mph in 2007, on an AIM R1 that was deliberately softer in engine and chassis tune than their normal British Superbike machine. Indications were that he would be on a sharper version for 2008.

An already strong sidecar class of established 'drivers' like Dave Molyneux, Nick Crowe, John Holden, Steve Norbury and former World Champion Klaus Klaffenbok were joined by three-times World Champion Tim Reeves. Between them they used a mix of Honda and Suzuki power units in Dave Molyneux Racing (DMR) and Louis Christian Racing (LCR) chassis. Like the solos, the sidecar men were keen to incorporate every new power-enhancing engine 'mods' that the regulations allowed. They also sought improvements in areas like the chassis, cooling, suspension, braking and streamlining.

NEW STARS
With solid previous TT placings, including a fine second in the 2006 Senior race, Cameron Donald probably missed out on being classified as a 'Young Gun' at twenty-nine years of age. However, the Australian was to be the star of the 2008 meeting, mounted on TAS Suzukis.

In the opening Superbike race he moved to the front on the fourth lap after earlier leader, Guy Martin (Honda), was forced to retire. Holding off a challenge from team mate Bruce Anstey, he rode to his first TT win, setting a new race average record of 126.82mph, with the fastest lap going to Guy Martin at a new record speed for the class of 129.54mph.

After the general record-breaking spree of 2007, it was perhaps not surprising that records in all other solo races remained intact in 2008. That is not to say the pace was slow, for 'Cam' Donald took his second win in the Superstock race at just 0.10mph below the record.

At thirty-five years of age, Steve Plater (Yamaha) was definitely too old to be considered a 'Young Gun', but his performances in 2008 justifiably saw him described as another new star of the Mountain Course. Putting in a stunning ride in the first Supersport race, he snatched victory at just below record pace, taking the win by 3½ seconds from John McGuinness (Honda), with another second-year man, Keith Amor (Honda), a further 8 seconds behind. The

second Supersport race, or to give it its full title, Relentless Supersport TT Race 2, went to Bruce Anstey on his gothic black-liveried 'Relentless by TAS Suzuki'. Bruce took the win from from Ian Hutchinson (Yamaha) and Ryan Farquhar (Kawasaki), setting a new lap record of 125.53mph. The four major Japanese manufacturers thus shared the podium placings across Supersport Races 1 and 2.

John McGuinness had won the Senior TT for the previous three years and he made it four in a row in 2008, taking his Padgett's Honda around at fractionally less than his own race average record pace to win from Cameron Donald and Ian Hutchinson. It was an action-packed race that saw the lead change several times. Early front man Bruce Anstey retired at the pits at the end of the second lap and his place as leader was taken by Cameron Donald. However, Cam's prospects of a hat-trick of wins in 2008 were thwarted when he was forced to ease the pace after

The massed-start racing on the Billown Circuit created close action. Here Chris Palmer leads Ian Lougher, Ryan Farquhar and Michael Dunlop into Castletown.

his Suzuki developed an oil leak. This was said to have been caused by repeated bottoming of the crankcases at the foot of Barregarrow. The win by John McGuinness was number fourteen and it put him into joint second place with Mike Hailwood in overall number of TT victories.

First place in both sidecar races went to Manxman Nick Crowe and, although he did not threaten his own lap record, he did set a new record race average speed in Race 1 at 114.37mph. Newcomer Tim Reeve showed his class with third and fifth places.

Down in the sunny south of the Island, a good entry delivered close racing over the Billown Circuit in the reinstated 125cc Ultra Lightweight TT and 250cc Lightweight TT. Chris Palmer won the former and Ian Lougher the latter. They were both Honda-mounted, as were the majority of the entry. There were other race meetings that still catered for the small two-strokes and there were enthusiastic owners and riders who continued to pursue their development, often at considerable expense.

Prize money in the Lightweight TT races, the overall result of which was decided by the best points total earned over two legs, was £900 to the winner of each leg and £1,300 to each overall winner, giving potential winnings of £3,100 for winning each race. By contrast, a start-to-finish winner of the Superbike or Senior TT races collected £22,000. That was a lot to race for, particularly as second place took a much-reduced £12,950. Supersport winners could earn £10,000 for the Lightweight TT, as could Sidecar winners. Top riders also relied on being paid substantial appearance/start money at the TT and for some, that money served to underpin their racing for the season.

TOO LONG

It was no secret that manufacturers, teams and many riders felt the two-week TT was too long. Indeed, the involvement was greater than two weeks for some of the teams with large transporters, for they had to cross to the Island in the week preceding the event and would not get away until into the week after it had finished. However, controller of the TT purse strings, the Isle of Man government, had no wish to reduce the timespan of the event, for that would see visitors staying for shorter periods and spending less.

John McGuinness tackles the flat-out right-hand bend at the end of the Bishopscourt Straight in 2009.

NOT ONLY THE RACERS

Competitors are not alone in seeking the thrill of speed over the TT course. For as long as the races have run, TT followers have sought to emulate the stars by riding the course at the greatest possible speed. Whether on belt-driven singles of yore or on the fully faired multis of the twenty-first century, for over a hundred years they have striven to copy the Mountain Course deeds of Harry Collier, Stanley Woods, Geoff Duke, Mike Hailwood, Joey Dunlop and John McGuinness. They do it with the roads open, dicing with each other and with everyday traffic, throwing caution to the winds as the speed bug bites and the only way they know to deal with it is to open the throttle wider.

Much of the riding over those years has been reckless, accidents have been plenty and fatalities not infrequent, but the majority survive and finish up with stories that they can tell their mates for years to come. Not surprisingly, in the telling, it sometimes becomes a case of 'the older I get the faster I was'.

2009: PUBLICITY

The organizers had done a good job of bringing the TT into the twenty-first century and their advance publicity for 2009 described it as 'The Greatest Show on Earth', while renowned motor sport commentator Murray Walker, who had links to the event stretching back over almost eighty years, called it 'The Greatest Motor-Sporting Event in the World'. Allied to such self-publicity, growing exposure was catching the imagination of the world at large and bringing more TT coverage, which also helped attract quality sponsorship of the event and its riders. Self-generating in a way, such increased publicity saw ever more people add the TT to their lists of things they must see. Some would make their pilgrimage as enthusiasts for the sport, often while strapped for cash, while others would take the easiest option to see this high-speed festival, being happy to pay whatever it cost to be part of the TT experience.

Many of the latter would be based around the Grandstand area, where everything was organized for them, while the former were more likely to seek out high-speed viewing points around the course. Unfortunately, the growth in restrictions on viewing points means that much of today's most exciting on-course action goes unseen.

The picture shown here illustrates the commitment required from those who ride to win at the TT. John McGuinness described the experience here with the words: 'You … get into top on the straight, then it goes left and right. Well that right-hander, you're a complete passenger … sat on a moving torpedo that's doing its own thing and you just have to let it do it'. He added, 'You're prob-

ably doing about 180, it's blind, you can't see through it'. McGuinness puts his life on the line here perhaps fifty times at each TT meeting during practice and racing, but the only people to see this supreme display of high-speed riding are nearby marshals, for spectators are now banned from the spot and even photographers, like Juan Cregeen, who took this shot, are no longer permitted there.

THE 'GREEN TT'

Among claims that the 'TT Festival' had a new look for 2009, one genuinely new event was a Time Trials Xtreme Grand Prix (TTXGP) race, for clean-emission race machines. This was described as 'providing an exciting opportunity for leading global innovators in racing and clean emission technologies to compete and prove to the world that being green does not mean being slow'. It was given the status of a genuine race for a Tourist Trophy, although it was to run over only one lap of the Mountain Course.

Seemingly there were not too many 'global innovators' wishing to take up the challenge, and after the small battery-powered field had done their lap, it was Rob Barber (Agni XO10) who was fastest at 87.43mph and thus headed the 'Best Buy Pro Class', while Chris Heath (Electric Motorsport) was first home in the 'Open Class'. Spectators were divided on the merit of the event, but just to remind everyone that the TT is a business, the Isle of Man government made a business-based decision that a place be made for the Green TT in future years.

HONDA

Honda may not have given direct works support to the TT in 2008, but the name was everywhere in 2009, in celebration of the fiftieth anniversary of the company's first competitive visit in 1959. However, the most important aspect of Honda's presence was that it came with increased support of the racing. Under the banner of HM Plant, John McGuinness and Steve Plater were down to contest the solo classes and Nick Crowe received engine support for his sidecar.

While the 2009 TT was not quite a Honda walkover, it gave the marque much cause for celebration, with wins and a multitude of new lap and race records. The biggest potential threat to Honda was seen as TAS Suzuki-mounted Cameron Donald, but after setting a blistering pace in early practice, he fell at Keppel Gate, damaged his shoulder and was out of the racing. There remained plenty of challengers, but Honda's John McGuinness took victory in the opening Superbike race, lifting the absolute race average speed to 127.99mph and the absolute lap record to 130.44mph. McGuinness was in control throughout, riding to his sig-

ABOVE: **Entries in TTXGP, like this MotoCzysz, carried a heavy battery load.**

LEFT: **Ian Hutchinson wheelies over the top of Creg Wyllies in 2009. A hundred years earlier, some riders had to get off and push their single-geared machines over the summit of this hill.**

Jenny Tinmouth is the fastest woman rider at the TT, having lapped at 119.95mph in 2010.

nalling boards and holding team mate Steve Plater at bay. He was followed by four more Hondas.

It was Ian Hutchinson's turn to fly the flag for Honda in the Superstock race, with a win and new lap record of 129.74mph. Staying with the big bikes, Steve Plater gave Honda yet another chance to celebrate with his victory in the Senior TT. Plater set a new absolute race record for the course of 128.27mph while John McGuinness rode to a new absolute lap record for the course of 131.57mph. Manxman Conor Cummins (Kawasaki) was second and Gary Johnson (Honda) third. The speedy McGuinness was denied a likely victory when his chain snapped leaving Ramsey on the fourth lap.

In Supersport Race 1, Ian Hutchinson (Honda) took the win at record-breaking pace with Bruce Anstey (Suzuki) raising the lap record to 126.54mph. Then, in only his second year at the TT and riding over damp roads in Supersport Race 2, Michael Dunlop (Yamaha) took the first of

many victories on his road to TT stardom. This was also the year in which Jenny Tinmouth took over from Maria Costello as the fastest woman racer around the Mountain Course, lapping at 116.48mph.

Sidecar Race A saw victory go to Dave Molyneux (Suzuki) after a challenging Nick Crowe (Honda) retired on the second lap. Far worse disaster was to befall Crowe and passenger Mark Cox in Sidecar Race B, when they collided with a hare on the approach to Ballaugh. The resultant crash inflicted injuries that ended their racing careers. Such was the scale of emergency support activity required at the scene that the race was abandoned.

Down at the Billown circuit, Ian Lougher gave Honda another two TT wins, beating the fastest lap of 2008 on his 125cc Ultra Lightweight and matching the 250cc lap speed on his Lightweight. When veteran Lougher opened his 2009 race week in the previous Saturday's Superbike TT, it had been his 100th TT start.

A NEAR MISS

Riding on the limit on the TT course means that, for much of the time, riders are only a moment away from disaster. The stretch from Ginger Hall to Ramsey has always been recognized as the bumpiest on the course and, at today's speeds, bikes are always fighting the rider for control. It was there that John McGuinness had a bigger than average 'moment'; in fact, it was close to a disaster. He recalled, 'There's a bit, slightly left and right by the Council Yard (Highways Depot) at Glen Duff. It looks nothing … but my 600 went lock-to-lock, big time. Smashed the clocks, bent the fairing stays, I ran over my feet and broke the brake lever.'

Such incidents are, literally, par for the course to those pushing the limits of their bikes' performance, because, as eleven-times TT winner and a man who always rode on the edge, Phillip McCallen said, 'You simply can't afford to ride well within your limits or you're going to be left behind.'

SAFETY

The concepts of safety and riding the TT course on the limit do not really go together, but the organizers put increasing effort into lessening the chance of a rider falling and also into dealing with the consequences should one do so.

Newcomers are encouraged to visit the Island as often as possible before racing. There they receive official support and tuition about riding the course, while being encouraged to fit in as many learning laps as possible. Away from the Island, many study videos of top riders and even play TT computer games in an attempt to glean knowledge. Come their first practice lap, they are guided around the course at speed, behind an experienced rider.

In further improvements to safety, the number of marshals and flag points were increased, with all marshals undertaking regular training in the job. Radio communications were extended with modern equipment. Medical support was available via helicopters, medics on the ground

There are twisty stretches on the Mountain Course requiring a knee-down style more often seen on short circuits. Here is Dan Stewart on the approach to Glen Helen in 2009.

This rider escaped injury when he tested the air-fencing at Ballacraine.

and from travelling marshals. Such facilities were as good as they could be made, and much money was invested in modern Reticell air-fencing on corners, which was better able to absorb impacts.

The organizers publicly acknowledge that the TT races are high risk, but do everything possible to manage the risk.

Mention is made above of Newcomers watching video laps to aid course-learning, but such is the unrelenting speed and commitment put into a lap by someone like John McGuinness that the picture it reveals could be discouraging to someone trying to find their way. However, for race followers who want to gain an impression of the speeds involved in TT racing, the constant changes of direction, the multiple places where bikes are airborne, the relative narrowness of the road in places, the uphill and downhill going, the lack of run-off, the frequent changes from light to dark and the constant crossing over white lines while cranked over – on-board videos offer an insight into what is involved. This is particularly so when accompanied by a soundtrack, for to hear the aural symphony as John

McGuinness seeks to keep his Fireblade delivering maximum revs, along with the associated upward and downward gear changes on a 130-plus mph lap, makes for an exciting 17-minute experience.

2010: NEWS AND NEWCOMERS

The swings and roundabouts of top road racers' fortunes were shown at the 2010 TT by the fact that Cameron Donald was fit again, but Steve Plater was injured. Otherwise, the recognized top runners were all present for what were the customary five solo races and two sidecar, plus the zero-emissions event. The latter was now called 'TT Zero' and a £10,000 prize was on offer for the first 100mph lap by a 'green' machine. The 125 and 250 Lightweight TT races, previously held at Billown, were dropped as TT events.

After being tried at the previous year's MGP, a 60km/h (37mph) limit was introduced in the pit lane, with time penalties imposed for speeding.

Pre-TT publicity told that good short circuit-riders like David Johnson, Dan Hegarty, Hudson Kennaugh, Dan

This is the way that Ian Hutchinson treated the course at Lezayre Church in 2010.

Cooper and Stephen Thompson were all hoping to make their TT debuts. Not all made it to the event, but it was indicative of the healthy interest being shown in the 'roads' from those racing the 'shorts'.

SPEEDS UP

Ian Hutchinson, a quiet-spoken thirty-year-old from Bingley, was in the form of his life at the 2010 TT. Showing his intention, his opening lap of practice was completed at over 129mph. Riding Padgett-supplied Hondas, 'Hutchie' carried his form into the races, achieving an unprecedented five victories across all solo classes. Not only that, but he broke race average or lap records – sometimes both – in almost all of them.

He warmed up with a win in the opening Superbike race at just below record pace, leaving Conor Cummins (Kawasaki) to set a new lap record of 131.51mph. Moving to the Superstock race, Hutchie grabbed the win with record-breaking race average and lap records of 128.10mph and 130.74mph. He won Supersport TT Race 1 at a record-breaking average speed, leaving Keith Amor (Honda) to break the lap record, and then repeated his winning ways in the second race, lifting the race average speed to 125.16mph, while Michael Dunlop (Yamaha) raised the lap record to 127.83mph.

With those four wins under his belt, Hutchinson came to the line on Senior race day with everyone asking if he could achieve an unprecedented fifth win in the week. The answer was yes, along with a new race average record of 128.60mph and the fastest lap of the race at 131.48mph, just 0.10mph slower than the absolute course record speed set by John McGuinness in 2009.

The complete dominance shown by Ian Hutchinson in 2010 is revealed by the list of names that filled the other podium places in the five solo races: Michael Dunlop, Cameron Donald, Guy Martin, Ryan Farquhar, Conor Cummins, Keith Amor and Bruce Anstey. A name missing from that list is John McGuinness. It was not a good year for McGuinness, who failed to finish two races and was restricted to fourth, fifth and seventh places in those he did complete.

As far as race wins were concerned, it seemed like almost a one-man show by Hutchie in 2010. However, on three wheels, Klaus Klaffenbok took a double victory at just under record pace, while in TT Zero, Mark Miller (MotoCzysz) gave an emphatic upward boost to electric-powered speeds, winning at 96.82mph, an increase of almost 10mph on the previous fastest.

TT Zero had echoes of the very first TT races, when competitors received a fixed amount of petrol and had to judge their pace to ensure that they had sufficient to complete the race. In 2010 it was limited battery output that meant that some riders had to restrict the speed at which they travelled on the flattish section of the course to Ramsey to ensure they had the power to cope with the Mountain climb and final downhill run to the finish. With a sound resembling a vacuum cleaner, TT Zero machines were beginning to impress with their speeds, but their race needed rather more participants than the nine starters and five finishers of 2010 if it was to grip the imagination of the thousands of watching petrolheads.

HUTCHIE

For all the bravado they show in racing over the Mountain Course at fantastic speeds, TT riders are only human. Ian Hutchinson said, when interviewed by Chris Moss after his five-wins-in-a-week 2010 TT, 'when you're coming down to the Creg on the last lap on the Friday, it's a relief to see the sea and know you're going back home on it'.

Hutchie was more than just a TT runner, for he also plied his trade as a professional motorcycle racer on the short circuits. Three months after his TT successes, he fell from his machine at Silverstone, was struck by another rider and sustained compound fractures to his left leg that were to prove a major setback to his racing career.

BALLAGAREY

Known to many as 'Ballascary', this fearsome wall-bound right hander before the drop into Glen Vine was in the news in 2010. It has always been a major test of courage, being taken at close to maximum speed. Back in 1938, Harold Daniell rode it 'full blast in top' during his record-breaking Senior win. Some twenty years later, multi-winner John Surtees described it as 'one of the most difficult to get right on the TT course'. Another thirty years on and Ray Knight said it was the only spot between Union Mills and Greeba Castle where a rider 'should allow any slack in the throttle wire'. In that same era, Steve Hislop reckoned to go through in top on a 600, but told how he hooked it back a gear on the big bike, enabling him to hold a tighter line. Today, John McGuinness approaches it 'mega flat out in sixth', before dropping into fifth.

The demanding nature of Ballagarey was shown in 2010 when, in Supersport Race 2, which was postponed until Thursday, the experienced Paul Dobbs fell there and was killed. The day after Dobbs' death, Guy Martin, a rider rarely out of the news, lost control there while challenging for the lead in the Senior race. In the ensuing 'off', which he rated a 170mph one, bike and rider disappeared in a fireball and everyone feared the worst. But, in the lottery that results from a high-speed fall on the TT course, Martin escaped with minor injuries. He did receive a whole lot of extra publicity, however, for film of the incident received worldwide viewing via the internet.

Before his accident at Ballagarey in 2010, Guy Martin powers his way down the Mountain.

2011: CENTENARY OF THE MOUNTAIN COURSE

The vision shown by the early TT organizers in moving racing to the more demanding Mountain Course in 1911 was responsible for pushing motorcycle design and developing reliability in the century that followed. In 2011, manufacturers were still using the same challenging circuit as a test-bed to prove their ideas, while competitors needed ever-increasing skills and courage to race 200-plus bhp machines over its 37¾ miles.

The centenary offered another publicity opportunity for the TT, with same-day transmissions of the racing increasing worldwide and ever more documentaries being made. All contributed to growth in interest and served to increase the number of visiting spectators.

It was a year in which several riders swapped saddles. A still-injured Ian Hutchinson signed for a Yamaha ride with SMR Racing, and Bruce Anstey moved to Padgetts Honda.

The latter were also to supply John McGuinness with a Supersport bike, while he rode a Superbike for the Honda TT Legends team, along with Keith Amor. Guy Martin moved to TAS Suzuki, while nurturing a growing career in television, and among Newcomers was British Super Bike star Simon Andrews. Regrettably, Ian Hutchinson's enduring injuries prevented him from actually contesting the TT in 2011 and past winner Steve Plater was no longer racing.

BMW had burst onto the world Superbike scene a couple of years earlier with their 4-cylinder S1000RR. A handful appeared at the TT in 2010 and twelve were entered in the 2011 Superbike race, making up some 15 per cent of the entry. With a claimed output of 193bhp straight from the showroom, no one doubted their straight-line speed. Keith Amor was timed at 189mph on one at Sulby in 2010 in the Superstock TT, but they were still to show that they were a threat over the Mountain Course. None of the top fifteen seeded riders were BMW-mounted.

Manxman Conor Cummins was among the fastest riders at the 2010 TT but suffered a setback to his career after a heavy fall at the Verandah during the Senior race. Here he puts on the power and the style as he leaves Ramsey on his McAdoo Racing Kawasaki.

In that same 2011 Superbike race there were eighteen Hondas entered, seventeen Kawasakis, fourteen Suzukis, nine Yamahas and one each of Ducati and Aprilia. Gone were the days when big Kawasakis had to be withdrawn because they did not handle over the Mountain Course. Now they were challenging for victory.

While the BMWs would have been virtually new bikes, the others would have been of mixed ages and specifications, for not everyone could afford new race machinery. In truth, even works bikes were unlikely to be new, because those built to race the 'roads' did a comparatively small racing mileage each year. Being so strongly built, after a winter overhaul and once fitted with the latest upgrades, they were ready for another season's competition.

TT SUPERBIKES

Back in the year 2000, David Jefferies set a new absolute lap record of 125.69mph on his Yamaha when winning the Senior TT. A decade later, and fastest lap in 2010 went to Conor Cummins (Kawasaki) in the Superbike race at 131.51mph, fractionally under John McGuinness' absolute lap record of 131.58mph, set on a Honda in 2009. The almost 6mph growth in lap record speed during this decade was twice that of the previous one and came from engines delivering outputs that had increased from c170bhp in 2000 to over 200bhp.

Contesting the TT was a fiercely competitive business, and while the machines brought to the event might still be referred to by the stock reference of Fireblade, GSX-R1000, ZX-10 and so on, apart from engine, transmission and major frame components, very little of the original bike remained after preparation as a top TT race bike. Among items changed would be forks, steering damper, rear shock, wheels, brake discs, calipers, master cylinders and hoses, radiator(s), oil-cooler, handlebars and clamps, clutch, exhaust system, chain, sprockets, quick-shift, fuel tank, fairing, seat, tyres, battery and all electrics/electronics. The replacement items would be the best that money could buy – or that the team could afford. Sometimes the best, say the suspension, came with a hidden cost, because it could be so 'trick' that it needed a specialist to get the best out of it. Today's suspension is five-way adjustable, with main elements like compression and rebound adjustments each having something like thirty-two settings. While most teams make use of the support of manufacturers' representatives in areas like suspension, they learned to be wary of getting out of their depth with too much adjustability, even though they and their riders recognized the supreme importance of achieving high-speed stability over the Mountain Course.

Where engines are concerned, all go through the hands

Derek Huxley fine-tunes a Jackson Racing Honda via his laptop.

of specialist tuners, who apply their blueprinting skills and bring specialized knowledge to traditional areas like pistons, valves, springs, porting and so on, with the aim of lifting output. Overriding the importance of those will be the correct application of the electronics package used. This is another area that can be both hugely expensive and difficult to get the best out of if too complicated. It usually needs a specialist within the team to use it to full advantage.

Before the introduction of electronic control, areas like ignition and carburation operated in a compromise mode. The restrictive effect of that would have been more pronounced at low revolutions, for the limited settings of which they were capable were generally utilized in gaining the best use of a racing engine's potential at full power. Philip Neill, of TAS Suzuki, explained how the use of modern electronics 'allow you to use finer increments of change'. Correctly applied, you could now achieve optimum performance throughout the engine's rev range by the precise tailoring of ignition and fuelling settings. Such refinement and control is what everyone strives to achieve from their electronic packages.

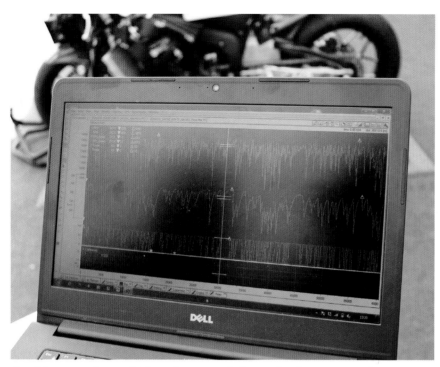

On this screen is overlaid performance information for two members of the same team, so enabling the team manager to spot strengths and weaknesses at particular points on the course.

The use of electronics extended to other areas, and by incorporating a GPS data-logging system, teams could see what a bike was doing at every point on the course rather than relying on riders to remember details such as the revs and gears they used at a particular corner. How much information was available depended upon the number of sensors fitted, and it was only accessible when the bike returned to the pits. It could take time to interpret and the resulting alterations to set-up might have to be varied for each rider in a team to suit their different riding styles.

Superbikes were still purpose-built for the demands of the TT course, but they were very close to those prepared for use in British Super Bike racing, perhaps sacrificing 10bhp at the top end to gain a little more performance in the mid-range. With few major changes to the course during the previous decade and with tyres easily able to last two laps, most of the increase in lap speeds at the TT since 2000 had come from faster bikes. While developments across all areas of the machine would have played their part in giving more speed, it was refined electronics that made the biggest contribution to increased performance. That may not mean greatly increased maximum speeds, it being more the case that the faster laps come from improved rideability and more efficient power delivery throughout the rev range.

RACING AND SPEEDS

Having written above about increases in power and speed, the only record broken during racing at the 2011 TT was in the opening Superbike race, where winner John McGuinness (Honda) raised the race average speed to a new high of 127.87mph. McGuinness also won the Senior race at slightly faster speed but below the Senior's records. Other Honda wins went to Bruce Anstey in Supersport Race 1 and Gary Johnson in Race 2, while Michael Dunlop rode a Kawasaki to win the Superstock TT.

In the sidecar races, Klaus Klaffenbok took Race A and John Holden Race B, while in TT Zero the seventeen entries saw nine starters and five finishers. Michael Rutter led the latter home on a Segway MotoCzysz at 99.60mph. Michael and the MotoCzysz were timed at an impressive 149.45mph at Sulby, with the fastest 'normal' solo being Michael Dunlop (Kawasaki) at 195.6mph and the fastest sidecar 145mph.

2012: LIGHTWEIGHT TT

A familiar race title returned to use in 2012, when the name Lightweight TT was applied to a new race, for bikes of 'Super Twin' specification. That really meant 650cc four-stroke, twin-cylinder machines based upon production models produced by Kawasaki and Suzuki, with engines boosted from a standard 70bhp to over 90, giving a top speed of 150mph. Already well established at other venues, particularly on the Irish road circuits, it would be run over three laps and, hopefully, would add interest to the race programme.

NEWS

Most of the familiar faces were back at the TT for 2012 and there were also entries from Newcomers such as Jamie Hamilton, Jimmie Storrar, Lee Johnston and Karl Harris. Young Lee Johnston said, 'the Isle of Man TT is the biggest and best road race in the world', while established star of the short circuits, Karl Harris, claimed he was taking to the roads to broaden his racing career.

An article in the TT programme surveyed the fitness level of riders. While the super-slim claimed to expend much energy on training, John McGuinness and Michael

The Norton team transporter in the TT Paddock.

Dunlop explained their more substantial physiques by saying 'they were not built for the gym'.

After a less than successful return to the TT a couple of years previously, Norton were back in 2012 with 2011 TT Privateer Champion, Ian Mackman, entered on their Aprilia-engined machine in the Senior race. The team certainly looked the part of serious contenders.

SAME AGAIN

As in 2011, the only record broken in 2012 was by John McGuinness, when riding to victory in the opening Superbike race, where he lifted the race average speed to 128.08mph. Perhaps indicating how difficult it was getting to go faster around the Mountain Course, McGuinness' record represented a reduction of just 10 hard-earned seconds in the overall time it took him to complete the six-lap, 226-mile race distance.

The remaining solo and sidecar races were all run at below record pace, some suffering postponements due to poor weather conditions. Those poor conditions extended to the customary Senior race day, Friday, and so its scheduled races were postponed until Saturday. With less than perfect conditions prevailing, the races were delayed through Saturday until, eventually, runners in the new Lightweight race were despatched at 6.30pm. Ryan Farquhar took victory in the mixed conditions, lapping at a healthy 115mph.

Then, in an unwanted first for the Tourist Trophy meeting, the decision was taken to abandon the Senior race without a wheel being turned. Officials had made inspection laps in cars accompanied by top riders and the joint opinion was that the 220bhp bikes would be impossible to race on slick tyres over the mixed wet and dry conditions of the Mountain Course. No other tyre was available to suit the mixed conditions.

The abandonment of the Senior TT was a disaster for all concerned. The organizers had taken a stance against racing in totally wet conditions some years previously. Since then the manufacturers had continued to increase the power of the machines from which the racers were derived, and tyre manufacturers developed ever more specialized tyres for use in the dry. The Mountain Course was renowned for its mixed conditions, but machine and tyre development for the Superbike and Senior races had reached a stage where they could not cope with them.

There seemed to be no way out of the dilemma and, given the changeable Manx weather, most recognized that the same situation will almost certainly happen again. Had sidecars been faced with the same scenario, they also would not have been able to run due to lack of suitable tyres. That meant with Superbike, Senior and both Sidecar races unable to run in mixed wet and dry track conditions, 50 per cent of the race programme was at risk. Riders' views clearly had to be respected on the issue of what the Superbikes could and could not do, but spectators were aware that 1000cc Superstock bikes, from which the Senior/Superbikes were derived, were lapping at only 1mph less on road-legal tyres.

Prior to the gloom cast by the abandonment of the Senior, the ten starters in the 2012 TT Zero had hummed around for their one-lap race. For the first time, John McGuinness had a ride in the class on a costly Mugen Shinden. However, Michael Rutter headed the four survivors home for the second year, with McGuinness in second place. Proving that this was the class where speeds were increasing, Rutter broke the 100mph barrier, earning the £10,000 bonus, and added 4 per cent to his previous best lap time, finishing with a speed of 104.06mph.

2013: THE COURSE

There were no major changes to the course for 2013, apart from it being subject to the usual cycle of repairs, where some stretches were relaid with super-smooth black-top, whilst others were surface-dressed with chippings. The former reduced rolling resistance and sped bikes on their way, while the latter increased it and slowed them. It is doubtful if the effects could be measured, although the smooth stretches, particularly if incorporating bends, probably gave riders increased confidence.

There were two new course-related items for spectators to get used to, and they were the application of names to two previously untitled bends. The right-hand sweep at the end of the Cronk y Voddy straight became Molyneux's, in honour of sixteen-times sidecar winner Dave Molyneux, while the left- and right-handers after the Twelfth Milestone, soon after Handley's, became McGuinness's, named after nineteen-times solo winner John McGuinness.

A few years before, McGuinness had revealed that those bends and the following straight were among his favourite spots on the course. Earlier stars, such as Peter and Charlie

John McGuinness (Honda, no. 3), Cameron Donald (Honda, no. 2) and James Hillier (Kawasaki, no. 1) in close company as they tackle the Mountain climb in 2013. The blue numbers on a white background indicate that they were riding 600cc Supersport machines.

Honda-riding Michael Dunlop was man of the meeting at the 2013 TT.

Williams, had told how working at those same bends gave them extra speed on the straight stretch leading to the top of Barregarrow, and John McGuinness agreed: 'It's little bits of the course like that – no one pays them much attention, but you can make up so much time if the bike's well set up, just by keeping up the speed.' As the time differential between winners and placemen was often close, attention to such detail could decide the outcome of a race.

THE RIDERS

Honda gave support to John McGuinness, Michael Dunlop and Michael Rutter under the Honda TT Legends banner for the Superbike and Senior races in 2013, while also assisting Simon Andrew, riding for Honda RAF Reserves Racing. Padgetts supplied McGuinness with Hondas for the other races and Michael Dunlop rode under his own MD Racing. Guy Martin was riding for Tyco Suzuki, previously called TAS Suzuki, and they also provided machinery for Newcomer Josh Brookes. He was an established star of the short-circuit scene and, arguably, the highest profile

one to tackle the TT in the current era. William Dunlop and Conor Cummins were fielded by Milwaukee Yamaha, while of interest in the Supersport race was the 675cc MV Agusta entered by ValMoto for rider Gary Johnson. In the second year of the Lightweight TT for 650 twins, David Johnson was entered on a Chinese-made WK650i, while Splitlath Redmond racing had the Chinese rider Cheung Wai On entered to ride their Kawasaki. Regrettably, complications with Ian Hutchinson's injuries from Silverstone in 2010 still prevented him riding the 2013 TT.

DUNLOP'S YEAR

The Dunlop name had a proud TT heritage and in 2013 it was young Michael Dunlop who kept the name at the forefront of the event, riding a Honda to victory and records in four races. Winning the Superbike, Superstock and both Supersport races, he arrived at the last day of racing with entries in the Lightweight and Senior TT. Deciding not to start the Lightweight, he concentrated his efforts on the Blue Riband Senior in an attempt to gain his fifth win of the week and thus match Ian Hutchinson's record of 2010. But it was the man who had made the Senior race his own in recent years, John McGuinness, who took yet another victory in 2013 and Dunlop had to settle for second place, 10 seconds in arrears. Bruce Anstey (Honda) was third and set the fastest lap of the race at 131.53mph, just fractionally under the absolute course lap record of 131.67mph, set by John McGuinness on his Superbike in the opening race of the week.

James Hillier took his first TT win in the new Lightweight race, while Michael Rutter (MotoCzysz) took another win in TT Zero, with John McGuinness (Mugen) less than 2 seconds behind. Rutter again raised the lap record by 5 per cent, leaving it at 109.68mph. There were eight finishers from ten starters, but the lap times of the last two were some 35mph slower than the winner.

The race average record for the sidecars had remained unbroken since 2009 and their lap record since 2007. The race regulations limited what changes could be made to their 600cc engines, and in 2013 the winning speeds of Tim Reeves and Ben Birchall were below record pace.

SPEEDS

Lap speeds of the 1000cc Superbikes grew from 125.69mph to 131.67mph between 2000 and 2013, representing an increase of 4.75 per cent in a period when output increased by just over 10 per cent, to approximately 220bhp. The speeds for 600cc Supersports went from 121.15mph to 128.68mph, an increase of 6.22 per cent, with their outputs increasing to 140bhp.

When looking for the fastest lap in a TT race, it is worth remembering that only the final one is a true flying lap. All the others are either standing start laps, like the first one and those after pit stops, or slowing down for refuelling laps. While the flying lap should offer the best opportunity of the fastest lap, for by then riders are well accustomed to course conditions and have a light fuel load, it does not always happen. This is particularly so if a rider has established a good lead, for he can then ride his last lap at a controlled pace, checking the time gap to his nearest opponent by way of his signalling boards. Many fastest laps are set early in a race, when riders are trying to establish a position at the front.

FUEL CONSUMPTION

Competitors usually try to gain an idea of fuel consumption during practice, but many find that it increases when they use the throttle harder under race conditions. Indeed, the number of top riders who have run out of fuel and lost a TT win is legion.

During the first two years running of the event (1907 and 1908) riders received a fixed allocation of fuel and their consumption figures were published. Chapter 1 told how winner of the Singles race in 1907, Charlie Collier, used fuel at the rate of 94.5mpg and winner of the race for Multis, Rem Fowler, averaged 87mpg.

By the mid-1930s, British single-cylinder machines refuelled just once in their seven-lap, and 264-mile races, using fuel at about 30–35mpg. Post-war multis were much thirstier, as were the two-strokes that followed.

Today, the race regulations restrict fuel-tank capacity to 24 litres, which equates to 5¼ gallons. This is, usually, just enough to complete two laps of racing before refuelling is required and gives a fuel consumption figure of approximately 15mpg.

TT GETS TOUGHER

The moment riders unleash the 220bhp of a Superbike around the TT course they are taking their lives in their hands. All know that they need every ounce of control and so recognize the need to show respect to other riders while riding in close company and when passing. But the often small time differentials between first and second place, the increased presence of short-circuit specialists, the riches to be won and just the overall pressure to win, saw tougher tactics coming into use on the course.

The organizers were selective in accepting entries and qualifying standards were based upon a percentage allowance over the average speed set by the fastest three riders in a class. However, there were big speed differences between top riders and those lower down the order, and the fast men were increasingly bullying their way past. It was a cause for regret for older riders like John McGuinness, but the newer stars took it for granted. Such tactics would certainly create worrying moments for those being passed, and it takes a degree of bravery to race with the really fast riders. Rising star Ivan Lintin remarked, 'the likes of Anstey and McGuinness will not give you any slack if you are paddling around – they will scare the living daylights out of you'. For his part, Bruce Anstey commented, 'catching a slower rider can cost you between ½ and 4 seconds'.

SET-UP

Electronic control packages now dealt with the set-up of engine performance, while another important area that riders spent much of practice getting right was suspension, front and rear. With components that allowed ever more adjustments, most teams relied on the support of specialists from firms like Ohlin and K-Tec to help get their settings right.

The experienced David Paredes (62) about to be passed at the 'K-Tree' by hard-chargers John McGuinness, Michael Dunlop and Cameron Donald in the 2013 Superbike TT.

Watching riders on a fast corner reveals those who have their suspension set up correctly, for they go round rock steady, while those without the correct adjustment are noticeably less stable. Something else to be observed is that some riders who are steady on the first lap will then lose that stability later in the race, as their suspension 'overheats' and loses performance. Those who pay the most for their suspension hope to avoid that failing.

Specialist support extends to other areas, for with every competitor wanting the bike tuned to suit their own riding style, areas like braking also benefit from the attention of

experts. Some riders like maximum stopping to be applied as soon as they touch the lever, while others seek progressive action. There are firms involved in developing brake calipers, pads, hoses and levers, who are capable of tuning each element to suit individual riders' styles.

2014: ANOTHER DUNLOP YEAR

Perhaps the biggest news on the run-up to the 2014 TT was that Michael Dunlop switched from riding Hondas to BMW S1000RR models in the Superbike, Superstock and Senior TTs. He remained on Hondas for the Supersport

At over 150mph through the bottom of Barregarrow, suspension is given its ultimate test. An airborne Conor Cummins shows (above) his suspension at maximum extension. A few yards later and (next page) it is on maximum compression, with the belly-pan about to scrape the road.

races. Ready to challenge the established names were rising TT stars James Hillier, Dean Harrison and Ivan Lintin, with hot-shot from the short circuits, Peter Hickman, about to make his TT debut on a BMW. Taking things very seriously, Hickman completed seventy learning laps of the course in a car on visits to the Island between January and April, plus many viewings of onboard video laps.

Changing his big bikes made no difference to Michael Dunlop's winning ways and 2014 saw him take another four wins in the week – Superbike, Superstock, Supersport Race 2 and Senior TT. Still only twenty-six years of age, Dunlop had started his TT winning ways on 600s and was now undoubted master of the 1000s. Nudging record speeds in all races, he broke the Senior TT lap record, raising it to

131.66mph. That was a little below the latest absolute lap record, set earlier in the week in the Superbike race by Bruce Anstey, who became the fastest around the course at 132.29mph.

Peter Hickman set the fastest lap ever by a Newcomer when he recorded 129.10mph on his way to eleventh place in the Senior, where nearly men Conor Cummins (Honda) finished second and Guy Martin (Suzuki) was third. It was a reversal of their finishing positions in the Superbike race.

Michael Dunlop's BMW wins were well publicized by the German factory, and they made much of the 'fact' that it was the first BMW win since Georg Meier's in 1939, which, conveniently, made it a seventy-fifth anniversary event. While it was certainly their first Senior TT win since

1939, for some reason they chose to ignore Helmut Dahne and Hans-Otto Butenuth's Production TT win of 1976 and Dave Morris's three BMW wins in the Singles TT in the period 1997–9.

Dunlop's performance had shown what a BMW could do at the TT, bringing the marque from the lower leader board placings, achieved by others on the S1000RR in the previous few years, to the top step of the podium. The only 'petrol' solo races not won by him in 2014 were the Super-sport Race 1, which went to Gary Johnson on a Triumph by a winning margin of just over a second from Bruce Anstey (Honda); and the Lightweight TT, where Dean Harrison (Kawasaki) took his first TT win. In one of those occasions loved by TT 'anoraks', the Sidecar A victory by Conrad Harrison (Honda) earlier in the week meant that he and

Dean were the first father and son to win in the same year. Dave Molyneux took Sidecar B and gave Kawasaki power its first win in the class.

John McGuinness came to the TT with a wrist injury that restricted him from riding with his customary vigour. However, he did achieve a win in TT Zero on his Mugen Shinden, lifting the lap record by an impressive 8mph to 117.36 and heading home the six finishers from nine starters.

ADVERTISING

A TT win always generated publicity from suppliers of components used on winning machines, usually the providers of tyres, brakes, chains and oil. After Bruce Anstey's record-breaking lap of 132.29mph in 2014, another concern to

One area where technology has not changed is in the mid-race refuelling process, where everyone uses the same basic gravity fillers. Here, the experienced Dan Stewart lets his crew get on with it in 2014.

take a full-page advertisement in the motorcycle press was HM Quickshifter. They claimed to offer 'revolutionary seamless shift technology with its clear performance benefits and overall enhanced ride experience'. The changing of gears had come a long way from the tank-mounted, hand-operated lever, via the positive-stop foot change and the first electrically assisted quick-shift to 'seamless' electronics. As in all areas, the latter may have represented the latest technology, but it would continue to be refined.

HOW LONG IS THE MOUNTAIN COURSE?

In working out lap times and speeds, it is crucial that the figure used for the lap distance is accurate. There are many who consider that the straightening of bends over a period of 100 years must have reduced the distance around the Mountain Course and it is a topic that has been subject to much debate.

From 1911 to 1914 the lap length was given as 37½ miles. The distance of 37¾ miles was first used in 1920, when the course was extended from Cronk ny Mona to include Signpost Corner, Governor's Bridge and Glencrutchery Road. The organizers' 'General Conditions for the International 1920 Auto-Cycle Tourist Trophy Races' described it as 37 miles and 6 furlongs, which equals 37¾ miles, a figure that seemed generally accepted.

Perhaps not everyone did accept it, though, for in its issue of 12 April 1923, *The Motor Cycle* said, 'The TT Course is to be measured accurately: to do this it will be necessary to employ a revolution counter attached to the sidecar wheel of an outfit driven slowly.' The figure that resulted was 37 miles and 1,299 yards. As ¾ mile is 1,320 yards, they obviously thought the course was 21 yards short of a full 37¾ miles. But did the sidecar take a central line or a racing line, and is a three-wheeler's racing line the same as a two-wheeler's?

From 1923 the organizers used a figure of 37 miles 1,300 yards and a speed/distance table was published based upon this, quoting an equivalent lap distance of 37.739 miles. After another official measure in 1937 it was declared to be 37 miles 1,291 yards, or 37.733 miles; the ACU used the figure of 37 miles 1,290⅔ yards to calculate lap times in the pre-war period, which they said was 37.733 miles. The race regulations for 1937 settled for 37 miles 1,290 yards.

Presumably there was more agitation over lap distance in the early 1950s, for assisted by TT winner Fergus Anderson, *The Motor Cycle* measured it in 1954 using a Smith's Instruments wheel-revolution counter and came up with a figure of 37.449 miles, which equates to 37 miles and 790 yards. So was it really some 500 yards shorter than in pre-war days?

It was the turn of *Motorcycle News* to have a measure before the 1978 TT. The method used was not declared, but its result of 37.195 miles (37 miles 343 yards) was. It seemed perfectly happy with its figure, which showed that getting on for 1,000 yards had disappeared since 1920, although the race organizers seemed equally content to continue calculating lap times based on 37.733 miles, as it had done for many years.

The next record of the course being measured comes from the centenary year of 2007, when Alex Coward, a veteran cyclist and official course measurer for Manx cycle trials, was asked to ride a lap and establish a figure. The line he took was generally 1 yard out from the left-hand kerb, with just the occasional cutting of a corner. After several hours of pedalling, Alex came up with a distance of 37.7224 miles, which is just 17½ yards (52.8ft was the actual figure quoted) short of the official 37.73 miles given in the current regulations for the race, although it is now shown in its metric equivalent, 60.70km.

The power put down by modern bikes sees them wheel-spinning under full throttle even in the dry, and they also spend more time than in the past with their wheels off the ground over bumps. So might those factors affect any conventional on-board recorded lap distances? Furthermore, do all riders cover the same distance, for the 'racing line' of tyre marks on bends can be 6 to 8 feet wide, which begs the question, do the fastest riders take the tightest line (and thus the shortest lap distance) or does their greater speed through corners mean they take the widest? So the questions go on. Perhaps after a century of use and in this age of on-bike GPS and data-logging, it should be possible to get a precise figure of distance covered. But what if the course is shorter than is officially stated, will TT fans be happy if current lap speeds are 'corrected' to sub-130mph figures?

2015: SPEEDS

In 2015 top riders were reaching 196mph on Sulby Straight. They had been nudging that figure for several years and people were beginning to think that 200mph was possible, a speed already reached on a longer straight at the North West 200. Also, Bruce Anstey's outright lap record speed of 132.29mph was completed in 17 minutes 6.6 seconds, so there was talk of a rider getting into the 'sixteens'. Former TT winner Nick Jefferies, thinking back to his early days, said in 2015, 'the speed increases of the bikes – it's mind-blowing'.

Over the winter of 2014–15, works of resurfacing and reprofiling were carried out on the bends at Keppel Gate and the results were expected to benefit the racers.

Wide of the 'racing line' and out on the loose stuff, this rider throws up chippings with his rear wheel as he exits Ballaugh.

IN THE NEWS AGAIN

Having ridden to four wins in 2013 on Hondas and another four wins in 2014 on a mix of BMWs and Hondas, the ever-restless Michael Dunlop came to the 2015 event on Milwaukee Yamahas. However, early in practice he decided that the new Yamahas were not for him, so he put out a call to his 2014 BMW winning team for help and they obliged with bikes for the three big races, while he located Hondas for the Supersport races. It was a headline-grabbing move, for no one could remember a top rider taking such action during practice.

Michael Dunlop's brother William seemed happy on his Yamahas, hitting over 170mph on Sulby Straight on his 600cc R6. However, he then crashed at Laurel Bank during practice and damaged his ribs, putting himself out of the racing. Michael stopped at the incident and helped carry the stretcher taking William to the rescue helicopter. If that was not newsworthy enough, Michael then tangled with another rider at the Nook on the last lap of the opening Superbike race, fell from his machine and was injured. Although he played down the seriousness of his injury, it affected his performances in the remaining races. Despite that, in a courageous ride, he set his fastest ever lap of the course in the Senior at 132.51mph, but his injuries meant that he could not maintain the pace and he finished in fifth position.

COMPROMISES

Long-established motorcycle dealers Padgetts supplied Hondas to two top runners in 2015 – John McGuinness and Bruce Anstey. However, unlike many teams, they did not believe in using on-bike data-logging, relying instead on feedback from their riders. The company was vastly experienced at the TT and knew the importance of getting the chassis and suspension right while building a strong motorcycle to cope with the rigours of the Mountain Course. But Clive Padgett explained, 'everything's a compromise on bike set-up – brakes, chassis, suspension, gearing – you have to work out where the biggest gain might be in your compromises'.

It was a time when road machines were being fitted with ever more electronics offering riders multi-modes to control the performance of engine, suspension and other features. Along with claiming 197bhp at 13,000rpm, Kawasaki's advertisement for its latest road-going ZX-10R mentioned three riding modes, five levels of traction control, ABS, quickshifter, wheelie control and launch control. By contrast, the TT regulations did not permit 'traction control,

Conor Cummins (Honda) stares into the setting sun as he tops Crosby Hill during evening practice in 2015.

launch control, anti-wheelie, closed-loop engine braking, corner-by-corner/distance-based adjustments, competitor adjusted trims'. A mode switch covering fuel and ignition settings was allowed, plus on-board data-logging, but no associated bike-to-pits telemetry was permitted.

SPEEDS OF 130MPH-PLUS

From being an elusive barrier, 130mph lap speeds had now become almost the norm for top runners in the Superbike and Senior races, with Superstocks not far behind. For many ordinary motorcyclists, even briefly reaching a speed of 130mph would be special, but the very best TT riders now expect to average that figure for the entire 226 miles of a six-lap race. They may not always look it, but in motor-

cycling terms those riders really are supermen and speed is what they live by.

Time was lost during practice week in 2015 due to adverse weather, but in improved conditions, Bruce Anstey opened race week with a win, taking his Honda CBR1000RR Superbike to victory at exactly the same race average speed – 128.75mph – as Michael Dunlop achieved during his winning ride in 2013. Anstey also set the fastest lap at 131.78mph, which was just under his own record of 132.29mph from 2014. The middle of the week belonged to a back-to-form Ian Hutchinson, who took three victories – Superstock and Supersport Races 1 and 2. His wins were at slightly under record pace, using a Kawasaki in Superstock and Yamaha in Supersport. Ivan Lintin broke race and lap

The number 1 rider and machine in the 2015 Senior TT, John McGuinness leans into Ballacraine on his Honda Fireblade.

records on his Kawasaki in winning the Lightweight race, with speeds of 119.93mph and 120.84mph. A few riders were being penalized for exceeding the speed limit in the pit lane, and Ryan Farquhar lost any chance of victory in the Lightweight race when he was hit with a 30-second penalty for speeding.

The Birchall brothers rode to victory in Sidecar Races A and B, setting a new race average record of 116.26mph, while Dave Molyneux set the fastest lap in both races, finishing with a new record speed of 116.785mph in Race B, just 7 seconds behind the winners.

John McGuinness did not have the best of TTs in 2015, although he did win TT Zero, raising the lap record to 119.27mph, to head home six finishers from nine starters. His Mugen Shinden team mate Bruce Anstey finished in second place. Now forty-three years of age, family man McGuinness admitted to nervousness each time he took to the Mountain Course, and when he lined up for the Senior race in his customary number 1 position, he was very aware of the strength of challenge from the younger riders behind him.

Unfortunately, the Senior race was red-flagged on the second lap after an accident to Jamie Hamilton on the drop to the Eleventh Milestone. It was a spot where thirty years ago the front went a little light on a downhill hump, but in 2015, on very much more powerful bikes, riders found their front wheels reaching for the air and had to work for control.

The Senior race was shortened to four laps and restarted. John McGuinness again gave his clutch the ultimate test, with searing acceleration off the line. At the end of the first lap he led Ian Hutchinson by just 1 second, but when he pitted for his fuel stop at the end of the second lap, he was 11 seconds up, for Hutchie lost time by overshooting Signpost Corner. With his usual slick pit stop, McGuinness went out to build on his lead, coming home victorious at a new record race average speed of 130.48mph and a new absolute lap record of 132.70mph. Second place went to James Hillier (Kawasaki) some 14 seconds behind, with Ian Hutchinson third, a further 6 seconds in arrears. On the second lap, eleven riders lapped at over 130mph.

Just part of the stock of Metzeler tyres brought to the 2016 TT – among them are slicks, treaded and wets.

It was an emotional John McGuinness who embraced his family after the Senior race. Drained after a fortnight of high-speed riding around the Mountain Course and all the associated demands made on his time as a top TT rider, he knew that his status had been under challenge. But he had dug deep to achieve his victory and had equalled Mike Hailwood's record of seven Senior TT wins. McGuinness knew his Honda was not the fastest bike on the track for it was an ageing model, but he gained huge satisfaction from his 2015 Senior TT win at record speeds, rating it as one of his finest victories.

So ended a weather-hit TT meeting that was attended by 42,000 visitors over the two-week period, an increase over previous years. More visitors was what the Island was seeking to achieve, for it meant more money into the Manx coffers, but TT enthusiasts noted a change in visitor profile, with some of the newer ones seeming to be there for the occasion rather than the racing.

2016: NEWS

Amidst the hustle and bustle of preparations for the TT challenge came a reminder that racing motorcycles could be a cruel sport. Two young men who had shown their talents with wins at the 2015 MGP, Billy Redmayne and Malachi Mitchell-Thomas, had entries for the 2016 TT, but both were killed in pre-TT race meetings – Redmayne at Scarborough and Mitchell-Thomas at the North West 200.

As ever, racing went on. There were minor changes to the Supersport regulations to bring them in line with

events at World level, while sidecar regulations were eased in respect of chassis and streamlining, with the aim of promoting development. The second sidecar race was moved from Wednesday to Friday of race week and the Lightweight race took the Wednesday slot. The Isle of Man government was looking for an external promoter to take over the organizing of the TT and to grow the event, so bringing more money into the Manx Exchequer.

There was the usual publicity about tyres, with several makers telling how they had spent the winter testing their latest ideas and Avon claiming to have been working on 'development of prototype rubber, with different carcass construction and compound mixes'. Everyone knew the importance of tyres at the TT, although they were maybe not quite so critical as in Moto GP, where tyres were the dominant factor affecting bike design. At the TT, riders now ran 120 front and 200 rear, a far cry from the cycle-sized tyres of the first event.

Spectators were always keen to see and hear something different in TT machinery and much interest was generated by the news that Padgetts were providing Bruce Anstey with a Honda RCV123, which was a limited edition road-going version of the V4 Moto GP bike. In addition, veteran Ian Lougher was to run a 576cc Suter MMX500 two-stroke. Most acknowledged that the Suter was a new machine and so expectations were not too high, but there was keen anticipation of what the Honda would deliver. Along with the distinctive sounds of those two bikes, Norton were back for another year with their Aprilia-powered machine, ridden by David Johnson. The Norton's unique exhaust note made it sound fast and 2016 was to prove that it was, with 130mph laps.

On the rider front, Guy Martin was absent, taking a year out, while Ian Hutchinson was to ride a Tyco BMW in the big classes and a Team Traction Control Yamaha R6 in Supersport. It was a machine choice mirrored by Michael Dunlop, but with different teams. Manxman Dan Kneen was looking to make a step up from his regular top-six placings, having earned a ride on top-specification Mar-Train Yamahas. However, a fall from a mountain bike on the run-up to the TT landed him with arm injuries and unable to ride.

John McGuinness was again on Hondas. He was supported by several different sponsors and wore different leathers

John McGuinness publicizes his EMC² 'cloud computing' sponsorship as he passes the Halfway House on his Superstock Honda in 2016.

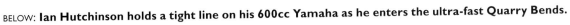

ABOVE: **There was no doubting the seriousness of Honda's support for the 2016 TT. Count the number of 'used' engines on the shelf, part-way through practice week. On the floor were a similar number of new engines, waiting to be issued.**

BELOW: **Ian Hutchinson holds a tight line on his 600cc Yamaha as he enters the ultra-fast Quarry Bends.**

to reflect this. McGuinness knew that in the big classes his Fireblade was slower than the opposition, but he still felt it to be a well-balanced bike for the Mountain Course.

READY AND WAITING

In contrast to the poor weather often experienced during practice, the sun shone throughout 2016's week of preparation. Getting underway on Saturday evening, riders were immediately on the pace and a few of the fastest put in six laps in their first practice session. By mid-week, stars like John McGuinness and Ian Hutchinson were saying that their bike set-ups were complete and they were ready to race.

By the end of practice all competitors had ridden more laps than usual, and the high speeds achieved created expectations of a record-breaking TT meeting. Arguably the most experienced of the top-level riders, John McGuinness, still rode a total of thirty-one practice laps, which was more than any other rider. Going on to ride twenty-five race laps, all together he put in 2,114 ultra high-speed miles at the 2016 TT.

Sidecars were usually sent out after solos and often did not get the best practice conditions, but they enjoyed those of 2016, although two passengers were unfortunate to fall from their very basic sidecar platforms and were injured. Past winner Conrad Harrison failed to find a passenger who could stand the pace, so withdrew from the races.

When interviewed, John McGuinness was complimentary about the course, remarking on the eradication of bumps at Tower Bends and new surfacing on some of the Mountain Road. However, he was critical of the condition of the Sulby Straight, saying it was 'beginning to feel like a Moto-Cross course'. Sadly, later that day, the experienced Paul Shoesmith lost control of his BMW at speed on the Sulby Straight and was killed. The Mountain Course was still so very demanding; later in the week it also claimed the lives of sidecar drivers Dwight Beare in Sidecar Race A, Ian Bell in Sidecar Race B and rider Andrew Soar in the Senior race.

FASTEST SPEEDS

Fastest speeds recorded on Sulby Straight during practice and racing in 2016 were:

Superbike/Senior: 196.8mph
Superstock: 191.2mph
Supersport: 173mph
Lightweight: 154.6mph
Sidecar: 146.8mph
TT Zero: 158mph

All figures were set in near perfect weather conditions.

The fastest riders were now timed at 175mph as they passed the Grandstand en route to the descent of Bray Hill.

Bruce Anstey's Honda RCV123 Moto GP-derived bike proved fast at its debut TT in 2016.

Dean Harrison's laurels for Supersport 1 race – amended to recognise his promotion to second place.

When first introduced in 1999, the timing clock showed a maximum speed of 165mph at the same point.

THE DUELLISTS

Practice performances showed that Michael Dunlop and Ian Hutchinson were the men on top form and their duels were to be the main feature of the week's racing in 2016. Dunlop leapt to the front of the opening Superbike race, held Hutchie at bay, set a new absolute lap record of 133.39mph and became the first man to complete a lap in under 17 minutes. He won by 20 seconds on his BMW from similarly mounted Ian Hutchinson, while John McGuinness (Honda) was third.

The next solo race was Supersport Race 1, and Ian Hutchison (Yamaha) led from the start to take victory from Michael Dunlop (Yamaha) by 15 seconds, setting a new lap record of 128.72mph in the process. Then, after post-race machine inspection, came the announcement that Dunlop had been disqualified 'for a technical infringement'. This brought Dean Harrison (Kawasaki) up into second place, with James Hillier (Kawasaki) in third.

Later the same day Hutchinson and Dunlop (BMWs) were fighting it out in the Superstock race, where Hutchie again took the lead with a record-breaking opening lap for the class of 133.09mph on treaded tyres. Michael Dunlop then retired with a broken gear lever and the win went to Hutchinson by 27 seconds from Dean Harrison and James Hillier on their Kawasakis. Come the Supersport Race 2 and Hutchinson confirmed his superiority in the class by leading from the outset, controlling the race from the front and winning by 17 seconds from arch-opponent, Dunlop.

The final contest for these two top runners came in the Senior race, where, over six laps, Michael Dunlop and his BMW were not to be denied. Leading from the outset, Dunlop broke the absolute course record, storming around the 37¾ miles in 16 minutes 53.93 seconds, at an incredible average speed of 133.96mph. Ian Hutchinson (BMW) was in second place and there he stayed, coming home some 30 seconds behind Dunlop in what was a record-breaking Senior TT, with John McGuinness (Honda) third.

It was nine years since John McGuinness set the first 130mph lap, back at the 2007 TT. Indicating how difficult it had become to increase lap speeds, it then advanced in only small increments, spending five years in the 131mph bracket, until Bruce Anstey's Superbike ride in 2014 took it through the 132mph barrier. Just two years later and

Michael Dunlop raised it to almost 134mph, leaving commentators searching for words to describe his outstanding Senior TT-winning ride.

Earlier in the week, Ivan Lintin won the Lightweight race at just below his own record pace set the year before, whilst among the three-wheelers, John Holden won Sidecar A, where Ben Birchall set a new lap record of 116.798mph before retiring. The Birchalls – Ben's brother Tom occupied the 'chair' – won Sidecar B after a close contest in the initial stages with John Holden and Dave Molyneux. It was a year when Honda power dominated the sidecar races, but their engines also had some notable failures. Seventeen-times winner Dave Molyneux did not start the first race and failed to finish the second with Honda power and he was publicly critical of their ageing design, declaring that he would use Yamaha engines in 2017.

The TT Zero-winning Mugen after the 2016 race.

A first-time win in TT Zero for Bruce Anstey saw him bring his Mugen home ahead of William Dunlop (Victory Brammor), at just under record pace. With five finishers from seven starters, this was the first year since the introduction of the class in 2009 that the electric-powered bikes had failed to record an advance in lap speed.

THE FUTURE?

This book on 'Speed at the TT Races' concludes with a repeat of the quotation that appeared in *The Motor Cycle* after the first races for a Tourist Trophy in 1907: 'It is useless to say that fast speeds are not to be encouraged, human nature being what it is.' One hundred and ten years later, it still provides a basic explanation of why riders strive to ride ever faster around the unforgiving Mountain Course. There have been many machine developments aimed at providing greater power, improved handling, better braking and increased reliability, all of which have combined to provide riders with faster racing motorcycles. Allied to that extensive machine development, even the most ardent TT follower has lost count of the countless improvements to the course that have aided the process of riding it faster. Another, more speculative factor, is that with the greater familiarity the human race now has with mechanically powered two-wheel devices, it is perhaps breeding even better riders.

Despite the developments on all these fronts, it is still hugely impressive that average lap speeds around the Mountain Course have increased from 50.11mph in 1911 to 133.96 in 2016. However, it should be remembered that the object of the first races was not to go ever faster, but to breed reliability in motorcycles that were still in the early stages of development. Thus riders competed for a 'Tourist Trophy'.

In the years that followed, there have been many instances when the motorcycle press announced that the motorcycle had reached the peak of its development in terms of power and reliability. They were repeatedly shown to be wrong, as advances continued to be made in all aspects of motorcycle design and use.

Today's large-capacity motorcycles come with performance that far outstrips what can be used on the open roads and, while the highest measured top speed of TT Superbikes is 196.8mph, they are probably hitting 200mph on the drop from Creg ny Baa to Brandish, which is, in round terms, 100 yards per second. Some may think that is fast enough, but the strong competitive urge present in TT racers will see them striving for even more speed from their two-wheeled projectiles.

At present there seems no desire to cap speeds, so they are set to continue onwards and upwards, albeit with smaller increments than in the past. Where it will all end is something that will be revealed to a future generation. Meanwhile, those special riders who risk their lives by racing over the TT Mountain Course will continue to go 'Faster and Faster'.

INDEX